Cinema Somnambulist

Richard Glenn Schmidt

Cover art by LeEtta Schmidt

THELEEMSMACHINE.COM

Copyright © 2016 Richard Glenn Schmidt

All rights reserved.

ISBN: 1516899253
ISBN-13: 978-1516899258

DEDICATION

To all of you that are still obsessed.
Don't ever stop.

CONTENTS

	Acknowledgments	i
1	Cinema Somnambulism	1
2	Nostalgia Loop	3
3	The Invasian	65
4	Franco Friday	121
5	The Theater Experience	193
6	Miscellany	217
7	1976	237
	Index	255

ACKNOWLEDGMENTS

This book would have been impossible without the assistance, patience, and support of my wife LeEtta and my editing team, Brad and Elizabeth Hogue. I also want to thank my parents for instilling in me a love of film that just won't go away. I'm also indebted to all of my fellow bloggers out there who inspired me to churn out a book's worth of content. You know who you are. I thank you all!

1 CINEMA SOMNAMBULISM

Do you dream in cinema? How about when something uncomfortable or scary starts to happen? Suddenly your perspective shifts to reveal that you're in a theater and watching a film where some uncomfortable and scary shit is happening to someone else. Do you ever dream of hanging out with Orson Welles? Have you dreamt of going through rare horror VHS tapes at a flea market only to wake up disappointed that those rare finds were entirely in your imagination? Do you walk through a labyrinthine mall that has a clearance DVD section full of cult movies that don't exist in the waking world?

My parents inspired in me a love of movies but I don't think that by introducing me to films like The Dirty Dozen (from dad) or Dirty Rotten Scoundrels (from mom), they ever imagined that I'd become quite this obsessed with film. Hey, that's funny. They introduced me to "Dirty" movies. My first memory of going to the movies is a hazy one but I'm pretty sure that my folks took me to see The Empire Strikes Back (1980). This could have been during either of its 1981 or 1982 re-releases because I somehow doubt they took me to it in 1980. I remember being enthralled but totally confused by the plot.

I didn't have a lot of friends growing up so I was always retreating to movies either on late night TV or on the video rental store shelves. Action movies were fun and all, but horror movies made me feel cool and brave. Then my teenage years happened and I moved away from horror (though it was always there, waiting) into the vast and utterly foreign oceans of anime and art cinema.

By the time I reached adulthood, a switch was flipped and I became so entrenched in rediscovering horror movies that even my nightmares became cool films that I would chase down until I woke up. But that wasn't enough. Suddenly there was an entire world of cinema at my fingertips. Say what you will about rampant consumerism and the ridiculous excesses of physical media (how many versions of Army of Darkness did we need exactly?), the 2000s were a great time to be a film fan. Some of us were complaining about aspect ratios and missing scenes but those of us from the VHS era and earlier were just astonished by the possibilities.

The book in your hands represents 7 years of blogging and writing about films. My website Doomed Moviethon was where I first entered the scene but it wasn't until I started my blog where I felt a sense of urgency to churn out fresh content. I also felt a sense of community among the bloggers which also helped spur me on as well. Without those wonderful people, I might never have gotten this far.

I've pulled material from the Cinema Somnambulist blog to try and capture my obsessive and scatterbrained approach to horror and cult cinema. Each chapter is organized chronologically by when I viewed each film discussed and not by release date. Why doesn't Cinema Somnambulist have more material that hasn't already seen the light of day online? Honestly, I'm very selfish and wanted this book on my shelves for myself and I hoped that there might be a few of you out there who get a kick out of it too.

So here I am, weary but very happy from battering my eyes on this ridiculously uncool journey through film watching, rare title scavenging, and DVD and Blu-ray collecting. I'm not done yet but I wanted to stop for a second and reflect on the insanity I've experienced so far. I promise that I'll never not be watching films, no matter how heavy my eyelids get. Even in my dreams, I'm a movie fan. I am the Cinema Somnambulist.

2 NOSTALGIA LOOP

I really don't think this will surprise you: I have a boring personality and I'm tedious to be around. How do I know this? The hours that I've spent (read as: wasted) scouring the weirdest corners of my cinematic memories are way more in number than I want to admit here. In order to save you, the reader, a lot of your precious time, I won't write out those exploratory hours in real time. Instead, I've attempted to gather in this chapter some of the key things that made me into the maniac that I am today.

Being a child of the 1980s, it's probably completely unsurprising how all of this turned out. Horror, science fiction, kung-fu, action, art films, animation, and more are all represented here. Like most film obsessives, my nostalgic streak is a mile wide and my fuzzy memories of flickering images are some of my fondest. Let's get this party started.

Richard Glenn Schmidt

The Sailor Who Fell from Grace with the Sea & More

I'm just sitting here and thinking about the film version of The Sailor Who Fell from Grace with the Sea, a novel by author and total nutjob, Yukio Mishima. I think I was probably 12 years old when my parents rented this 1976 film (or it turned up on cable), and they totally kicked me out of the room when the demented kids in the film decide to kill and dissect a cat. Because I was a stealthy ninja at the time, I decided to pull a fast one on my folks and hover in the hallway leading to my room and watch the scene.

Now I didn't really want to see an animal killed onscreen even if it was staged but my curiosity was overwhelming. Because I was as inconspicuous as a drunken mountain lion with Tourette's syndrome, my dad yelled from the couch, "If you're going to be a sneak just get out here and watch the damned thing!" So I come out sulking like a moron just in time to see the very vague and blurry cat surgery scene. I think what my parents were really disturbed about was these kids trying to prove through 'objectivity' that they were capable of anything. Having seen this, I thought it was a great idea so I went out and killed every house pet in the neighborhood.

Okay fine, I was disturbed by the idea too. These English schoolboys killing both a cat and Kris Kristofferson reminded me of Lord of the Flies and how when the chips are down, kids suck. At the time, I was creeped out because I figured that all the shitty bullies at school were going to be the first ones to turn into soulless cannibal dicks when society crumbled. Obviously I know now that anyone can crack under similar pressure and that everyone has the potential for evil inside them somewhere. It's what makes life great!

Which obviously leads me to "Headbangers Ball". Wait, what? You see, I wasn't exactly forbidden from watching this ragtag metal video show but if my dad caught me up after "Saturday Night Live" had ended, he'd give me shit. So I would pretend to be tired and go to my room (WHERE THERE WAS NO CABLE! SO UNFAIR) until I thought my folks were asleep. Then I'd sneak out, turn the TV on, put the volume at the lowest possible level and bask in the metal goodness. This was at the time when hair metal was at war with death metal and thrash for supremacy of HB so it wasn't easy to sit through the whole show. Of course, I always got caught and never got to watch the whole show anyway. My dad would always come storming in with the "What the hell are you watching?" bit and that would be that.

And now I'm thinking of one of the strangest double features I ever accidentally had. Had I not stayed up way, way past my bedtime, I would have never experienced the joys of Deadly Friend (1986) and Surf Nazis Must Die (1987) on good old cable TV. Watching horror at 2AM and eating

Easy Cheese right out of the can... This was pretty much the most amazing night of my life. When I finally revisited these two flicks years later, I found out how awful they are. In defense of Surf Nazis Must Die, at least it was meant to be bad. Deadly Friend has no such excuse (though it does have one spectacular death scene.)

So what does any of this mean? I don't know. My parents were kind enough to give me their old VCR back then so I could rent Hellraiser (1987) and The Brood (1979) to watch alone in the privacy of my own room. Yet they were totally brainwashed by all the bad press heavy metal was getting at the time and were convinced their son was at risk. When I was a full blown metalhead a few years later and my folks were accusing me of smoking dope, I tearfully tried to explain to them that I just had bad taste in music and fashion. Good thing they never snapped and sent me off to boarding school in England, that's where the true evil lies. See, I tied it all back together!

Richard Glenn Schmidt

Horror vs. Sports

You can either be a horror fan or a sports fan. You can't be both. It's impossible. Okay, maybe you can but I can't. I blame my father. No, seriously. My dad's motto was "put the game on". It didn't matter what my mom and I were watching, when it came time for the game, we had to give up the TV. My dad would watch football, baseball, and basketball primarily with bowling, tennis, and golf as backups. His other motto was "I gotta check the scores" which was actually "put the game on" but under the pretense of quickly seeing how 50 other games were going. This was impossible. We would sit and wait for him to get these little tidbits of information and then the next thing you knew we were watching the fucking game. This is back before there were 11 different ESPN channels and all those On Demand games on 24 hours a day so I imagine that life with dad would be significantly more sporty nowadays.

So I have to be careful when I have kids. (God help us all.) If I dominate their entertainment, they'll turn on me and hate horror movies. Or worse, they'll just hate movies altogether. That is a frightening concept. (But me having kids? That's just terrifying!) My dad and I had a few similar interests. We both had a passion for comedy shows like "Saturday Night Live" (the Dana Carvey era), "SCTV", "The Monkees", "Monty Python's Flying Circus", old reruns of "Laugh-In", and "The Carol Burnett Show". There were also the war movies such as The Longest Day (1962), Midway (1976), Tora! Tora! Tora! (1970), and our favorite: The Dirty Dozen (1967). These flicks would usually drive my mom from the room but it was just so hard to find movies that he and I could agree on. I hope she didn't mind too much. I have no idea if my father even liked horror flicks, but yeah, it always came back to goddamn sports. If he was trying to get me to get interested in them through saturation, he failed miserably. Or maybe he just didn't give a flying fuck what I wanted to watch.

The funny thing about sports (football especially) is that you can totally nerd out on them. Obsessively following what players are being traded to what team, coaches' strategies, weather conditions, injury reports, and even the personal lives of the players is just as geeky as any horror fan's useless trivia mastery. I love my friends who play fantasy football. That shit is like football fan fiction or something (but with less sex, I guess).

I see this kind of passion for detail when I go to the cigar bar. I sit there rereading Spaghetti Nightmares or checking out the new Videoscope while a bunch of dudes (some of them my age) are debating the relevance of Derek Jeter or Brett Favre or some fucking shit that makes me sleepy just trying to recall and I just get jealous. That's the one thing I long for from sports talk. That camaraderie among dudes who are total strangers. They always have something to go on about. It's an easy subject that even if you totally disagree, you can still have a blast arguing about. You can always debate who would win in a fight between Freddy and Michael Myers. Oh wait, was I talking about sports or horror?

So yeah, my dad was a great guy but he and I were from different worlds when it came to our entertainment obsessions. The method was the same. We both put blinders on and focused on our genre. He had sports. I have horror. I wish he were alive today so that I could try and find some horror movies he liked. Obviously, we'd do other father-son bonding stuff too if he were to return from the grave (unless he came back as a flesh-eating zombie) like boogie boarding or building model ships together. Keep in mind, this is the guy who introduced me to Blade Runner (1982) and The Blues Brothers (1980). Wait a minute! There's a sport I like. Hunting replicants! See, I'm practically a jock.

I'm sure that during the holidays, I would have to suffer through some football with him but I'm pretty persistent. I can wear people down on horror movies. I can change the subject without the person even knowing it. Easiest thing to do is start extracting their favorite (or sometimes least favorite) horror movie memory. Nothing pleases me more than hearing someone's tale of how such and such movie scared them as kids. Next thing you know, I'm showing them Hausu (1977) or Messiah of Evil (1973) and they just don't know what hit 'em. My mom says that I remind her of my dad so much. No argument there. So what is my motto? "Put the gore on".

Richard Glenn Schmidt

Freddie Cougar

One magical Saturday night in 1985, my sister Lora was given the arduous task of babysitting me. I was 9 years old and I was actually excited about it. As far as siblings go, we got along pretty well and with my parents out at a party or whatever, we could kick back and have fun. Unfortunately, my sister's creepy boyfriend and his buddy were allowed to come over which made me a little jealous. Now that she was a cool teenager, I saw her less and less.

In a recent email to Lora, I inquired about this particular evening and this awful duder she was dating and she says she doesn't remember either. He wasn't the nerdy comic book geek she dated for a while (a guy I worshipped but who turned out to be a stalker-ish creep) and it wasn't the awesome king of sarcasm that she eventually married. No, this was some rebound jerk that she probably went out with for a week or something. Hopefully, it was less than that. With his perfect hair, sharp features, and ridiculous ego, he just seemed like a total sleazebag to me.

Anyway, this jerky guy and his dumbass friend were there spoiling my evening but they did bring along some very important entertainment. The VHS was something called A Nightmare on Elm Street (1984). Lora immediately said I couldn't watch it because I was too young. This blew my mind. How could a movie be that scary, offensive, etc.? Keep in mind, this was the same girl who woke me up in the middle of the night so we could sit up and watch the thoroughly twisted and bizarre, Fantastic Planet (1973). If you ever wondered where my hardline political views on our giant overlords come from, there you go.

Her creepy boyfriend and his bud had their hearts set on watching Nightmare on Elm Street so they started arguing on my behalf saying that I was totally old enough. Then the urban legends about the film were brought up. According to my sister, a teenage friend of hers had to sleep in her mom's bed for 3 months after watching Wes Craven's film. Somebody chimed in that Nightmare was so scary that it had driven a bunch of kids insane because they were afraid to go to sleep after seeing it.

So before they would agree to start the tape, I had to promise Lora that I wouldn't freak out and if I did, I wasn't allowed to tell mom and dad. She would disavow any knowledge of letting me watch such a scary film. I was also instructed to bail out if I got too scared. I agreed to everything and begrudgingly accepted the challenge to watch this film. At this point, my imagination was running wild. What the hell kind of a horror movie is so scary to force teenagers to lose their minds?

When my parents came home later that night, I spilled the beans about being allowed to watch a horror film of such an intensely graphic and scary magnitude, and they couldn't have cared less. R-rated movies were not forbidden to me and hadn't been for a long time. My folks were selective about my viewing but some real doozies slipped through once in a while. The funniest thing was trying to communicate to the people who had brought me into this world just how brave their son was and how I was exhilarated but not traumatized by the experience.

The actual experience of watching A Nightmare on Elm Street through my nine year old eyes (especially after all the hype perpetrated by my sis and her friends) was thrilling but definitely not the sanity erasing experience I was prepared for. The profoundly terrifying concept of a man who could kill you in your dreams just kind of went over my head. When I was 12 years old, I revisited the film and it scared me silly. The image of Tina's walking corpse in a body bag leaving a trail of blood everywhere she went really got to me the second time around. For some reason, as I got older the film got scarier to me.

A Nightmare on Elm Street did eventually give me a nightmare. When I was around 14 years old, Freddy Krueger invaded my mind. In this nightmare, I was at a long table in a mansion having dinner with a posh family. All of a sudden the forks lifted themselves off the table and chased everyone out of the room. "It's Freddy!" someone screamed as they disappeared out the door. I was left alone with the butter knives which came to life and started following me around the room. I woke up to the sound of my own laughter. I haven't dreamed of Freddy Krueger since.

Richard Glenn Schmidt

Night of the Living Duder

In 6th grade, my fascination with horror was still going through its growing pains. My mind had already been poisoned by a number of accidentally amazing moments. Catching Girls Nite Out (1982) in the middle of the night while I was supposed to be sleeping, seeing A Nightmare on Elm Street on video with my sister Lora, going to the drive-in with Lora and her future husband to see Creepshow 2 (1987) are just a few important things that happened to me. Another monumental event took place on Saturday, October 31st, 1987. All day I had been seeing commercials advertising a midnight showing of Night of the Living Dead (1968) on TV. I don't know why but something told my 11-year-old brain that this was a must-see.

We had just moved into these creepy apartments in Jupiter, Florida called Jupiter Sound Apartments. The place is one of those motel style dealies that was designed to make me uneasy for no reason whatsoever. I only had two friends which I made relatively quickly in the whole neighborhood. Oops, make that no friends. One was Timmy who had just moved to Alaska and the other was Jeff who I caught stealing $10 (my life savings) from my dresser while we were hanging out. My older sisters were now both married and out of the house. So needless to say, my Halloween night was wide open.

Staying up late was no problem. I was already wired from inhaling untold amounts of candy. Just before midnight rolled around, my parents called it a night and I was left alone to face the black and white terrors of George Romero's classic film. From start to end, I ate up Night of the Living Dead. The downer ending where Ben survives a zombie plague but falls prey to dickhead rednecks was truly shocking. But the two scenes that affected me the most were when Tom and Judy met their fiery fate at the gas pump and when Karen takes a trowel to her mother. I was totally fucked up about Tom and Judy's death scene. This cold feeling in my stomach came creeping in like when Travis shot Old Yeller. It seemed totally unfair to me that they got blown up and then consumed by the zombies.

Karen killing and then devouring her mother on the other hand, scared me in the best way. I was exhilarated and oddly happy during that moment. Don't read into that one, Mom. It was also apparent to me that the scene was kind of weird and beautiful. I don't think I had a word for it then but thanks to the freaky sound design, Helen's death is pretty friggin' surreal. Her sped up screams opened up a part of brain that I didn't know existed. Ever since then, I have appreciated directors who use horror as a place to air their freaky cinematic ideas (whether intentional or not) and push the limits of what a typically low brow genre like horror can be used to express.

So yeah, that was a magical night. It was indeed a big turning point. The next day, all of my G.I. Joes were no longer fighting Cobra and vice versa. Instead, these two warring factions had to unite in order to fend off a zombie horde. Soon I would be sneaking peaks at Fangoria magazine at the drugstore, reading Stephen King novels by the truckload, and eventually renting as many horror movies on VHS as humanly possible.

VHS Covers of Doom

This story does not have a happy ending. You know what though? I'm not even sure that this counts as a story. As my childhood came to an end (the first one, the actual one, not the one that I keep perpetuating now), my parents gave me their old VCR and carte blanche in Video-X-Tron (which became a Blockbuster Video in 1990) to rent pretty much whatever I wanted.

No, they weren't letting me get stuff from that little room in the back with the curtain over the door (but don't think I didn't peek back there a few times)! Thankfully, my folks were letting me rent any horror movie that caught my eye. My goal of seeing every horror movie in the store had just popped into my brain one day and I couldn't let it go. But there were some things that were just too much for my young brain to take. One cover that managed to frighten and sicken me at the same time was Color Me Blood Red (1965).

To this day, I can still remember the feeling of nausea that passed over me when I beheld the lurid and ghastly artwork for the film. I think the air conditioning was broken and it was suddenly stifling inside the video store. Plus, there was this smell of something rotten wafting through the store and everything started to swirl around me. I almost, almost puked. This story would have been better if I had tossed my cookies all over the floor right at the foot of the shelves. Forget renting it, I was afraid to even touch Color Me Blood Red to see what was on the back cover. However, I was brave enough to rent 2,000 Maniacs (1964) -even though I had no clue the two films shared the same director- but fell asleep before any of the good stuff happened.

The saddest part is, I've still never watched Color Me Blood Red. Sure, I've read about it but I kind of want to preserve this unpleasant memory because it's still pretty special to me. The fact that cover art alone could drive me to the brink of projectile vomiting is very magical. Or maybe I'm still scared... Okay, fuck it, I'm putting this on my Netflix queue right now. Thanks, you guys. I knew you'd help me get through this.

Juan Piquer Simón's Pieces (1982) has become one of my favorite pieces of trash but when I was a young lad, holy shit, I did NOT have the courage to even consider renting this bad boy. And I can almost blame it entirely on the cover art. I had recently watched Flesh for Frankenstein and the whole stitches-tearing/guts spilling out thing had totally wrecked me. So based on the VHS art for Pieces, I assumed that the film was about a girl who was made up of hastily sewn together parts who walked around while falling apart.

This assumption freaked me the hell out, and I always passed on Pieces. My morbid imaginings didn't turn out to be true when I finally watched the

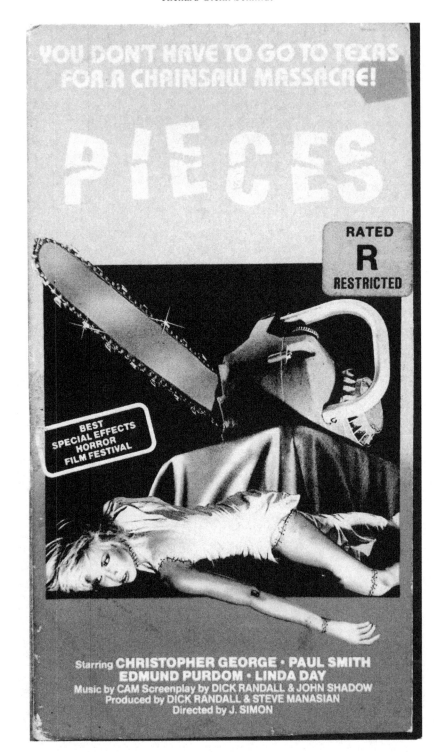

film 15 or so years later. It turned out to be one of the most outrageously hilarious and ludicrously gory slasher flicks I've ever seen, but the girl on the box art doesn't split her seams. She does mangle a dude's junk and that would have freaked me out even more, probably. Either way, somebody's genitals are getting ground up!

Speaking of genital grinding (not the good kind), it just occurred to me how the cover for Color Me Blood Red managed to disturb me so much. Something told me that the man in the picture was collecting his victim's "lady parts" and that's what made me feel so sick. It seemed to my 11 year old brain that this was some kind of sexual mutilation and that really made me ill.

For some reason, I was a total wuss as a kid and this is probably the most pathetic of my VHS scares. I've been staring at images of the Texas Chainsaw Massacre Part 2 (1986) VHS cover and I can't figure it out. All I know is that the idea of renting this film petrified me. At 12 or 13 years old, I had handled the original film just fine. In fact, I really hadn't found it all that scary, just loud. So what in the damn hell was it about the lame ass packaging for the sequel that freaked me out so much?

Years later, when my friend Tim insisted on renting Texas Chainsaw Massacre Part 2, I was finally ready. I was also 19 years old and somewhat less of a wimp. After the end credits had rolled, I was ashamed of myself. Not for being too scared to even watch this film when I was a kid; no, I was more ashamed for having waited so long. I loved and still love Part 2 very, very much. It's such a fucking great movie!

I guess you could say that my kidself was more afraid of the concept of the sequel than of the actual video content that the VHS cover was purporting to contain. Or you could say that I was postmodernally (I wish that was a real word) terrified by the very act of unimpressive representation that the VHS cover was doing all too well. Damn it. I have no idea why the hell I couldn't bring myself to rent TCM2 back in the day. Maybe I was just a stupid ass idiot dumbass moron. Either way, most of the poster art for this film is better than what ended up on the VHS.

Some things are becoming clear to me. As you may or may not know this true fact about me, I'll spill this here. For a very long time, Dario Argento's Phenomena (1985) was my favorite horror movie of all time. I've spent a fair bit of time thinking about and yet I never really put much thought into how that movie entered my life. It was just there. However, while I've been sorting through my strangely disjointed childhood horror movie memories, something revelatory happened. I remember very distinctly going straight to my local video store looking for Creepers, the truncated form of Phenomena. I found it, rented it, and there you go, end of story, right? WRONG, duder, WRONG!

The night I rented The Creepers, I was supposed to be renting Creepers.

Since I was such a young idiot, I didn't know anything about anything and rented a totally different film. So I'm sitting there in my room, watching schoolgirls getting sexually assaulted and strangled by a madman (who I thought was French) and I kept thinking "This ain't right, y'all. This very, very ain't right at all, damn it!" The next day, I took the tape back and was able to get Creepers. Finally, I was able to witness my first Dario Argento film.

But wait, there's more! Man, this is boring. Anyway, not only had I found out that I did not enjoy watching women being raped; I also discovered my first taste of Euro-sleaze. Thank you, The Creepers AKA In the Devil's Garden (1971) AKA Assault AKA Say Goodbye to Your Innocence, Richard. But wait, didn't I get a free rental out of it? That's true, I did. Okay folks, my memory is coming to life here. The Creepers was in the Creepers box at the store. So I got to rent the proper film for free AND I'm totally blameless for the mishap. This is my primal scream therapy. ARRRRRRGH! Nothing self-indulgent going on here, I promise.

So there you go. Forget everything you know about how I came to find the magic that is Phenomena. Seriously, forget it. I did. Gee, do you think something may have led me to go searching for Creepers in the first place? Could it have been a little something called "Stephen King's World of Horror" AKA "This is Horror"? OMG! Will I be talking about that very program at length in this very book? ROFL! Thanks, this has been very fun. BRB!

Richard Glenn Schmidt

Fuzzy Kung Fu Memories

In that decade of greatness, the 1980s, some TV station (can't remember which) would dedicate most of their Saturday programming to kung fu films. From around noon until midnight, they would play cheap junk fu like it was going out of style. I would spend the entire day in the darkness of our den absorbing these masterpieces as well as flailing around the room attempting to imitate the masters' moves. My mom offered to let me take karate lessons but I knew they would be too much work, so I respectfully declined. Besides, the piano lessons were more than I could handle anyway.

One of these fabulous kung fu Saturdays, my parents were gone all day and into the night. They came home just in time to interrupt the climax of an excellent flick where the team of good guys had finally reached the hideout of the lead villain. Suddenly, as the final battle began, the main baddie's hair turned white and then he flew at them. I had seen a lot of crazy shit that day but this fucker could fly!?!? I was told to go to bed so I missed how it all worked out but it's probably better that I've never been able to identify this film. Why mess with my imagination?

It wasn't any individual film that made the magic happen. It was the moviethon that had done it. I was in a hyper-elated state after an epiphany of a kung fu bender. Man, I wish that I could remember those flicks. Scott, a friend at work with a cult film obsession and a much better memory than mine, helped me track down one of the films that played on that fateful day. It was called Chinese Super Ninjas. In this one, the good guys travel around fighting ninjas who use the elements (earth, water, fire, etc.) as the basis for their skills.

So yeah, I still can't remember what the film was where the bad duder's hair turned white and then he proceeded to fly. The other one that day ended like this: Another team of good guys goes against a bunch of bad dudes. All but one or two of the good duders is killed. At the end, our hero (or heroes) walks over a hill to see that the enemy's reinforcements have arrived. There are like hundreds of soldiers running towards him. He just says 'fuck it' and runs screaming into them, sword drawn and ready to die. There's a freeze frame and it ends. We assume he is marching into his certain death. I still haven't tracked this one down.

Shortly after high school (1994-ish), I rented a couple of kung fu flicks for a drunken night at home (my folks were out of town). My friends came over and we watched something wonderful called Against the Drunken Cat Paws (1979) AKA No One Can Touch Her. My friends and I were glued to the screen for its entire running time and then we were fucking robbed! The climax was cut down so badly that we knew we'd been ripped off.

Because I'm a thorough book researcher type guy, I found the VHS rip of Cat Paws and discovered that the fight scene is 9 minutes shorter than it

Cinema Somnambulist

is in the original version. Nine fucking minutes. Was there a shortage of VHS tape in North America that year? Unbelievable! So anyway, what made things even worse that night was the second film I had selected was so boring and of such inferior Kung fu quality that I still can't remember what it was. Do you have any idea how much that damaged my social life? It was a disaster and I've never had any friends since then.

The Horror of the 1990s

My horror obsession was totally dormant during most of the 1990s. That usually pisses me off but when I think back on things, it's totally understandable. I was a little busy being emo and chasing chicks to really care about horror movies. I was such a jerk! There were still moviethons (usually of the Charles Bronson, Steve McQueen variety) but my goal to rent every single horror movie in the video store became pointless once Blockbuster Video started ditching older titles so that they could have 90,000 copies of Pretty Woman and Forrest Gump in stock.

One of my fondest horror memories during this time period was when my friend Tim rented Texas Chainsaw Massacre 2. As a kid, I had been too scared to rent Tobe Hooper's sequel. I was 19 or 20 years old and I still had that anxious feeling in my gut that I was about to have the shit scared out of me. Of course, TCM2 is pretty friggin' genius and is still one of my favorite 80s horror flicks. It's scary and silly and awful and great. After the flick was over, I pledged my love to Stretch and was ready to go back to the video store and clean them out. I didn't. I wasn't ready. Not yet.

There were a lot of great flicks that came out in the 90s but you had to dig deeper to find them. Most of the really great horror films of that time period had abysmal or nonexistent marketing, and I was too much of a vacuous, self-absorbed angst-ridden moron to go hunting for these things. And much like today, I was very obsessive (about ska music, anyway) and I could have been plumbing the depths of obscure cinema. I did have a few very close run-ins with greatness during this time period.

The first was at my local used record store, Sound-X-Change (RIP) in Jupiter, Florida. There was this gorgeous punk rock woman there who I asked out frequently (even though she was 21 years my senior) and oh yes, she was cooler than cool. One day, she lent me her tape of Seconds (1966) starring Rock Hudson. This film was pretty obscure at the time, and it's actually quite a bizarre little gem. She had taped it off of cable one night and so I made a tape of her tape and then proceeded to watch it over and over again; you know, in case she quizzed me on it later. This could have been the start of something big. I could have challenged her to a rare movie hunt and then a moviethon and then marriage. None of that stuff happened.

The next and most pathetically wasted opportunity came around 1998. My girlfriend at the time lived in Port St. Lucie, Florida. Trust me, it's a magical place as everyone who has ever lived there will tell you. As usual, we were bored out of our skulls and headed to the even more enthralling Stuart, Florida where there was a video store in the downtown area called Groovy Movies-A-Go-Go. How fucking awesome is that? And yet, I didn't appreciate it. I walked in, browsed, got bored by all these "weird" movies I'd never heard of (yes, that's how I actually felt at the time), and rented

The City of Lost Children (1995). That's kind of cool, I guess, but this guy had tons of shit from Something Weird Video and rare gore movies aplenty. Fuck, I'm really ashamed of myself right now.

The third and final incident occurred when my friend Rocky (real name) and I were at a porno store. Before you get the wrong idea, this was (presumably) the first porno store in North Palm Beach so it was something of an event. On Northlake Boulevard, the same street as my mom's antique store (who am I, Lane Kim?), they opened up a freakin' porno store! We had to check this out, so my friend and I went there to marvel at the horror that is "porn shopping". While I was perusing the tapes, I found something called Shatter Dead (1994). A switch was tripped in my brain and that deafening call of horror was momentarily awakened. There were gallons of blood on the artwork for this tape and it was such an anomaly to find in a porno store that I almost bought it right there on the spot.

Rocky talked me out of it. He said that they had that movie at Groovy Movies-A-Go-Go and that if I really wanted to see it, he'd rent it for me. The store was just a couple blocks from his house and he went there frequently. For God's sake, what the hell was wrong with me? The keys to the castle were right there. I was in that area nearly every weekend to visit my girlfriend or hang out with Rocky and I couldn't see how special any of this shit was. Now that nearly all of this type of awesome store is long gone, I feel really, really stupid.

Instead of talking about the really great horror movies from the 1990s, I want to ramble on about the really average or horrible stuff that came out during the era and/or the really cool stuff that I didn't like because I didn't think it was good (even though it was). These are just titles (mostly) off the top of my head that helped facilitate the dormancy of my love of horror. Some of these were theater experiences but most were rentals.

In the friggin' awful category is Nadja (1994). I rented this artsy fartsy vampire flick and was awestruck by how boring and shitty it was. I have not and will not return to the Nadja. It might be good with a little more patience but no thank you. There's also The Good Son (1993) and that ill-fated Psycho remake (1998). Both were complete shit. Stephen King got raped on "The Tommy-knockers" and "The Stand" TV adaptations but he'll never be able to sit down again after Sleepwalkers. Sweet boxcar Jesus, that was totally terrible. Oh and Jack Nicholson in Wolf (1994). WTF? Ugh… and Wishmaster (1994). I can't think of a more bland horror franchise than this. It's like they tried to take Pinhead and mix him with Freddy Krueger. Well, maybe it's more original than I'm giving it credit for. Either way, it just doesn't work for me.

The Craft (1996) was one of those movies that took me a long time to appreciate. When The Craft came out, the ultra-Christian girl I was dating called me in tears after having seen it with her friends and had had the wits scared out of her. I tried to calm her down but it turned out that she was more afraid FOR ME than of the film. Now I had and still have no affiliation with any Satanic cults or covens and yet, this chick had been convinced by The Craft that my soul needed saving. Like fucking IMMEDIATELY! Well, we got into this huge argument and broke up on the spot. Years later, when I finally watched The Craft, I found it very enjoyable. It's a pretty great 90s teen horror movie and it helped get me out of an awful relationship. Bonus!

Whoa, 1998 was a big year for horror. It looks like the genre was trying to come back from the dead. Urban Legend is still a favorite of mine though not exactly inspiring. While The Faculty and Disturbing Behavior were okay, each of them could have been better/more memorable. Blade (1998) was definitely a movie. Revisiting it recently I noticed that it's holding up pretty well. Blade II (2002) is awesome but I'm still not too hot on this series.

And finally, there's Sleepy Hollow (1999) which is either a love it or hate it flick. I hated the piss out of this one when it came out and couldn't figure out what the hell Tim Burton was thinking. Now, I love it and I can't figure out why I didn't adore this flick the first time around. It's cheesy, it's gory and it's funny. What's not to love? (A lot of people hate this one but they still might come around like I finally did.)

Richard Glenn Schmidt

My Life with Demons

My friend Shawn was the first of my friends to come from a 'broken home'. His parents were divorced! This alien concept was a struggle for me to accept at first, but as time passed, I realized that kids from homes with divorced parents are people too. Shawn's cool redneck dad lived next door to me so I only got to see my friend every two weeks or so. Okay, maybe "cool redneck" is an oxymoron. He had a really racist dog named Shiloh who he gave to us. She would bark like mad at black people. Not cool. Not cool at all. So anyway, one weekend when I was ten years old, I managed to convince Shawn that I had to spend the night at his mom's house. She had remarried several years before and for some reason, I imagined that Shawn's life at her place was some kind of Shangri-La.

I was right. I swear to you, this kid had every friggin' G.I. Joe figure and vehicle ever released and we spent so much time choosing our forces and setting up the battle that the battle never even took place. The next day, with only two short hours left before I had to leave Heaven, his mom reminded Shawn and I that we hadn't watched all the movies we'd rented. There were two left: an action movie I can't remember and Lamberto Bava's Demons (1985).

The horror bug had already crawled into my brain and was laying eggs (which are still hatching to this day) so my vote was for Demons. For some reason, the hideous creature on the box art was strangely hypnotic and I couldn't stop staring at it, even as the movie played out. Obviously, I had no idea who producer Dario Argento was or who director Lamberto Bava was. I had no idea that Italians made horror movies. That revelation was a long time comin'.

There has rarely ever been a more perfect entertainment. My ten year old brain devoured Demons. The film is about a movie theater full of patrons who get possessed by murderous and slime-spewing creatures from hell. Luckily, there are samurai swords and motorcycles lying around to enable all kinds of nonsensical mayhem and gore-soaked action setpieces. The only scenes that truly frightened me were when the survivors finally get outside the theater to find that the city is overrun with possessed people. I have this thing about society breaking down. Very scary.

So the hero guy and the survivor girl hitch a ride with some heavily armed parents and their kid in a jeep who are trying to flee the city. As they're cruising along and we expect the ending credits to roll, the girl suddenly starts growling and we see that she was scratched by a demon at some point. While she's turning into a demon beast, the kid (who was Bob in House by the Cemetery (1981), by the way) nonchalantly turns around in his seat and shoots her with his shotgun. Point fucking blank. She goes flying and my jaw hit the floor. After all the gore and pretty much relentless

insanity of Demons, the last thing I expected was this kid to be a bad ass.

Shawn and his mom were nonplussed by this monumental event. Shawn thought that the kid was dumb for taking so long to react. You see, I always identified with kids in movies so to see one actually kill someone (even someone possessed by a demon) was very shocking (and empowering) to me at the time. I would be similarly bowled over by Hob, the kid drug kingpin in Robocop 2 (1990). Demons would pop up again a year later when my sister and her husband were looking after me. This time, something truly scary happened: I accidentally kicked over my brother-in-law's chaw-spit can. I know that the cigars I smoke are disgusting and all but my God, the toxic waste that came slowly oozing out of that Coke can was truly odious.

When the sequel to Demons hit the video store, I was more than a little ecstatic. Some people have claimed disappointment with Demons 2 (1986) but I have to say, I was completely satisfied the first time around. In this film, the demons go after the residents of an apartment complex. It may not be the most memorable or inventive film but for my preteen brain, it was magic. The scene where the demon comes out of the television… Genius! And of course, the fight scene in the weight room where a bunch of roid-raging lunkheads are no match for the demons is freakin' awesome.

I guess the most frustrating thing about Demons and Demons 2 is that I had to grow up (don't believe it). Back in 2003, when I revisited these flicks from my childhood, they just didn't measure up. Call me crazy but the first film drags. I wasn't friggin' BORED with Demons when I was 10! What fucking horrible trauma happened to me between 1986 and 2003 that made me into such a lame-o? Oh yeah, that's right. I worked at Pier 1 Imports. Its sequel is just kind of redundant and mostly disappointing. Thankfully, I can still appreciate these films for their killer soundtracks and Italian oddness but alas, most of the magic is gone. Boo hoo.

UPDATE: Any criticism on Demons is now null and void. I hate to step in like this and retract my statements but I recently revisited Demons and Demons 2 YET AGAIN in 2015, and man oh man, I loved them both. I admit that Demons 2 is pretty weak but it's still fun as hell. Demons is a dang masterpiece. It just goes to show you how revisiting a film multiple times will reveal untold treasures. So yeah, I don't know what giant item was jammed up my butt when I wrote about my previous disappointment but it has since dislodged itself and been long forgotten. Viva Lamberto Bava (or "Lambava" as Brad and I call him)!

Anything but the Exorcist

One of my earliest memories of a horror movie almost scaring me was around the time when The Exorcist (1973) was making its debut on a local TV station. I'm pretty sure I was 8 years old when one night, my dad and I were watching TV and I was dumbstruck by an ad showing a couple of highlights from this classic terrifying film. I flipped out. The sight of Linda Blair as Regan staring off into space with goo dripping from her face freaked me the fuck out. About 5 minutes later, my dad reminded me it was time for bed. I begged and pleaded not to have to sleep in my room upstairs. The house seemed so creepy all of a sudden that I couldn't even think about ascending the stairs. He agreed to let me sleep in my sister's room next to the den. She was staying at a friend's house so I retreated there and left the door open.

My logic was unfortunately flawed. You see, I could still hear the TV from my sister's room and my dad was still watching TV on the same channel that was playing the ad. So every 10 minutes or so, I could hear the demon's threatening voice, the shouting of the priests, and the screaming of Regan's poor mother. Worse still, my sister had these cheap closet doors that wouldn't close completely. I had to keep getting up to try and close them. Every time it seemed they would stay closed, they would come unlatched and slowly open again. I just knew there was a possessed girl in there about to jump out and kill me at any moment. I called my dad into the room about 10 times and he finally had to yell at me to get me to chill the hell out.

It wasn't until many years later that I got up the nerve to rent The Exorcist and finally watch it. I think I was 13 or so when I finally confronted one of the most horrifying films ever made. We picked up the VHS at the video store, and I watched it alone in my room. This experience was anything but disappointing. I was mortified, exhilarated, and shaken to the core. My only option was to check out the sequel. Woops, that didn't work. To this day, I still haven't managed to sit through Exorcist II: The Heretic (1977). I have read a few reviews that have highlighted the film's good points but seriously, I find it interminably boring. I promise to give it another chance sometime (especially since Ennio Morricone did the score).

Now The Exorcist III (1990) is where it's at, y'all. I didn't see this film until it had been around for quite a while. One of the last ma and pa video stores in Jupiter, Florida was going out of business and I managed to score this and Blue Velvet on VHS for $1 apiece. It was during this time period in my life when I would watch whatever few films I owned over and over again. My love for Blue Velvet eventually waned (stupid mechanical bird) but I still love Exorcist III. William Peter Blatty brought the pain by pretending that Exorcist II never happened and assaults the viewer with all kinds of crazy craziness. The film gets under your skin with some truly scary scenes and a severely angry George C. Scott yelling at people (and demons). Plus, Brad Dourif delivers one of the finest monologues of his career.

In 1998, The Exorcist came stumbling drunkenly back into my life and featured even more abominations. Kim, my girlfriend at the time, and my best friend Scott were psyched beyond belief to catch the movie re-released in theaters. This was a very bittersweet experience. The film looked great but some asshole had added new cheesy sound effects, digital touchups, and outright lameness. When it came out on DVD dubbed as the 'Version You've Never Seen', I was pretty pissed off. Several of the film's scariest bits are telegraphed to the audience via digital images hidden behind doors and slapped onto tense scenes that don't fucking need any help being creepy. One thing I did learn about the original Exorcist is that the more I watch it, the more it scares me. Knowing what is coming next only makes the wait more unbearable

Somebody gave me a copy of Exorcist: The Beginning (2004)but I haven't watched it yet. For some reason, I'm not in a hurry. Oh yeah, I know why, I'M TOO FREAKIN' BUSY WATCHING ALL THE RIP-OFFS! I doubt I will ever be able to articulate what it is about all of the films that rip off the 1973 classic but for some reason, they fascinate me. First, it started with The Antichrist (1974). This is one seriously demented film when a grown woman gets possessed by a demon and all kinds of Satanic hilarity ensues. Next came what is probably the best and most infamous of all the Exorcist clones, Beyond the Door (also 1974), which has some very chilling and mind-bending moments of insanity. I also enjoyed the Spanish flavored clunky Exorcismo (1975), starring the great Paul Naschy.

The list of good rip-offs is pretty short but the list of bad yet entertaining is quite long. Here in the states, there is the blaxploitation take on the phenomena called Abby (1974) and the very uneven Piper Laurie vehicle, Ruby (1977). Spanish horror genius Amando de Ossorio directed his own half-hearted attempt to cash in on the phenomenon with Demon Witch Child (1975) AKA The Possessed, and some damn fool named Mario Gariazzo directed a dull monstrosity entitled The Eerie Midnight Horror Show (1974) -a title cooked up to get some of that Rocky Horror cash- AKA Enter the Devil starring the one and only Ivan Rassimov as the devil himself. This movie sucks, but oh man, it's friggin' outrageous. There's one lame latecomer called Satan's Wife (1979) that I strongly dislike and good old Werewolf Woman (1976) has some possession scenes in it that couldn't have just happened on their own.

I guess when it comes down to it, the original Exorcist is a lot of work for me and is anything but a popcorn movie. It's a grueling film experience, a beautiful and painful endurance challenge that requires patience and a strong constitution. Plus it's over 2 hours long! When I need my demonic possession fast and cheap (and trust me, I always do), I turn to the Italians (or the Spaniards). These films are a delicate balance between the genuinely scary and the delightfully tacky. I still have a special place in my heart for the original but nobody ever had a crisis of faith while watching The Eerie Midnight Horror Show! Well, I mean, I hope no one did because that would be some sad shit right there. Oh yeah, I almost forgot The Night Child (1975). Now that's a weird one!

Richard Glenn Schmidt

Do Robocops Dream of Robosheep?

Robocop (1987) and Bladerunner (1982) are very similar films and I am going to make a list of how they are similar. 1) They both take place in a city. 2) They both take place in the future. Those are the only two I can think of right now. Well, that didn't pan out. I guess I'll just blab on and on about why Robocop is still one of my favorite movies of all time, but first, I have to talk about how I almost got to see it in theaters.

The summer that Robocop came out, I was taking swimming lessons. I was nine years old and I did not yet know how to swim. It was for that reason (and partly because of Jaws) that I was scared of the deep end of the pool. However, unlike my breakdancing lessons from the previous summer, I was taking to swimming quite well. It was only a mildly humiliating experience. I was one of the older kids there (if not the oldest) so the learning process actually made me feel dumb because I should have already been swimming like a dang fish. So anyway, my mom promised me that she would take me to see Robocop if I passed the class.

Robocop was the hottest movie that summer. The buzz in my mind promised me that it eclipsed the awesomeness of Transformers: The Movie. This was essential viewing and the promise of seeing it made me all the more determined to learn how to swim. On the last day of class, my mom stayed on the benches, watching, and was ready to pick me up, take me to lunch, and then whisk me off to the movie theater. My tenth birthday was just a few days away, I was going to see Robocop, and some 7 year old kid was playing with his snot in the pool. I was having the time of my life. That's when the swimming instructor announced that our final test was to jump off the diving board into the deep end of the pool.

It was like a slap in the face. It dawned on me that in order to pass the class and get to see the movie event of the century, I had to risk drowning. Like, really drowning. I watched other kids (some of which were half my age) jump off the diving board and into the deep end. Each time they sank like a stone and my stomach seized up. Then they rose to the surface laughing and confidently swam to either the edge or the instructor waiting in case something went wrong. I was going to fucking die. I just knew it.

I immediately got out of the pool and went over to my mom and tried to talk her out of making me finish the class. She was not amused. I begged her not to make me jump into the deep end and explained that I knew how to swim so there was no reason for such a pointless act. She told me that if I didn't jump off that diving board, she wouldn't take me to see Robocop. I lost it. I wasn't really a tantrum kind of a kid at this point. I never swung my arms around, banged my head on the ground, or squealed like a beast. I just shook and wept. I'm sure it looked like my dog had just died or something. I was in one of those impossible quandaries. I knew that crying wasn't going to get me what I wanted. I knew that I was going to have to do the scary thing I had to do. I knew that by crying, I was making things worse, but I couldn't stop.

After five (or ten or twenty) failed attempts to get up the courage to jump into the deep end, I finally did it. Now granted, I was crying when I jumped in and I had the instructor catch me when I hit the water. And I came up choking and flailing like a drowning cat. Yet I rose from the pool triumphant and went over to my mother who was just staring at me. Smiling (and strangely proud), I said something to the effect of 'see, I knew I could do it, now take me to Robocop'. She calmly said, 'no' and we left the pool. I don't remember if we spoke on the way home or not. I probably tried to reason with her and failed. I didn't get to see Robocop that day and I'm glad. I had proven myself to be a sniveling wussy coward and God only knows how I would have turned out if my mom had given in. So Robocop came and went. It was in theaters for what seemed like forever, and I didn't even try to convince my mom again to take me to see it. I had failed in my quest to grow up even a little bit that summer.

The following summer, my parents took me along to a Tupperware convention in Orlando, Florida. It was a week's stay in a nice hotel (probably the Marriot) with a game room and a swimming pool (uh oh). The best part about the trip was that my parents would be in meetings all day and I would be free to roam around the place to read, draw, and waste some cash at the arcade. It was late afternoon when we checked in, hauled our bags upstairs, and went up to our room. Something caught my eye immediately: there was this little cardboard promotional thingie on top of the cable box showing the Pay-Per-View movies the hotel offered. At the top of the list was… that's right, friggin' Robocop! I danced a jig and showed my mom the good news. For a split second, I could see that she was remembering last summer's Robo-swimming misadventure. But she just smiled at my enthusiasm and said that I could watch it the next day while she and my dad were at their meetings.

The wait was agony. I had already waited a year to watch Robocop and now I had to wait one more night? Shit. I could barely sleep a wink that night. Of course, I had already wasted a third of my week's videogame budget that evening (they had Space Harrier!) so my mind was already racing, and the promise of the single greatest film of all time waiting for me in the morning made it almost impossible to sleep. At six in the morning, I got up with my parents. I tried to help them get ready to pass the time. The next showing of Robocop was at 8:00am. After a quick breakfast with my folks, they went on their way and I was finally alone. I shut the curtains, plunging the room in darkness, and watched some morning cartoons while keeping an eye on the clock. When it was finally time, I turned to the Pay-Per-View channel and there it was: ROBO-FUCKIN'-COP!

So I'm sitting there, all alone in the dark, watching Robocop. My short 11 years on the planet suddenly meant nothing. This was the apex of my life and I knew it. At the first sign of gore (a hapless executive getting shredded by ED-209), the realization that my disastrous swimming lesson freak-out that prevented me from seeing the best film ever made WITH MY MOTHER was a blessing in disguise. I knew that my mom would have flipped out and I wouldn't see Robocop until I went off to college. If only my Space Mountain spaz-out had some secret happy outcome. All that really accomplished was making my father ashamed to call me his son. But that's another story.

When the film was over, my mind was swarming. I couldn't calm down. You'd think that I had snorted about 50 lines from that coke factory Robocop busted. I went down to the arcade with a fistful of quarters and played Rolling Thunder until I was broke. Once my parents were done with their conferences for the day, I chewed their ears off about Robocop. I just couldn't shut up about it. However, I was very careful not to mention anything about people getting shot in the privates, their hands blown off, stabbed in the jugular, shot in the kneecaps, etc. I did mention the toxic waste bit. How could I resist grossing my mom out by detailing a scene where a man is dipped in toxic chemicals and then explodes when he gets hit by a car? I just couldn't.

When you just couldn't get enough Robocop (and believe me I just couldn't), then you just had to check out Marvel's comic adaptation of the film. It is seriously one of the worst fucking comic books ever made. Obviously, all of the cursing is absent, as is the extreme gore. The worst part, of course, is the terrible artwork. Certain scenes from the film are drawn pretty good, the rest of it is just awkward and lackluster bordering on pitiable. This lame garbage put me off so much that I didn't even know there was an actual Robocop comic book with its own storyline. I'm assuming it sucked too (though it probably doesn't suck).

The following Christmas, after I thought I had opened all of my presents, I noticed that there was one for me left unopened. Judging by the shape and the weight, it was definitely a VHS tape. When I peeled off that paper, you could have knocked me over with a feather. It was Robocop! I owned very few movies in those days and my parents had just given me the most ultraviolent thing I'd ever seen.

I think I've watched Robocop somewhere between 20 or 25 times thanks mostly to that tape. This was one of the very rare films that I could actually watch twice in a row. I prided myself on knowing every line of dialogue by heart. (Yeah, that's one useless talent I no longer possess.) Unlike the comic book adaptation, I found the network TV version quite amusing with all the curse words replaced and jarring editing to cover up the violence, so I usually watched it when it was on. Obsessive behavior is

so much easier when you're a kid. No one's keeping track of your free time.

When the trailers for Robocop 2 (1990) started popping up on TV, I couldn't contain my excitement. I actually started writing my own novelization of what I thought Robocop 2 was going to be about just based on what I gleaned off the trailers. I don't remember how far I got or what the exact plot was of my little fan fiction, but I was 14, so I imagine it was pretty friggin' dumb and hilarious. Or maybe just pathetic.

I have a vague memory of my mom taking me to the theater to see Robocop 2. I know she just bought me a ticket and dropped me off. I'm glad she didn't come with me to see the film because there were several things about this awesome sequel that would have probably caused her to bolt with me in tow. For instance, there's that kid, Hob (played by Gabriel Damon), a drug pushing, murderous psychopath, who was my freakin' hero. My mom would have noticed the obvious glee and admiration on my face during scenes of him blowing people away and cursing up a storm and it would have been all over, right there and then.

Even then I knew the sequel wasn't as good as the original but I was more than pleased. The things that I loved about the first film were even more pronounced here. The urban decay, fake commercials and newscasts, the cartoonish levels of violence, etc. It was all there. A bad guy like Cain (played by the terrifying Tom Noonan) made me forget all about Clarence Boddicker. Of course, seeing Dan O'Herlihy in a hot tub... that wasn't so good.

So apparently, the Robocop phenomenon continued without me. When I heard they were making Robocop 3 (1993), I had only two rules: it had to be rated R and it had to have Peter Weller. Well, they screwed that up and did neither of those things. No disrespect to Robert John Burke but dude ain't Robocop. I will never accept him. Of course, the PG-13 was the final nail in the coffin of my interest. I was a dickish 16 year old at this point so there was no way I was going to waste my precious (yeah right) time on this crap. I've still never seen Robocop 3.

Then there was a TV series which I didn't even know about until the toys were available for purchase at Kay Bee Toys at the University Mall. This was in 2002 and the show had been off the air for 8 years. Another strange thing: Kay Bee never had the Robocop figure. It was always the supporting characters. Had they had at least one friggin' Robocop, I would have bought the dang thing. But wait, there's more. A mini-series? A Japanese rip-off? A slew of videogames? (No wait, THAT I remember.) A Frank Miller comic book? And now, word on the street is that a 3D Robocop might be in the works? I'd buy that for a dollar! You knew that was coming, didn't you? Not surprisingly, at the time of this writing, I still haven't bothered with that Robocop remake (2014).

I did pick up the DVD back in 2002 and had a tearful reunion with my

Robobro. It was still an exhilarating film, and I remembered so much dialogue from it that I annoyed everyone in the room (nothing new there) by telegraphing the best parts. But I haven't watched it since. I guess it's time to get reacquainted with an old friend. I probably need to get down with this unrated cut I keep hearing about.

Richard Glenn Schmidt

I Want to be Happy

I was just sitting here, trying to think about movies. The first thing came to mind was Nell (1994). That movie is so funny. It's got Jodie Foster talking gibberish for two hours, and Liam Neeson has sex with her. At least that's how I remember it. That's a pretty sweet deal for all parties involved, right? I don't know. I think that movie makes me uncomfortable because it's sad. I mean, it may have been uplifting and all but the whole concept was depressing. I don't like that. It's okay when a horror movie makes me depressed but not when a drama does it. When a horror movie provides that gory ennui that I crave, it's usually a bittersweet sensation not unlike eating circus peanuts. Or is that just sickeningly sweet?

How deranged was I when I watched Breaking the Waves (1996)... FOUR TIMES!?!?! It wasn't in a row or anything but what the fuck was I looking for with those repeat viewings? Lars von Trier destroys Emily Watson for 2 and a half hours and I couldn't look away. When it's not making you cry, Breaking the Waves is a gorgeous and joyful movie (for approximately 3 minutes of its running time). I did manage to come away from that film with... what? A healthy hatred of the Scottish Highlands? An irrational fear of Stellan Skarsgård? I even gave The VonTrierMeister another shot with Dancer in the Dark (2000). How's that old saying go? "Fool me once, shame on Danish dudes. Fool me twice, that's not so nice."

A few years later, I decided to ruin my life with Requiem for a Dream (2000). Why would anyone watch this shit? I finally broke away from my fascination with drug culture movies. Once you realize that drug movies make drugs look really fun for about an hour or so before people start dropping like flies and/or losing limbs and/or becoming prostitutes. Okay, Trainspotting (1996). I think I watched that maybe 5 times. Why? Why would I ever have wanted to watch that? Hooray for charming and hilarious junkies! Even the poster for that movie gives me the chills now. I'm Ewan MacGregor! There's a baby crawling on my ceiling! Waaaa! Waaaa! I stood up and applauded at the end of The Basketball Diaries (1995) when the credits rolled. I think being a dumb idiot may have helped with that.

I'm trying to think of some other shit that is just agony for the soul. Recently, I watched This is England (2006) and I just wanted to crawl into a hole and die. Oh, these films are poison. Like American History X (1998) which I watched twice or Romper Stomper (1992) which I must have sat through like half a dozen times. These are gut-wrenchingly depressing movies. Obviously, the anti-racist message of these movies appeals to me and one has to stare in the face of monsters, especially disturbing and perfectly portrayed ones. But I would get so morose after watching these films. I can only imagine what a friggin' unendurable bore I used to be (still am). Geez.

Like, I would watch Rumble Fish (1983) over and over again. Who does that? Was I ever in a gang? No. Was I ever in a Nazi gang? No. Did I have such a tremendous heroin/cocaine addiction that I could relate to the characters in these movies? No. IFC or Sundance or whatever played Bully and I followed it up with freakin' Elephant (2003). These aren't movies for human beings. They are movies for donkeys named Eeyore. Suddenly, Kids (1995) just popped into my head. I watched it with this chick and then we made out afterwards. You see what Portishead can do to a person? Who watches Gummo (1997)? I mean, besides me at 22? Why the fuck have I seen The Pillow Book (1996)!?!?! I can't vomit hard enough right now.

For a short time I was obsessed with Arizona Dream (1992). It's a momentarily fun and quirky flick that gets really dark and bizarre (in a bad way). Of course, this leads me to Vincent Gallo which leads me right into Buffalo '66 (1998). I pretty much overdosed on this one. Why would I watch such a bleak (though momentarily hilarious) film populated with horrible, horrible people? Also, why would I buy the DVD and proceed to watch it over and over again? The only thing I got from this movie is a healthy appreciation of Yes (which some would say is unhealthy). Shit, what the fuck? I can't even imagine being in the frame of mind where I would rent Slacker (1991), Floundering (1994), and The House of Yes (1997). Sure, I watched Krzysztof Kieślowski that one time and it did get me laid with an actual girl but don't you try that at home, kids. Hey I know what would be fun, let's watch A Woman Under the Influence (1974). Now that's a happy movie!

None of these are terrible movies, really. And I'm really glad I watched them to develop my tastes. Cinema people seem to always harp on the negative side, so of course wildly depressing stuff is going to be somebody's classic. For some people, these are going to be classics because they're the films that got them through their awkward teenage (or awkward early to mid-20s) years. I guess they did for me. Part of me growing up cinematically was watching things that made me want to kill myself. Nowadays, I watch horror movies. Some of them are dark and depressing like Martyrs (2008) but most horror flicks are uplifting like Crazy Lips (2000). I went from one form of depravity to another and somehow I'm more stable. Weird, huh?

So I guess what this ramble is really about is this, if I had to live my life over again (well, at least from 18 to 26), I would put down that VHS of Leaving Las Vegas (1995) and just watch Night of the Demons (1988) again. "Shut up, Richard."

Richard Glenn Schmidt

Last Tango in Palm Beach

My recent ramble about depressing movies got me thinking about Last Tango in Paris (1972) which I think I've watched about a dozen times. What is Last Tango in Paris exactly? Is it a darkly hilarious sex tragedy? Is it artsy couple's porn? Sure, why not? Sometime in the late 90s, I was a pretentious bag of tears and I was drawn like a moth to a blowtorch to Last Tango. I knew I was going to love it even before I popped the VHS into the player. And you know something? I don't give a shit about Paris or France, and I don't even know how to tango. Maybe it was all that Henry Miller I read. I'm shrugging my shoulders right now. It's like that thing people say, "I don't know much about art but I know what I like." Yes, people really say that and I have to agree with them; especially when it comes to this film because I don't know what I'm talking about. I'm probably missing the point but here I go anyway.

The film is about two selfish and unlikable people: Paul (Marlon Brando) and Jeanne (Maria Schneider). Paul's wife just committed suicide, and Jeanne is about to get married to a pretentious filmmaker. I still don't know who is worse off. Completely by chance, they go to rent the same apartment and start up a love affair. This is a bad relationship from the get-go. They don't tell each other their names, they just get it on a lot, and talk all the time. Doesn't this sound like a fascinating film? Isn't this the most riveting plotline you've ever read about in a crappy book in your life? Well, it gets better. Paul decides to take their freakish relationship to the next level. Jeanne says "Screw you, tugboat!" and blows him away. The end.

This movie tries to be shocking. It features two characters doing and/or talking about things (SEXUAL THINGS!!!!) that must have been shocking and/or groundbreaking to the arthouse audiences that this film was made to reach. I'm just guessing here but this film probably didn't give much of a thrill to the grindhouse crowds. They might have just found it odd that Brando was wallowing in their genre. This is a trashy movie but it's also a beautiful trashy movie. I have tried to get into other films by director Bernardo Bertolucci and it just didn't work out. The Sheltering Sky (1990)? No. No. No. No. And also no. I'm not going to think about that. The Dreamers (2003)? Please, I'm getting a little nauseous now. Maybe The Conformist (1970) will save me. I'll check it out soon, I promise. (I actually kind of loved The Conformist. Thanks, Brad!)

Anyway, why the fuck is Brando in this anyway? Duder was getting weird, that's why. He wanted to be totally self-indulgent (on camera, for a change) and Bertolucci gave him that chance. Brando isn't acting here. He's just being himself, brutish, crude, sardonic, cruel, and brilliant. His obsession with death would pop up again in Apocalypse Now, another movie where he stopped acting and just started being himself on camera.

Bold or incredibly lame? I don't care. I'm a huge Marlon Brando fan but I don't know if it was this movie that started my fascination with him or if I was already into this guy's work beforehand. For instance, I love One-Eyed Jacks and I sat through The Young Lions just for one brilliant Brando moment ("I have killed no one.").

Paul's wife's suicide reveals to him that he didn't really know her at all. It gets even worse when he meets the man she was having an affair with; a man just like Paul. His wife even bought the guy the same dang robe for Christmas. The greatest and most morbid moment in the film, and probably my favorite of all of Brando's monologues, comes when he goes to view his dead wife's body. He delivers a eulogy like I've never seen before. This scene is funny, jaw-dropping, profound, and insanely depressing.

The funniest thing was comparing the censored version of this movie to the uncut (which I was more used to). In the uncut version, we see an overhead shot of Paul having anal sex with Jeanne using butter in a way that butter was never meant to be used. It isn't erotic so much as it is terrifying, boring, and unpleasant to watch. In the censored version, this scene is obscured by a lamp! The editors superimposed a fake lamp over the shot of Brando doing the donkey donkey to Schneider! I remember watching this with my girlfriend at the time and we got a big laugh out of trying to see around the lamp on the TV. See, I told you it was a couple's movie! The scene in the hall with the ballroom dancers more than makes up for this awfulness. Paul and Jeanne are the only people truly alive while the mannequins that inhabit their dead world twist and turn around them.

So this sex/death obsessed film appealed to me at the time, and I'd probably still get a kick out of it now. It's a celebration of life in the face of death, a tango in the face of misery, and it's also a real downer. It's the physical world painted with bold strokes and in achingly painful detail. When Jeanne kills Paul at the end and then practices what she'll tell the cops (that she has no idea who he is), does she do it to free him? Does she do it for herself? Can she really not handle their relationship on a realistic level? Is Paul a sacrifice so that she can be happy in her new life? Or is she just setting herself up for a life inside a world of secrets like the kind that Paul's wife lived in (which ended in tragedy)? Who knows? Maybe Paul deserves to die. Maybe this movie is so indefensibly pretentious and full of itself that I shouldn't even be talking about it. But this comes from a period in my life when I had the patience for bleakly passionate shit like this. What can I say?

Richard Glenn Schmidt

Ricky Horror Science Fiction Picture Show

At some point in one's childhood, one either stops being nerdy -and goes boogie boarding or learns to enjoy beer- or one just gets nerdier and rents Evil Dead II (1987) for the fifth time and watches it alone again. As you can see, I chose the latter and I'll never recover. What I find interesting is that I could have become a total comic book nerd or a sci-fi nerd or a horror movie nerd or an RPG nerd. I had enough nerd points gathered for any of those nerdy categories. For some reason (which I have explored thoroughly), horror won out. Science fiction was the easiest genre for me to give up on but there are so many fun things that made my friggin' head explode with their bizarre ideas, insane plotlines, and/or total cheese.

All of the movies I'm going to blab about have a common thread, each have mated with multiple genres in order to reach multiple markets. The most common genre blended with science fiction in the following is action. Horror likes to sneak in there once in a while but mostly, action seems to be the easiest of sci-fi's bedfellows. Like most horror children of the 80s, I think my sci-fi-ness really got started with something as obvious as Alien (1979) and then several years later with Aliens (1986). But there were other things that influenced me as well. I'm starting to realize that my voyage through science fiction was a doomed one from the start.

I remember a strange show that came on after "Monty Python's Flying Circus". It was called "Doctor Who" and the theme song scared the hell out of me. All I remember about the show was a cheesy looking robot walking on (what I thought was) the surface of Mars and a guy with crazy hair who dressed like a British schoolboy. There was "Buck Rogers in the 25th Century" but all I remember from that is BEE TEE BEE TEE BEE TEE BEE TEE BEE TEE BEE TEE BEE TEE. And what kid didn't watch the original "Battlestar Galactica" and revel in the tedium? Down, Muffit, down! Bad dog!

As for science fiction movies, I guess I'll start with The Black Hole (1979). I remember seeing this movie at a very young age and being amazed, terrified, and immensely bored all at the same time. My mom bought me the toys for V.I.N. CENT and Maximilian. They mixed very well with my Star Wars toys. A few years later, I would attempt the same cohabi-toy-tion between my G.I. Joes, He-Man toys, and a Tupperware container full of Legos that failed big time.

Another science fiction film I remember seeing at a very young age (that wasn't Star Wars or Flash Gordon (oh, that theme song)) was a freaky little number called Android (1982). I couldn't sleep one night so I snuck out of bed and put on HBO just in time to catch the opening credits. What awaited me is a nihilistic and perverted little film starring Don Keith Opper as Max 404, an android who just wants to love (or kill if he doesn't get to love, whatever) and Klaus Kinski as Dr. Daniel, Max's creator as well as a total dick. Some space pirates show up, take control of the space lab, and things end pretty badly for everyone involved. There are sexual situations, awkward android emoting (or lack of emoting), and a genuinely depressing atmosphere that hangs over the entire movie. SPOILER: Max gets his own love droid. Isn't that cute? No, it's creepy and fucked up! Of course, vastly important things like Blade Runner (1982) and Planet of the Apes (1968) - when some network started playing all 5 movies on TV incessantly- came along shortly after this and made me even more afraid of the future. Android made me afraid of people. And androids. And Klaus Kinski, who is neither.

Recently, I remembered Eliminators (1986)! When I saw that amazing poster art staring back at me on my computer screen, I jumped for joy (while remaining completely still in my seat). This silly ass movie has cyborgs, a team of mercenaries, a ninja, and a time machine. What more could a kid want from filmic entertainments? I loved this movie when I first witnessed it 24 years ago. But the funny thing about Eliminators is that I rented the tape again a few weeks later and couldn't sit through it. Not even an almost boob shot from Denise Crosby could hold my interest the second time around. Now that I have a copy of it again, I'll be able to judge it properly.

A year or so after the amazing Robocop entered my life, I got to see Cyborg (1989). My parents and I were staying at a fancy hotel for another Tupperware convention and I was allowed to stay up late and watch Cyborg on the Pay-Per-View thingie. While my parents slept, I sat at the edge of our beds in complete darkness and had my mind torn in half by the awesomeness of Jean-Claude Van Damme. Now keep in mind that I was only 12 when this happened and please take pity on how lame I was (am). While I can't confirm this (as I haven't watched this film in a very long time), I swear there was some brief nudity in Cyborg. I remember some boobs flashing and I was like "OH SHIT, LADY BOBBINS!" Anyway, I friggin' loved this movie and I'm kind of scared to watch it again for fear of it turning out to be a complete piece of shit. Update: I have this on Blu-ray now, and it's still fun as all heck.

Uh oh, I'm getting a little loopy now. Two movies that will be forever entangled in my mind are Trancers (1984) and Nemesis (1992) from the same guy who directed Cyborg. Even though they were released 7 years apart, I saw them both around the same time and it just gets confusing. Both films have phenomenal cover art and they both have Tim Thomerson! These are great films but I can barely remember them. I know they are both better than Slipstream (1989) with Mark Hamill and Bill Paxton. That movie is about wind but it also features an android. There's always Hardware (1990), a movie that is so friggin' disturbing that they needed the music of Ministry mixed with video footage of Gwar (as if either of those bands aren't scary enough on their own). I seem to remember a long sex scene and a perverted fat guy peeping tom watching through the wall. Then a robot designed to kill humans reassembles itself and starts fucking shit up. Unfortunately, I remember Enemy Mine (1985) all too well. Not that it isn't a great film or anything but it was on cable CONSTANTLY. A film like that loses its power after you've seen it 900 times on cable.

There were some also horrible disappointments that helped steer me away from the genre for years. Did you ever see I Come in Peace (1990)? It answers the age old question: "How could anything with Dolph Lundgren be bad?" For some reason, I forgot to mention Robot Jox (1989). Oh wait, I remember why. It sucks! Poor Stuart Gordon went from Re-Animator (1985) and From Beyond (1986) to friggin' Robot Jox? It's an unbelievably annoying movie despite being ahead of its time. The western world just wasn't ready for live action mecha just yet. I had just gotten over mourning the death of my happy thoughts thanks to The Adventures of Buckaroo Banzai Across the 8th Dimension (1984). That baffling and stupid (now cultish) movie answers the age old question: "How could anything with Peter Weller be bad?" I'm not even going to go into The Ice Pirates (1984) or Megaforce (1982).

Skinemax Nights

I really don't know how I can talk about Single White Female (1992) without first talking about the Playboy channel and a bunch of other bullshit. My parents went all out with the cable back in 1995 and so we had every dang movie channel and the stupid Playboy channel. Of course, this was before there were 18 HBOs and 50 Showtimes but hey, we were living the good life. I've always been obsessed with the bizarre shit that cable channels used to fill their late night programming and I was sometimes richly rewarded (Wicked City) or sometimes horribly destroyed (Mask of Death (1996)). I probably shouldn't just hint at the amazing cinema of Lorenzo Lamas. The guy was in Terminal Justice (also 1996), probably the best movie cable television has ever transmitted. The story involved those oh so important elements that make our lives in the future -the film takes place in 2008- tolerable: gratuitous nudity and virtual reality.

The Playboy channel was (and probably still is) friggin' genius IN A BAD WAY. They had a talk show called "Night Calls" about sex that was completely bogus and pandering to sex-starved morons. The most hilarious thing was when they would show porno movies and then cut out the bits that made them pornos. The forbidden and magical channel of my youth turned out to be a bunch of silicone crap and a complete waste of time. My mom still accuses me being "a real sneak" about watching Playboy back in the day but I'm pretty sure I didn't care if she knew. The few occasions where I actually had friends over and my folks were out late or out of town, I'd put on the Playboy channel for a laugh. I was quite the entertainer. I eventually fled from Playboy to see what was on HBO, Cinemax, and Showtime. And oh boy, there were some surprises, yessireebob.

This all begins to make more sense when you take into account the fact that I worked the night shift as a security guard back in the day. Sometimes I worked 10pm until 6am but most of the time I worked from 6:30pm 'til 6:30am! Needless to say, on my days off I would stay up very, very late. The graveyard shift affects your mind and you don't see the world as other people do. Things that would not normally entertain anyone suddenly become strangely fascinating. Like The Doom Generation (1995) or Full Eclipse (1993). Don't forget that I'm also a dude so of course when my friend Scott and I saw they were going to play Malicious (1995) with Molly Ringwald, we were pretty psyched. You know the movie? The one where she plays a psycho and gets nekkid. Well, we just had to check it out. The only embarrassing thing about that is I actually liked the movie. Go Molly! Go Molly! It's (actually not) your birthday!

One of my favorite films from this sleazy time in my life was Poison Ivy: The New Seduction (1997). Now I don't mean to diss Drew Barrymore or Alyssa Milano's finest performances in the first two films but seriously,

Poison Ivy III is awe-inspiringly stupid and totally genius. Obviously, Jaime Pressly is totally awesome as Violet (the sister of Ivy!) but this movie, written by the mind behind The Skateboard Kid II (1995), is wildly entertaining and only slightly insulting. The most surprising thing is the person who steals the movie: Megan Edwards. She plays Joy, a tennis playing, uptight, and sheltered rich girl. Violet comes in and wrecks her life. Why? Because she's a friggin' psycho, that's why! But Joy is such a great character. She's kind of like this oppressed gothic heroine. And those tennis outfits! Oh my goodness. Terrible shit just keeps happening to her and finally, she's left all alone in the world which is better than how she started. The film just stops with her running out of the house with dead bodies all over the place. Perfect. I imagined myself there, in the driveway (in my 1976 Ford Granada), just waiting to rescue her.

Shit, I was just thinking about the films that nearly ruined dirty movies for everyone everywhere, all over the world. Of course, the most offensive (and not in a good way) is Basic Instinct (1992). Thankfully, Stephen Chow parodied it in Fight Back to School III (1993). Then there's the wretched Body of Evidence and The Temp (both 1993). These movies are so darn soul-destroying. Oh no, I just remembered Jade (1995). William Friedkin was quoted as saying, "Hee hee hee hee, I made a sexy thriller!" Did you know that there was a time when David Caruso was kina awesome?

You could take Jade and -before throwing the DVD in the garbage- make it a double feature with The Last Seduction (1994). I think I just died a little. Poor little Linda Fiorentino wouldn't properly recover until Kicked in the Head. Go figure. Of course, The Last Seduction has Peter Berg. I don't trust that guy. He totally creeps me out. Plus, he directed Friday Night Lights (2004). Lame.

Okay, so I'm talking about these corny ass adult thrillers, right? Are there any good ones? Well, yeah. More Skinemax filler comes in the form of Romeo is Bleeding (1993) -not to be confused with Romeo Must Die (2000)- but this one blows all the bullshit out of the water. The fact that it comes from director Peter Medak (The Changeling (1980)) might have a little to do with that. And when you get a classy duder like Gary Oldman (don't mention Lost in Space (1998), please) and the stunning and frightening Lena Olin, you got yourself a winning combination. Throw in some neo-noir stuff, a very, very dark story, some amputee fetishism, and whammo! Instant classic!

Have I talked about Single White Female yet? No? Well, I'm going to. Right now. It is hard to imagine a trashier or more ridiculous film than this Bridget Fonda/Jennifer Jason Leigh vehicle. Have either of them ever been in a movie better than SWF? No? I didn't think so. To illustrate how evil Jennifer Jason Leigh's character is, they have her kill a puppy! Like, whoa dude, that's foreshadowing. There's a shower scene and legitimately steamy sex scenes and murders and a gay neighbor and- DAMN IT! That puppy scene is still disturbing even after all these years. Being a guy, I tried to imagine what I would do if crazy Jennifer Jason Leigh was my roommate. Like how far would I let her crazy behavior go on before I was all like "Hey look, this isn't working out. You need to stop dressing like me." But then again, who doesn't want to have sex with themselves? Right? Who's a doppelganger banger? Doppelbanger? Hello? Uh oh. The important thing is that of course, I knew I was the one who could save poor old crazy Jennifer Jason Leigh from herself. Isn't that romantic? SHE KILLED A PUPPY!

Repo Man Sauce

One lazy summer day, my plans fell through. Take my hand and mourn with me! You see, I was 16 years old and I had failed my driving test (a huge blow to my gigantic ego) so I was pretty much stuck. I might as well have been 12 years old in my worthlessness (as you'll soon see). It feels so wrong not being able to do jack squat on a Saturday when your buds are out doing God knows what and giggling maniacally at the very mention of your name. Friend 1: "Should we call Dicky?" Friend 2: "Har har, that's a larf. Let that loser soak in his own loser juices until Hell freezes over." Wow, some friends! Am I right or am I right? Paranoid delusions aside, I was having a pretty lame day.

I tried but couldn't sleep in. I called my friend who was to be my ride to whatever event was going on that day and found out about the cancellation. I called some other friends that I couldn't reach (no cell phone in 1993, y'all). I found out there was no food in the house. I called my mom to see what she was up to and found out she wasn't going to be home until later that night. My dad had been dead a month or two so his ghost was kind of lingering around the place but was no help whatsoever. Oh yeah, one more thing: I had stupidly dumped my girlfriend a few weeks before but don't think I wasn't tempted to call her to try and patch things up (at least so I could get a ride somewhere).

So I did what any lame-brained teenager would do. I poured some Ragu pasta sauce into a bowl, heated it up in the microwave, threw in some chunks of cheddar cheese, and ate it with a spoon. Sounds delicious, right? Well, I thought it was. See, there was no macaroni and cheese in the house so I didn't really know what to do with all that pasta. To give you an idea of how dumb I was, I had no idea how to prepare pasta for myself. Macaroni and cheese? No problem! You boil the macaroni and then add the sauce. Simple. But what about pasta? How does that shit get magically transformed from its hard form into its soft form? I shit you not, dear reader, I had no clue.

So I turned on the TV and there was a movie called Repo Man (1984) about to start on TV. To this day, I can't remember what channel was showing it. It may have been TNT or something. It was definitely a channel that edited out cursing, that's for sure. But anyway, I had never heard of this movie before so I just left it on. Suddenly, the punk rock credits kick in and I was glued to the spot. In the desert, a cop pulls over a guy named J. Frank Parnell driving a 1964 Chevy Malibu. The man is singing to himself and is almost totally oblivious to this cop's presence. The cop knocks on the window and asks to see what's in the trunk. J. Frank Parnell says "Oh, you don't want to look in there." The cop takes the keys and walks around to the back of the car. As he opens the trunk, J. Frank Parnell's eye, reflected in the rear view mirror, widens with anticipation. The cop is instantly vaporized. The car speeds away leaving only the cop's smoking boots and his lonely motorcycle behind.

That's how Repo Man begins. Basically, every scene will knock your socks off. This is what I discovered, eating spaghetti sauce and cheddar cheese. I can't imagine a better film for a boring Saturday morning. Nearly every frame of this movie is hilarious, quotable, and just supremely awesome. Since then, I have watched this film more times than I can remember and can quote pretty much every line for you, if you'd like. No? Okay, I won't. "You wanna be a hero or rather be a chicken-man? You ever see a farmer's wife?"

Okay, the movie is actually about a loser punk named Otto (Emilio Estevez) who is full of angst and can't hold a job to save his life. After his "best friend" steals his girlfriend from him at a party, Otto goes on an all-night drinking binge. While walking home the next morning, he is approached by Bud (Harry Dean Stanton), a repo man who tricks Otto into helping him repossess a car. At that very moment, he is hired by the "Helping Hand Acceptance Corporation", a sleazy repo outfit. Otto quickly discovers that the life of a repo man is a dangerous one. He gets a new girlfriend, Leila (Olivia Barash), a member of UFO (United Fruitcake Outlet) who is desperately searching for some proof of life from outer space.

When word comes down that there is a Chevy Malibu worth $25,000, every repo man in the city and various government agencies goes after it. What's with this mysterious car? Are there decomposing aliens in the trunk? Is that a crazed scientist behind the wheel? This is Repo Man and it's all you ever needed to know about the 1980s.

Obviously, Repo Man made me aware of both Harry Dean Stanton and Tracey Walter, two gentlemen who rule the Earth as brilliant character actors, but the film's other major accomplishment is introducing me to the amazing Fox Harris as J. Frank Parnell, the man with the aliens in his trunk, inventor of the neutron bomb, and victim of a botched lobotomy. I tell ya, this actor is so over the top in his scenes that you can almost feel him burning right through your fucking television. Harris made a few appearances in some pretty decent B movies and just about every one of those appearances is totally unforgettable. The guy died in 1988 and his picture can be seen next to the term "underutilized" in the dictionary. He did get his chance to shine in the totally bonkers Dr. Caligari (1989) and the obscure horror anthology Dark Romances (1990).

So what did I learn on that fateful Saturday? I learned that eating nothing but pasta sauce for an entire day can give you massive amounts of life-altering heartburn. I learned that Ecco the Dolphin gets way too difficult after a while, so just give up. I learned that life is long and boring

Richard Glenn Schmidt

and that Repo Man will only get you through 90 minutes of it (or 2 hours if it's on network TV). I eventually bought the movie on VHS and played it for everyone who would sit still long enough to enjoy it.

    A few years later, I dated a girl whose family ran a repo lot. The first night hanging out with her and her folks, her mom asked me if I had ever seen Repo Man. I, of course, said yes and they didn't believe me! Well, after I telegraphed the dialogue for the first 10 minutes of the film, they conceded that I did indeed have proficient knowledge of Emilio Estevez's finest work. Somehow, that nerdy act got me the girl and even earned the respect of her family. How many times has a movie done that for you?

Richard Glenn Schmidt

The Hills Have Eyes Part II Made Me Puke!

It shouldn't surprise the average horror fan that a film as pitiful and lame as The Hills Have Eyes Part II could inspire me to a very long night of reverse peristalsis. Other than that friggin' awesome cover art, THHEP2 totally sucks. But in Wes Craven's defense, his ill-conceived coke binge in the desert (that's just my speculation on how this POS came to be), isn't the only thing behind one of the most nauseating nights of my life.

It was a Saturday evening in my tenth year of life and my TV promised me some scary delights with The Hills Have Eyes Part II. My parents ordered pizza from my favorite place in town. This was Peachtree City, Georgia, by the way, and the quality of pizza available was probably not what one would call "gourmet". This particular pizza place (whose name I can't recall; though I doubt it was one of the majors) had pretty strange pizza. The cheese always looked like it had melted and set several days before its arrival at our front door. The sauce was strangely tangy and very, very salty. While I beheld the non-magic of THHEPII, I gorged myself on this stuff (pepperoni to be precise).

Then I noticed that something was wrong. That dizzy feeling which I had mistaken as hunger wasn't going away. It was getting worse. I stopped in mid-chewing to run to the bathroom and puke my guts out. I stayed in the bathroom for a while. Once I was sure I was empty, I brushed my teeth and staggered out to the living room. My mom threw a blanket around me and I laid out on the couch. Lucky for me, THHEPII was still on! Thank you, commercial breaks.

So I'm lying there, in a flu-inspired fever and still rather nauseous, and trying to make some sense out of this fucking lame ass movie. The film is still a blur to me. I remember some traps, some hill people, motorbikes, and a dog. One could argue that I should probably watch this film again without the extenuating circumstances of pizza vomit and raging fever but really, who gives a shit? Deep down in my heart, I know that The Hills Have Eyes Part II blows. So what?

Bad Drugs, Bad Zombies, & Bad Pesticide: Toxic Zombies

A shady government agent and his crony decide to wipe out some marijuana growers by dusting them and their crops with an untested herbicide. This turns the dirty hippies into bloodthirsty and fleshhungry (okay, how is that not a word? WTF?) zombies who go on a rampage. It's up to one fish and game inspector named Tom (played by Charles McCrann) to um... well, I was going to say "save the day" but really Tom was just going fishing with his wife Polly (Beverly Shapiro) and kooky brother and happened to be there when all those mellows got harshed.

In the same movie, a very special young man named Jimmy (Kevin Hanlon) and his sister Amy (Judith Brown) are orphaned when their parents get all kinds of devoured by the zombie horde (there's like 4 of them). Tom and Polly rescue the "kids" from danger thus endangering themselves and there's lots and lots of running around in the woods. The four of them take shelter in a shack in the woods filled with a crazy loner named "Hermit" (Dennis Helfend) but things go awry when the zombies miraculously learn how to light torches and bring on the siege. Do I have to go on? Blah blah blah, everyone is killed except for some people who aren't.

My dogged pursuit of every single darn film from my formative years has led me to another dud. While Toxic Zombies (1980) isn't all bad, but I have to wonder what kind of super perfect attention span I had back in the day because this movie has too many of those dangling (and hope-murdering) plot points to fill out its running time. This flick also has too many characters which are introduced very quickly and are given time to speak their thoughts aloud because the writer doesn't trust the viewers to figure out what the fuck is going for on themselves.

I first encountered Toxic Zombies on TV one Saturday afternoon and I think it was followed by the absolutely wretched, The Loch Ness Horror (1981), when I was probably pretty young. I saw this shambling zombie mess shortly after I'd seen Night of the Living Dead (1968) but years before I caught Dawn of the Dead (1978). And despite my difficulty sitting through this film now (horrible head cold notwithstanding), I can see why this little indie zombie flick stayed in the back of my head all these years. The gore is pretty wet in some places (they cut almost nothing for TV) and the overall mood is surprisingly bleak.

Well, the hammy performances do illicit some laughs and I was particularly charmed by Beverly Shapiro as Polly, the whiniest human female ever captured on film. I feel slightly different about the somewhat less enigmatic Judith Brown as Amy or as I call her "The Amy". While this helluva strangely alluring old teenager is out looking out for her very special brother, I just can't seem to take my eyes off of her. Director Charles McCrann gave each of these lovely ladies plenty of screentime and saved the movie. Toxic Zombies is no lost classic, that's for sure. It's got that Super 16 charm, plenty of cheap gore (nothing over the top or anything), a cheapjack piano and synthesizer heavy score, and a little nudity. I love this film's alternate title, Bloodeaters.

"This is Horror" Redux

MTV aired a series called "This is Horror" (AKA "Stephen King's World of Horror") back in 1989, and it could be responsible for my development into the freakish man that I am today. Had it not been for this collection of interviews and gruesome clips, I may never have developed my Linnea Quigley fixation and pursued Night of the Demons and Sorority Babes in the Slimeball Bowl-O-Rama (both 1988) so doggedly. I was also introduced to the world of Sam Raimi. After watching the segment on the Evil Dead series, I immediately went out and talked my parents into renting Evil Dead (1981) and its first sequel. Then I proceeded to watch Evil Dead II (1987) about 5 times. Luckily, they didn't watch them with me or my horror smorgasbord would have been over before it started.

"This is Horror" was a rallying cry to horror fans. It confirmed what my 12 year old brain already loved about the genre and it opened my eyes to an entire universe of insanely sick and creepy stuff. Unfortunately, this series has been neglected by the DVD age so far. Some kind souls have placed 4 episodes on YouTube but it's hard to track down on home video.

I can't stress how important "This is Horror" was to my burgeoning horror movie fandom. This show was stretched out over several Saturday nights on MTV (it was on before "Headbangers Ball" if I recall correctly). My curiosity about the genre had already been stoked by Elvira, Mistress of the Dark, Commander USA, Jason, and Freddy but "This is Horror" gave me some direction. The next time I was at the video store (Video-X-Tron had already been bought out by Blockbuster by then but they still had a good selection), I beheld the horror aisle and I made the proclamation that I would watch every single horror movie in the store.

Most irritatingly, I still haven't found the entire series yet. Apparently, it was on Japanese laserdisc at one point but all I have right now is this one VHS tape ("This is Horror Archive I" according to the cover). First things first, the whole description on the back of the box is bullshit. To be fair, the description might be for the entire series but the person buying this single tape is in for something slightly different.

I'm shocked by how much Dario Argento is on this tape. Most (if not all) of the footage of the "Italian Hitchcock" comes from the Michele Soavi directed documentary, Dario Argento's World of Horror (1985). This is quite interesting for me because it seems as though this may have been the impetus for me to seek out old Dario. So this show might have been why I marched into the video store and demanded me some Creepers.

There's some talk with director Brian Yuzna and special effects designer Steve Johnson. There's lots of good stuff here. I'm glad that films of my youth, like the very disturbing Society (1989) and the very fun Dead Heat

(1988) were mentioned. There's a weak and rather half-assed section on vampire movies. They show clips from Vampyres (1974) which was very surprising (never found that one on VHS as a kid!), the comedic vampire scenes from The House that Dripped Blood (1971), and friggin' Vamp (1986) which I remember renting but still can't remember anything about.

And that pretty much sums up what's on the tape. I finally got a little tiny slice of what was an extremely influential part of my growing up. All of this took place in Jupiter, Florida so you can imagine how important having a world of fantasy to escape to was for me at the time. I wasn't what you might call a "popular kid" (does that shock you?) so many of my weekends were spent alone in front of the TV with the VCR buzzing away. Horror movies were my best buds, and they continue to warm my heart even after all these years.

Update: I've been watching the episodes on good old YouTube and I've got to say, Stephen King in this era is annoying as balls. You can tell that he was just goofing off and very likely being interviewed for something else when the footage was cut up and interspersed throughout this series. His segments couldn't be short enough for me.

A bearded Lloyd Kaufman pops up to talk up all things Troma Entertainment which is probably how I ended pursuing both The Toxic Avenger (1984) and Class of Nuke 'Em High (1986). Funnily enough, an extended clip from Blood Simple (1984) did not encourage me to seek out the Coen Brothers' feature film debut. My obsession with Hellraiser (1987) and Hellbound: Hellraiser II (1988) most certainly got started here and a ton of time is devoted to those two films!

Richard Glenn Schmidt

G.I. Joe: The Movie and the S-Word

When I was a kid, I played with toys. Pretty freaky, huh? I had Transformers, He-Man (is the plural of that He-Men?), Star Wars, and Legos. I guess it's pretty obvious that I was a spoiled kid. How else would I have grown into this adult-sized man-baby that you see before you today? But back in the day, nothing came close to the fury and obsession over G.I. Joe that gripped me from age 9 through age 12 (when I stopped playing with toys altogether).

After having my brain melted by the amazing Transformers: The Movie (1986), rumors of G.I. Joe: The Movie (1987) were putting me right up to the edge of heart palpitations. But luck was not be in my favor as the film was never released in theaters. I had to wait until it came out on VHS before I would get to see it.

Having no idea when it was supposed to come out, I was surprised as hell to see it on the "New Releases" shelf one night while my dad and I were at the video store. I remember that my mom was out of town on business so I was legit disappointed that she was going to miss the movie! Yeah, my excitement for G.I. Joe at the time was so insane that I often forced my parents into partaking of such things.

Dad and I had dinner and I put the tape on. Less than 5 minutes into the movie, my dad bailed. He said he was going to read a book or watch a game on the other TV or something. I was shocked. How could anyone walk away from my most anticipated film of all time (that month)? So anyway, I got back to the movie and... and... Honestly, I was disappointed.

In fact, I barely remember G.I. Joe: The Movie at all save for two things. One of them is someone said "shit" which blew my mind. I had never heard someone curse in a cartoon before (maybe a robot said "shit" in Transformers: The Movie?). I was so glad that my mom was out of town because she probably would have been mad if she had heard it. My dad was a bit more lenient but I paused the movie when it happened and looked over my shoulder just to make sure he wasn't in the room.

The second thing is actually pretty horrifying and to this day, pops into my head randomly. For reasons that I can't remember, Cobra Commander gets turned into a snake. As he slowly devolves into a creature, he keeps hissing "I was once a man! I wassss once-ssss a man!" This completely freaked me out and actually made me feel bad for Cobra's charismatic leader. Okay, this is as far as I can go without actually re-watching G.I. Joe: The Movie. Hold on. Let me go watch it.

Hi, I'm back! Well, sadly, one thing didn't change, I'm still disappointed in G.I. Joe: The Movie. The story (which loses steam way before its conclusion) is that during a battle in the Artic, the forces of Cobra retreat into a strange oasis filled with an ancient race known as Cobra-La. These creatures are plotting to take over the world by launching spores into the atmosphere that will mutate mankind into anamorphic cavemen or something. G.I. Joe decides to stop them. There's more to this but I want to get the hell out of here while I still can.

I do like how the movie added even more elements of science fiction, fantasy, and even a little more horror to the Joe universe. Anyone familiar with the TV series can tell you about some wacky and totally fucked up episodes. I even like how we get a brief glimpse of Cobra Commander's face shortly before he turns into a wiggly reptile. And there was blood spilled when Duke gets injured. You never saw that in the show even with all the grenades, missiles, ninja sword-fighting, and laser blasts. As for someone saying "Shit" in the dialog this time, I think it was edited out. Maybe I'm thinking of Transformers: The Movie. Is this the nerdiest thing I've ever talked about? No, probably just the laziest.

What is surprising is how much anime is packed into this film. Back in the day, anime or Japanimation (as some used to call it) was so scarce that every tiny bit of it was special. I think G.I. Joe: The Movie subconsciously planted an insidious anime parasite in my brain that would grow and eventually destroy everything in my head. Don't believe me? Look at the frickin' crew on this film (which was listed hilariously under its UK title Action Force: The Movie on IMDB for a while there).

Cutie Honey, One Piece: The Movie, Fist of the North Star (series 2), Dragon Ball Z, Sailor Moon: The Movie, Galaxy Express 999, Final Yamamoto, Mobile Suit Gundam, several Mazinger movies, Full Metal Alchemist, Saint Seiya, etc. are just a few of the titles that the Japanese members of this crew had their hands in over the years. Their influence on the look of this film and even some of the plot elements are impossible to ignore. Don't get me wrong, a huge crew from the US and other countries were instrumental in bringing this film to life but yeah, it's films like this that helped make me an anime fan for life.

Richard Glenn Schmidt

Why I'm So Messed Up: Laughter in the Dark

One day in the late 1990s, I was reading a book written by Vladimir Nabokov in 1932 called Laughter in the Dark. That isn't really special. If it was the late 1990s, I was either reading Henry Miller, Nabokov, or the wildly underrated Heinrich Böll. Anyway, as I got to the end of the book, I had a massive wave of déjà vu when the amazing climax started to unfold. Sometime as a kid, I had seen the film adaption of Laughter in the Dark on cable and that ending had been buried deep in my brain just waiting for me to remember it.

Years later, I found the listing for the film version of Laughter in the Dark that was directed by Tony Richardson and was released in 1969. Finding the film proved to be another matter entirely. Forget DVD, I couldn't even track down a damn VHS copy. Then I turned to my usual sites for a download. Nothing. Son of a bitch! Other than some lobby cards and a poster, I couldn't find the film.

Now here's where complaining online helps. (I've been an advocate of online complaining since the first time I did it back in 1998.) I blogged right here on this very blog about how I couldn't find Laughter in the Dark. Then, in the summer of last year, someone read my post and contacted me. It was Rand C. He offered to send me a copy of the film if I promised to review it. Of course, I said yes. What Rand didn't know is that when I'm really excited about a film, I put it off. And since I'd been looking for this film since the end of the last century, my excitement was so huge that I didn't watch Laughter in the Dark for 6 months. What can I say? I'm quirky.

Nicol Williamson plays Sir Edward More, a wealthy art dealer who is bored with his family and work. One day, a female usher named Margot (Anna Karina) catches his eye at the cinema. He becomes obsessed with the beautiful young woman and attempts to woo her while using an assumed name. Margot reverse-stalks Edward once she catches sight of his fancy car and chauffeur. Edward was hoping for an easy lay but Margot has got plans for this fool. With a well-timed telegram and a three day sex binge, she destroys his marriage and invades his life.

Unfortunately for Edward, Margot proves to be impossible to please and she's quickly seduced by his colleague Herve (Jean-Claude Drouot), a much younger and more dashing fellow. Margot convinces Edward that Herve is gay and encourages him to include the rogue on their vacation in Spain. When he finally catches on to the affair, Edward goes ballistic and demands that she never see Herve again. While driving through some mountain roads, he and Margot's arguing causes a car accident that leaves Edward blind.

Margot and Herve concoct a scheme to bleed Edward dry while

continuing their affair. She rents a remote villa with a secret room where Herve will live and where they can get it on at night. As weeks go by, the embezzlement of Edward's money continues as she has the poor bastard signing blank checks. Worse still, Herve begins to get stir crazy to keep their twisted game going and plays tricks on the blind man for amusement. The cruelty escalates and -don't worry, I won't spoil it!

Director Tony Richardson was no stranger to adapting literature for the big screen but there's two things working against him. 1. Vladimir Nabokov's characters are total dickheads and 2. Richard Burton was an alcoholic. Burton was fired for being too drunk to work and was replaced by Nicol Williamson after filming had begun. Williamson, who's played everyone from Merlin to Hamlet to Sherlock frickin' Holmes is a fine actor and does a great job here. But man oh man, his character is hard to sympathize with, especially with the word "SUCKER" tattooed on his forehead like that.

Transplanting Nabokov's novel from 1930s Berlin and Switzerland to 1960s England and Spain is easy when you throw miniskirts, hippies, inflatable furniture, and cacti into the mix. Cinematographer Dick Bush (Tommy, Sorcerer) brings some serious talent to the table which makes the fact that this film hasn't landed on Blu-ray yet even more frustrating. I love the setting in the Spanish mountains in the latter bits of the film. I kept waiting for Paul Naschy to show up and wolf out.

I think the film would have been served better if Margot hadn't been such a blatantly manipulative jerkwad and been more sly and seductive to the viewer. Anna Karina is lovely but the moment she started whining, I wanted to shut the movie off. Edward too should have been more likable right out of the gate but if memory serves, the screenplay follows Nabokov's version of these characters pretty closely aside from making them British. But if all of the blame landed squarely on the handsome but devious Herve, it would hurt the film. These three assholes kind of deserve each other.

How does the old saying go? "A fool and his money are soon parted shortly before that fool is destroyed by the brazen malice of two psychopaths." Edward's treatment at the hands of Margot and especially Herve is heartbreaking. Even if you despise the guy for his simpering foolishness, you still root for him by the final reel.

Before we get to the finale, let me just talk about how Laughter in the Dark affected me. There's a cool scene right at the beginning of the film where Edward is at the cinema. The film that the packed house is viewing is never shown but the sounds of a woman in peril and gunfire can be heard through the theater. These sounds cause uproarious laughter in the audience and Edward looks rather disturbed for a moment. Then he lays eyes on Margot for the first time. This brilliant piece of foreshadowing is how I knew I was in for a treat even though it would be a painful one.

When this film ended the other day after seeing it for the first time after all those years, I was left with a profound sense of dread and a renewed fear of human beings. Though it's not as good as the book, I think Laughter in the Dark absolutely deserves to be seen by film fans and Nabokov fans alike. The ending is a real crackerjack of a scene that I won't spoil here since this film is still unavailable on home video and I'm hoping people will seek it out. It occurred to me that maybe I only caught the end of this one when I was a kid. But it's entirely possible that I saw this whole movie which explains why I'm so messed up.

Movie Memory Mining

While I continue to mine the depths of my memory (without leaving any reliable support beams or adhere to any safety regulations as I go), it dawned on me to try and recall what my very first memories of watching movies are. The first film that I have a very tenuous memory of catching in theater is The Empire Strikes Back (1980). Since I was only four when that film was first released, it was likely during its 1981 or 1982 re-release. This sticks out for me because I remember being really confused how the empire was able to reattach Darth Vader's head after Luke cut it off. This plot confusion didn't get cleared up for many more years than I'd like to admit.

I asked my mom if she remembers taking me to this film. All she recalls is something loud and scary happening. I was much too young to have seen Star Wars (1977) in the theater but my parents got me The Story of Star Wars record which I listened to constantly. I remember very distinctly getting to see The Return of the Jedi (1983) in the theater because this was when my ravenous collecting of Star Wars toys was in high gear but I'm getting ahead of myself.

Now I can't confirm the following but I believe that my family enjoyed cable television while I was little lad in Montana. I asked both my mom and my sister Lora about when we got cable and they don't remember. Lora says it was probably after my folks had an addition added to the house which was where our den was located. Why am I harassing my family with this asinine bullshit? It's called book research, y'all!

The first movies I remember watching were Popeye (1980) and Clash of the Titans (1981). I don't know if HBO (or whatever channel or channels we had) still does this but when they had a new movie, they would play it all day long. So if memory serves (unlikely), I watched Popeye and Clash of the Titans over and over again all weekend long. I also remember that they played Hardware Wars (1978) and I laughed my head off after my dad explained to me why it was funny.

In the vein of things cinematically tragic, I was utterly freaked out by another short film called Recorded Live (1975) which is about film reels that come to life and devour a guy. This poor bastard shows up to a movie or TV studio looking for a job and dies horribly. This could be a metaphor for my social life and how it has been utterly decimated by my love of movies. Or it's about how I feel about showing up for work.

Robert Altman's Popeye is just grotesque and weird. I tried to sit through it once many years later but I was struck by how wrongheaded it seems to be. Maybe it captures the spirit of the original cartoon too well. What is the spirit of the old cartoon, you ask? Imagine if you cut open the rotting carcass of a bull, climbed inside, and did push-ups on your knuckles while listening to the 1812 Overture on 78rpm. That's how I feel about it.

So anyway, I have a feeling that if I put the 1980 film on right now, I might actually enjoy it just because it's so goddamned weird. Chances of me actually doing that are around 12%. Lora says that she definitely remembers watching Popeye around this time.

Leave it to something as silly as Clash of the Titans to introduce me to the magic of Ray Harryhausen. Later, I'd have my mind blown by his work on the Sinbad movies but this epic 1981 um... epic was just what the doctor (I assume a pediatrician) ordered. My fondest memory of this film is the nighttime scene where Calibos sneaks into Perseus and his crew's camp in order to kill them. This sequence haunted me in the best way and is the closest thing to that European horror vibe that I love coming from a fantasy movie. I recently bought Clash on Blu-ray and haven't revisited it as of yet. However, I have been listening to Laurence Rosenthal's score while writing this. I've seen the 2010 remake but all I remember is that it wasn't terrible. Oh and Medusa was truly lame.

3 THE INVASIAN

Before I get started let me just say that I believe I have a pretty (un)healthy obsession with Asian horror films. As anyone who has noticed the path that Doomed Moviethon and Cinema Somnambulist has taken over the years, my focus has almost always been Italian horror, gialli, and slashers. Running pretty much parallel to that has been Asian horror though I've always had trouble articulating what it is that makes this stuff so great. I was astounded while putting this chapter together by just how much I've already seen. What was even more astounding —no, mindboggling- to me was discovering how I've only barely scratched the dang surface.

My love for Asian horror films began as generically as possible. It all started in 2002 with The Ring. And I'm not talking about the original either. I'm talking about Gore Verbinski's version of Ringu (1998). Mr. Pirates of the Caribbean himself and screenwriter Ehren Kruger were able to take a beautiful and frightening Japanese horror film and crank it up for American audiences. Some of the subtleties of the Japanese film were abandoned for us silly gaijin but the end result was well worth it.

While LeEtta and I were dating it was imperative that we go to the movies ALL THE TIME. Some couples get drunk together and some go boogie boarding. LeEtta and I went to the movies. Sure, we saw some terrible shit (I'm looking at you, Ballistic: Ecks vs. Sever) but The Ring was one that I did not want to miss. You see, I had no perspective on this film, other than "Hey, this looks interesting". All I knew about the film was from the TV trailers. You watch a cursed videotape and then you die 7 days later. Sounded like a pretty awesome urban legend type of flick, so we went. I had no idea it was a remake until a few days after I saw the film.

The horror bug, having been dormant since the 90s, was just about to awaken within me. So you see, I wasn't hip to anything just yet. I wasn't making my bimonthly trips to the bookstore for the newest issues of Rue Morgue, Videoscope, Shock Cinema, etc. just yet and I was only just beginning to check out some horror movie review sites (mostly for nostalgia's sake). This is funny to me now. I had absolutely no idea that I would be focusing practically all of my energy on horror movies very soon. The idea for Doomed Moviethon was still a couple of years away.

So anyway, LeEtta and I head to the theaters to check out The Ring. It was a packed house which is totally alien to me now. I never, ever go to the movies on a Friday or a Saturday night! Amateurs! So the movie starts and things start getting really scary really friggin' fast. The moment that had me climbing out of my seat was the dang horse scene on the ferry. Jeez!

I recently revisited this remake for the first time in nearly 8 years and I'll get into how it stacks up to the original as well as how I feel about it now later. Long story short (too late!), LeEtta and I were completely and utterly terrified while we clung to one another in the darkness of the theater. To add to the mayhem, pretty much everyone in the theater was screaming and freaking out. I don't care what anybody says, this is a scary ass movie. Verbinski took a great story, some haunting imagery, and altered what he needed to alter for American sensibilities. It certainly worked on us. I'll never forget when we went to bed that night, we could still see little Samara lurking in the dark corners of the room.

But wait, wasn't there something else? Oh yeah, I suppose horror anime did get to me first. The very first anime I ever purchased on VHS was the original Vampire Hunter D (1985) way back in 1994. I had purchased Appleseed (1988) that day for $35 and after discovering how horrible it was, I begged the guy at the comic shop (Past Present Future on Northlake Boulevard) to let me exchange it for something else. He agreed and out of sheer desperation, I grabbed Vampire Hunter D. I've never regretted that purchase. I encountered many horror anime series as the years went by but never once did it ever cross my mind that there might be horror movies from Asia. In my defense, I was also not actively pursuing horror movies at this time. I was all like "Evil Dead and Hellraiser are enough for me!" Silly fool. The world was out there just waiting for me.

My first Asian horror film proper was the splatter/sex/sci-fi epic Wicked City (1992). I had seen the anime years before but the live action version left me so gob smacked that I didn't even know what hit me. I thought it was just some fluke, some random Japanese freakout (yeah, I know it's a Hong Kong flick, forgive my ignorance). I was kind of dumb back then and not nearly curious enough!

Fast-forwarding back to 2002, my friend Nafa encouraged me to check out Kwaidan (1964) from the library and it was an amazing atmospheric masterpiece. I also managed to get my hands on a grubby copy of Kuroneko (1968) from the library as well. This chilling little tale is about a mother and daughter who are raped and murdered by a pack of travelling bandits. The two return from the grave to get their revenge on samurai who cross their path. Simply awesome.

While the waves of remakes like the disappointing The Ring Two (2005) and the unwatchable American version of Pulse (2006) were slowly starting to roll in, I was busting my hump to try and see as many Japanese horror films as possible. This was pretty frustrating and it was before Netflix; so in order to watch decent movies, I had to buy them unseen. Fun! In fact, this was just true for all fans of obscure movies for a long time. I hope all you young whippersnappers out there don't get all spoiled and shit with the sheer brilliance of Netflix and YouTube. Being able to get 90% of the awesome and weird crap that's out there sent to your mailbox (or watch on Internet thingies) is totally insane.

Things changed completely in such a serendipitous way that I can only call it a miracle. After work one evening, I decided to stop off a little videogame store (that used to be on over on 56th Street). They had a decent selection of games and even some anime for rent. On this particular day, I walked in and noticed that an entire section of the wall was dedicated to Asian freakin' horror movies! I wish there had been a camera recording my reaction because I'm sure it was pretty amusing. There were titles I had never heard of before. And there were Chinese DVDs! Wait a second, other countries besides Japan make horror movies too!?!?

It was then I met Steve of Unearthed Films. He was working the counter and was very patiently explaining to some neighborhood kids how the store's trade-in policy worked. I waited until he was done and then I exasperatedly erupted. I grilled him about how long had the store been carrying all these great titles, how long he'd been working there, etc. Thankfully, the poor guy didn't throw me out of the store right then and there. Instead, we shot the shit about horror movies for a while and I rented some films. I think I rented Ebola Syndrome (1996), and The Cat (1992) that time.

With that, I expanded my search to include Chinese horror films. Eventually, I would discover Korean, Thai, and Indonesian horror but first I got a taste of Category III (the Hong Kong equivalent to NC-17) films and the wild and dark territories that that leads to. Ebola Syndrome was the first and is still one of the most disturbing films I've ever had the happy displeasure of viewing. Other titles like Dr. Lamb (1992), The Untold Story (1993), Human Pork Chop (2001), Devil Fetus (1983), and its sequel in name only Devil Fetus 2: The Rape After (1984) have graced my eyes with their sleaziness and splatteriness. Steve also introduced me to the disturbing Battle Royale (2000) and the Evil Dead Trap movies.

In just a few short years, I think that Asian horror became overexposed and (most annoyingly) over-remade here in the States. It was impossible for horror fans not to get burnt out. I know that I started feeling the draw of European and Italian horror even stronger after that awful Pulse remake. Don't get me wrong, I liked The Grudge remake (2004) at first -weird I know but I just really wanted to like it for some reason- but it's nothing compared to the original. And like any genre, there's going to be mediocre and outright terrible shit that gets big promotion and cool artwork to mislead any unsuspecting horror fan.

I think the craziest thing is that I know I could just dedicate this entire book to Asian horror and be done with it. Would I ever run out of films? Hell no! And just for the record, I'm going to try very hard to just focus on places other than Japan and Hong Kong. It won't be easy but I think I can manage to give those two monstrously prolific horror hotspots some competition in this chapter.

So you, dear reader, are going to go on this journey with me. I always just assume that the immersion process will do all the work for me. Of course, I could be setting the stage for a magnificent failure but who cares? It's just movie watching, right? Bring me Asian horror; be it awesome, painfully mediocre, or just plain awful. I'm ready.

Pray (2005)

Two losers, Mitsuru and Maki (played by Tetsuji Tamayama and Asami Mizukawa) kidnap a little girl and take her to an abandoned school. When Maki calls the parents demanding the ransom money, they inform her that their daughter has been dead for over a year. But that's only the beginning as the school seems to be inhabited by a very angry and murderous spirit.

Pray is a weird one. The plot seems too simple at first but a couple of plot twists come along to help keep things popping. A generic story (even with the surprises) and leisurely pace don't help this film at all but it's just strange enough to be interesting. I'm glad the reviews I'd read beforehand were so awful. They inspired me to seek it out. (Reverse recommendations, y'all!)

While you won't have to strain your eyes, most of Pray is pretty murky; filmed in a dark location at night with mostly drab tones. It's almost a relief whenever someone flicks the dang lights on. Overacting from some of the cast and a schmaltzy passage near the end aren't going to win any points with anyone. But on the plus side, the ghostly action is fun and the soundtrack is eerie and suspenseful with some beautiful passages.

The Queen of Black Magic (1979)

A wedding party falls under a black magic curse. The bride has horrific visions and the entire ceremony is in shambles. The groom, Kohar, took Murni's virginity and then spurned her for his new woman. Now he accuses her of casting the curse upon his fiancé. Kohar encourages the villagers to capture Murni, set her mother on fire, and then throw her off a cliff. She is rescued from death by a witch doctor who teaches her the arts of black magic. Murni uses her newfound abilities to get vengeance on Kohar and the people who tried to destroy her.

The Queen of Black Magic has excellent direction and pacing. The movie flies by as we are treated to one wild scene after another. Somebody please, buy me this soundtrack! The score for The Queen of Black Magic is some wild synthesizer action mixed with a killer string section and awesome percussion.

"All men are traitors!"

Obviously not big on women's lib, Murni (played by the lovely Suzzanna) is first manipulated by the man she loves and then becomes a pawn of the evil sorcerer. Thankfully, Kohar, the unrepentant prick gets what he deserves. Permana, the holy man, comes preaching that prayer is the best defense against black magic and he's right. The ignorance of the villagers and their refusal to pray will spell out their doom.

The gore effects are simple but gruesome with some wicked splatter moments. One evil bastard is killed when giant blood-filled boils appear on his body and burst all over the place. Another choice scene comes when someone rips his own head off. The head starts flying around and bites a strip of flesh off the leader of the village. Frankly, it's brilliant.

This was my first foray into Indonesian horror and it won't be the last. The story reminded me of a 70s Shaw Brothers gore flick but more conservative like an Indian horror film (just without the musical numbers). Other than the crazy gore and Murni's wacky training montage, the most outlandish aspect of The Queen of Black Magic is a totally unnecessary melodramatic twist at the end that just makes the story a little more confusing and even a little stranger. Overall, this is a fun flick that folks with a taste for international horror will go bonkers for.

Art of the Devil (2004)

After her married lover gets her pregnant, dumps her, shares her with his buddies, and slaps her around, Kamala (Krongthong Rachatawan) turns to black magic to get revenge. After killing the dude and his family, she is further enraged when she discovers that the guy had kids with another woman and they are in line to inherit all of his wealth. To get her hands on the dough, Kamala marries her lover's illegitimate son Boom (Supakson Chaimongkol) and starts destroying the family, one member at a time. Only Boom's sister Nan (Arisa Wills) and a curious journalist (Somchai Satuthum) figure out what Kamala is up to but are they too late to stop her?

This Thai horror film doesn't really do the genre justice. While watchable and suitably gross, Art of the Devil didn't exactly blow me away. The biggest problems come from the stiff acting, uneven direction, and the generic plot. There are plusses for the film features some very cool moments that balance out the cheesy ones. And yes, there are some bloody, freaky, and nasty setpieces that must be seen to be believed.

The cast is led by two lovely ladies, Krongthong Rachatawan as the villainess and Arisa Wills as the heroine. Unfortunately, Nan is a shrill and dopey party girl character and kind of unlikeable. Kamala on the other hand, though flatly written, is 5 kinds of crazy. At least her reasons for revenge and her terrible greed are solid. Of course, the scene where she dances and sweats profusely and sexily during a black magic ritual will improve any actress's performance in my book.

So this film isn't perfect by any means but is worth a look for its great gross out sequences including black magic shenanigans with some not-so-fresh corpses and a show-stopping scene including a whole bunch of eels and a few gallons of blood. The gross-out bits don't get started until the halfway mark, so a little patience goes a long way with Art of the Devil. Oh yeah, someone should have told the director that albinos aren't scary. The non-menacing little albino ghost girl jumping up and down on the bed was hilarious, not scary.

Art of the Devil 2 (2005)

Two years after graduation, six high school friends reunite for a little get together in their home town. But these kids share more than just friendship. A bond formed after they used black magic to rid themselves of an evil and horribly abusive teacher. This terrible secret comes back to haunt them during their reunion and one by one, they succumb to terrible curses.

Hey kids, be sure to bring your barf bags for Art of the Devil 2. While it does have a similar theme of the perils of black magic, this is a sequel in name only to the first film. In fact, part 2 is an improvement over the 2004 film in almost every way. A better and more original script, great performances, beautiful scenery, better cinematography, and wildly disgusting gore make me wonder why they even bothered connecting this to Art of the Devil at all. Oh yeah, duh, the first one made money!

I really loved this film but there are a couple of problems. First of all, why does the baddie resort to torture if that person can just conjure up some spirits to cause the carnage? Or is taking some pliers to toenails and teeth part of a really complicated ritual? While I really appreciate a certain blowtorch scene (which I had to pause and take a break from for a few minutes), I still don't understand why the magic itself couldn't have caused all the mayhem.

Secondly, I think the teen angst angle was a little heavy handed. While I thought the kids were driven to seek out retribution, I couldn't help but laugh at their incredulity as the same horrors they caused came raining back down upon them. Isn't that the nature of black magic that whatever evil you cause will revisit you threefold? Hello, watch a horror movie, you dang fools!

Cannibalism, amateur dentistry, eye violence, fish hooks where fish hooks should never be, lizards crawling out of places that lizards should never be, and a pickled head; oh yes, it's all here! Even I was shocked by some of the outrageous grue on display and I'm a sick bitch. I'm wondering if Thai black magicians wrote the script because all the blame falls on Cambodian black magic. Is Thai black magic less hardcore than their neighbor's version? Anyway, Art of the Devil 2 proves once and for all that pointless torture and black magic go together like teen angst and pickled corpses.

The Machine Girl (2008)

After her parents were wrongfully accused of murder and committed suicide, high schooler Ami (Minase Yashiro) has been taking care of the house and her younger brother Yu (Ryôsuke Kawamura). When Yu and his friend are murdered by the son of a local yakuza, Ami desperately tries to get revenge. When she is apprehended by the yakuza, her left arm is hacked off. Ami escapes and her life is saved by Miki (Asami), the mother of Yu's only friend, whose husband builds Ami a machine gun arm to replace her lost appendage. These two bloodthirsty and very angry young ladies take on the yakuza, ninjas, and even the parents of their victims.

First things first, this neo-grindhouse flick delivers on all of its promises. The film sports great camerawork, muted colors (except for the blood), and an excellent soundtrack. There is obvious and cheesy CGI in some of the over the top action sequences but its combination with practical and latex effects make up for the obvious budgetary restrictions. The imaginations of the filmmakers rule the day with this one. And then there's the blood. Holy fuck, this movie is bloody as hell.

"I'm a demon! I've turned into a demon!"

The Machine Girl revels in both a gleeful madness and a campy attitude that will surely earn this a cult following for years to come. This film is a delightful gore spectacle with a formulaic plot taken to hilarious extremes. You know how the old saying goes: when life hands you lemons... KILL EVERYONE! And watch out for that drill bra, yo.

Tokyo Gore Police (2008)

This flick comes from the same production team behind The Machine Girl but this is a whole different creature, my friends. Director Yoshihiro Nishimura channels everything from Robocop to Blade Runner to Wicked City here as the dystopian elements and the perversity come packed in along with the insane violence and gore. Eihi Shiina of Takashi Miike's Audition (1999) plays Ruka, a cop in the future hunting criminals called engineers. These genetically enhanced baddies can grow bio-weapons wherever they are seriously injured. There is lots more to the plot of this movie but it will take me a couple of years before I can process what I've just seen.

Needless to say, Tokyo Gore Police is even more outlandish and insane than The Machine Girl. This candy-colored nightmare is an offensive exercise in explosive grotesquery and sleaze. Gross-outs include but are not limited to genital mutilation (resulting in an impressive penis cannon), bug eating, and a woefully disconcerting vagina flower (did I just type that?).

"Thanks a lot for telling me. You insane bastard..."

My only complaint of Tokyo Gore Police is its running time. At 109 minutes, I have to admit that I started squirming in my seat a bit. The scope of this film is quite grand and it's certainly never boring. However, some of the plot threads got a little thin. That being said, TGP is some seriously badass and jaw-droppingly repulsive entertainment (with acid-squirting nipples). And just like The Machine Girl, if you can accept some of the glaring budget shaving and CGI tomfoolery, you will have yourself a great time with this film.

Love Ghost (2001)

This film is based on the manga by horror manga master Junji Ito (the creator of Tomie) so my expectations were high. In it, there is a legend that if you go to a certain shrine in the middle of town, cover your face, and ask the first stranger who comes by if you will be lucky in love that you will receive some honest to goodness love advice. But the legend also says that the shrine is cursed and a vengeful spirit will appear out of the fog and say you will be unlucky in love. This unwanted news is much more than just a bummer, man, it will lead you to commit suicide.

I didn't mind Love Ghost though it definitely encouraged me to doze off several times. Unfortunately, the budget couldn't handle the unbridled insanity that Ito's original storyline devolves into. The filmmakers also forgot to exploit what makes the manga so good; it's freakin' scary! Worst still, instead of keeping things simple story wise, the movie shoots itself in the foot with a major plot twist that makes the confused conclusion anything but satisfying. First time director Kazuyuki Shibuya does a pretty good job with the film even with the screenplay problems but this is a tough flick to recommend. Some arterial spray and pretty girls in schoolgirl uniforms just aren't enough to make Love Ghost worth checking out. If you're going to watch every Japanese horror movie ever made, you could certainly do worse but that's not saying much now is it?

Wicked City (1992)

One of my strangest movie theater experiences happened in the mid-90s when I saw the animated film Wicked City (1987), directed by Yoshiaki Kawajiri. It was at the old rundown theater somewhere in West Palm Beach where the Rocky Horror crowd would congregate. Wicked City is an action-packed, gory, and kinky anime with some hilarious dubbing. It was a packed house and a fairly lively crowd until a wee bit of tentacle rape happened. Then we all sat in stunned silence for the rest of the film. I don't know how many anime fans were among the folks there that night but I'm going to go ahead and guess that most of the attendees had never seen anything like that before.

One night, a couple of years later, I was watching HBO, Showtime, or Cinemax (I don't remember which) and they announced that they were going to play Wicked City. I decided to watch it again but opted to pass on recording it to VHS. I was pretty sure that one more viewing would probably be more than enough. When the film started, I got a little confused. It wasn't animated! I had no idea there was a live action version of Wicked City. And it was from Hong fucking Kong! Other than kung-fu films, my only exposure to Hong Kong cinema was John Woo's The Killer. I was in for another surprise and luckily, there was much less tentacle rape involved.

Tokyo has quite a crisis on its hands. There are monsters disguised as humans walking the streets and there's an epidemic of people addicted to a drug called Happiness which has some seriously bad side effects. Taki (Leon Lai) is a member of an elite anti-monster taskforce who has a lot of issues. His partner, Kai (Jacky Cheung), is a half-monster full of angst and his ex-girlfriend, Gaye (Michelle Reis), is a full-blooded monster who is also full of angst. Taki's boss has put him in charge of capturing Daishu (Tatsuya Nakadai), a monster who he believes is responsible for bringing the Happiness drug into Tokyo (and who also happens to be Gaye's lover). All hell breaks loose when Daishu is captured by the anti-monster squad and Daishu's son Shudo (Roy Cheung) decides to destroy the city. Can Taki and Kai save the day or will the differences between monsters and humans be too much for them to handle?

That's approximately 33% of the plot of Wicked City (or as I like to call it, Wacky City). This movie has so much going on that it still baffles me after multiple viewings. Double crosses, triple crosses, and a duder humping a living pinball machine, this one has it all. Director Tai Kit Mak brings us a visionary splatterfest in primary colors that can barely sit still long enough to tell the viewer what the hell is going on. But then again, it's also childishly simple in terms of character motivations and it's pretty obvious that the writers (one of which is director Tsui Hark) don't give a double goddamn about wallowing in the cheese in order to get this wild ass story told.

Oh, this cast is awesome. Leon Lai is great as the conflicted hero and Roy Cheung of Fight Back to School is perfect as the creepy evildoer. Jacky Cheung of A Chinese Ghost Story III gets all mopey and emo (waaa, I'm half monster, waaa!) but rises to the status of hero when the going gets tough. Prolific Japanese actor, Tatsuya Nakadai (Illusion of Blood), tries to steal the movie as the wise and completely badass 150 year old monster, Daishu. (But what about those lovely ladies? First up is Michelle Reis (A Chinese Ghost Story II) who kicks 100 different varieties of ass. She makes me want to find my own Happiness-addicted monstrette to call my own. Carmen Lee of Forbidden City Cop squeezes into her tight white dress oh so nicely which is probably standard issue for female anti-monster squad agents.

If you can look past the convoluted plot, great magic awaits you. The word 'spectacle' barely does Wicked City justice. I can pretty much guarantee you've never seen anything quite like this before. Wicked City is the bright green mango cherry Slurpee version of Blade Runner. When you need your fix of eye-popping gore sequences and hyperactive fight scenes, give this one a spin. Oh yeah, be sure to watch the dubbed version for even more insanity and I also suggest you watch Wicked City as a double feature with Johnnie To's ridiculous epic, The Heroic Trio (1993).

Sweet Home (1989)

A TV crew goes to an abandoned mansion in the woods to investigate the rumors of a lost fresco by a famous artist. While restoring the painting, the crew begins to notice strange things about the house. It turns out that the mansion is the home of a vengeful spirit who uses the shadows to consume and burn anyone who is foolish enough to cross its path. The surviving members of the crew must solve the mystery of the terrible tragedy that took place there if they want to get out alive.

Director Kiyoshi Kurosawa has given us horror fans some seriously awesome films like Pulse (2001), Cure (1997), and Retribution (2006). He's also given us some unfairly obscure things like The Guard from Underground (1992) and friggin' Sweet Home. This film is quite a product of its time but is driven by imagination and an off kilter sense of humor. Think of this as The Legend of Hell House (1973) combined with Evil Dead (1981) by way of Poltergeist (1982). And while Sweet Home isn't nearly as insane, it's artificiality and otherworldliness make it a great double feature with Nobuhiko Obayashi's Hausu (1977).

"The shadows are alive!"

I found Sweet Home in its entirety (in five parts) on YouTube. But you know what? That's not good enough for me. I want to own this deliriously beautiful and wildly entertaining movie, damn it. This film is genuinely eerie and delightfully campy with a few excellent gore sequences thrown in. The writing is also very sound with some well-developed and likable characters. If you are at all into Japanese horror and fun 80s horror then you need to check out Sweet Home. It might just end up being your new favorite flick.

Séance (2000)

Junko (Jun Fubuki) is a medium who is very sensitive to the spirit world. This connection to ghosts makes it impossible for her to even hold a regular job. She sometimes holds séances to help others come to terms with the dead. Her husband Sato (Koji Yakusho) is a sound engineer at a TV studio who, through a very strange twist of fate, accidentally kidnaps a missing girl that his wife was trying to locate. Instead of turning the girl over to the police, the couple cooks up a scheme to make Junko into a famous medium. Of course, their plan goes to shit and tragedy ensues.

Director Kiyoshi Kurosawa (Cure, Pulse) knows how to deliver the scares and he also knows how to deliver chilling, thought-provoking, and painful horror films. Séance is no exception. It is less about ghosts and more about what happens to good people facing a moral dilemma. The film features an amazing score by composer Gary Ashiya that is both haunting and threatening with a drab, off-white palette from cinematographer Takahide Shibanushi.

Performances by Jun Fubuki and Koji Yakusho are superb. The way these two characters interact and the way that the supernatural has become a commonplace and dreary thing. In fact, Junko is so worn down by the physically and emotionally taxing world of spirits that she can't hold down a normal job. Both characters are so well written and both of these talented actors give believable, dynamic performances.

Séance is an excellent film with a bleak atmosphere and genuine dread hanging over the whole storyline. The plot keeps taking turns for the worst and it's just a darkly beautiful and sad thing to behold. The only thing really wrong with this movie are the cheesy effects used on one of the ghosts, revealing this film's made-for-TV origins. So if you can forgive that one instance of silliness, you're in for a treat. Turn off the lights, crank up the speakers, and dig Séance.

EDIT: Hey there. My good friend Brad just asked me if I'd seen Séance on a Wet Afternoon because it sounded very similar to Kurosawa's Séance. I had seen the 1964 film and then it dawned on me like a ton of bricks riding on a flaming snowplow: Séance is a remake of Séance on a Wet Afternoon! The films are quite different but they do share many of the same plot elements. Wow, I'm pretty dense.

Forest of Death (2007)

A remote section of forest in Thailand is known as a popular place for suicides and bonus, it's also said to be haunted. Detective Ha (Qi Shu) is trying to close an unsolved rape/murder case that took place there. May (Rain Li) is a reporter on a sensationalistic TV news program is interested in the forest. She shows up with a camera crew to film a reenactment with a murder suspect in the forest. During the recording, a detective drops dead on the spot for no discernable reason. May's boyfriend, botanist Shum Sho-Hoi (Ekin Cheng), is called in to see if he can provide any answers to the strange phenomenon. The mystery deepens as the freshly dead bodies of people who have been missing for 40 years start to turn up.

Forest of Death has some problems. The story is really muddled and none of the characters are all that interesting. The romantic triangle subplot can't seem to get off the ground and the music score is really over top, nearly ruining some potentially great scenes. I liked the urban legend behind the forest's mystique (wouldn't that be a rural legend?) but the film never comes together. Somewhere around the 45 minute mark, I started losing my patience but the film got just strange enough for me to stick it out to the end. Still, it was a chore to get through this one. And the weapon of choice for suicides and murders: box cutters, always the box cutters. There are a few cool (and some corny) ideas about plants feeling pain and fox spirits but they're not worth sitting through this one for. The Pang Brothers have done much better.

Kuroneko (1968)

A gang of battle-hardened and starving samurai invade the home of Yone (Noboku Otowa) and her daughter-in-law Shige (Kiwako Tochi). The two are raped, murdered, and their house is set on fire. The two sell their souls to a black cat to gain supernatural powers so that they can get revenge on the samurai. Yone's son, Gintoki (Kichiemon Nakamura), returns home from the war to find his wife and mother missing and their home burned to the ground. Gintoki's boss, Raiko (Kei Sato), a powerful general, informs him that a number of samurai have had their throats torn out in the woods and he wants him to investigate.

Okay, what idiot let this film slip into obscurity? Why isn't Kuroneko part of the Criterion Collection*? Hello? Anybody? Kaneto Shindo's masterpiece rivals his own classic, Onibaba (1964). Kuroneko is a tragic, dreamlike, haunting, and near-perfect film full of quiet tension and bursts of beautiful madness. The sound design, the music score (a hypnotic mix of bold percussion and minimal strings), and the cinematography are all razor sharp. All of the actors are superb and turn in flawless performances.

My only criticisms are pretty nitpicky. I think the film might be too dreamlike. Out of the three times I've watched Kuroneko, I've managed to dose off twice. The plot is insanely simple so it's not like I woke up and didn't know what was going on. This is a sensual and eerie film filled with quiet moments that come packed with loads of foreboding. I suppose the other problem is the melodrama between Gintako and Shige and then later between Gintako and his mother. But honestly, it's like Shakespearean quality stuff so I'm not really complaining.

The film's black and white cinematography and kabuki theatre style direction and staging make this film feel older than it is. You might find yourself thinking that this film feels like it was made in 1938 instead of 1968 but there is always some bizarre visual just around the corner to grab you and shake you down to your core. One of the eye-opening moments in the film is when Shige is making love to a samurai and then, out of nowhere, she digs into his throat like a Shriner digs into the taco meat at Golden Corral. It's startling and it really snaps you out of the trance-like and deceptively soothing scene that has been unfurling before you.

I first watched Kuroneko on an old and beaten up VHS I checked out from the library. I loved it. Several years later, I was overjoyed when I noticed that IFC was playing it one night because I was able to replace my grubby copy with a better one from the broadcast. However, I have to say that this film not being remastered and treated with some respect is fucking bullshit. The Region 2 DVD looks pretty good but come on, it's probably going to be out of print soon. I live in The United State of America, bro! And I simply will not tolerate films not being available in my region!

*Someone at Criterion got the memo and eventually released this!

Ghost Ballroom (1989)

Okay, let me try and do this as painlessly (for me) as possible. Mei is a prostitute junkie who owes her employer and lover, Master Condon, a great deal of money. Condon and his cronies throw her out of her apartment window and she dies. When she shows up and starts making some serious supernatural trouble for her killers, Condon hires a monk to get rid of Mei's spirit. Knowing that she can't do it alone, Mei approaches her living friends to help her gain the strength to take her revenge on Condon.

The kooky circus/pop opening credit music should have been enough to tip me off to what I was in for when Netflix sent me Ghost Ballroom. The plot is as dumb as a bag of rocks and the tone is all over the place. Director Wilson Tong tries to blend gritty urban drama, comedy, horror, kung-fu, and magic in one film and he almost pulls it off. The biggest problem is that Ghost Ballroom is so spastic that it never develops any of its characters. There is no main character to follow. Instead of 2 or 3 leads, this film has 5 or 6 main people who are never painted in anything more than a superficial light. All of the characters are hookers, drug dealers, gamblers, gangsters, junkies, etc. so it is kind of tough to find anyone to relate to.

Where Ghost Ballroom does succeed is in its energy. Once it gets going, the pace never lets up. For the benefit of my Western eyes, there are multiple moments lost in translation that are worth a laugh or two. There are also some genuinely funny parts (some clever, some straight out of the gutter) but the constant tone problems I mentioned make it difficult to really enjoy them. The horror and magic sequences are cool enough but are usually pretty weak. Thankfully, the sleazy sex is kept to a minimum as well. Had director Tong pushed the envelope in either direction, this film might make a little more sense, entertainmentally (not a real word!) speaking. It's not the worst I've seen from that wild planet called Hong Kong but it certainly could have been much, much better.

Richard Glenn Schmidt

Put a Ringu on It

The Ring was one of the things that helped jumpstart my seriously neglected love of horror movies. That October was when I started to raid the shelves at the video store again for some horror delights. This very profitable remake also helped spark the fiery love I have for Asian horror. So it's a big deal for me. In fact, it was such a big deal that I didn't watch The Ring for nearly 8 years. I've had the DVD for a long time but I just couldn't bring myself to watch it.

I don't know why I did this. I know that it wasn't because I was too scared. After consuming countless horror movies between 2002 and now, it's safe to say that I was ready to revisit the flick. Honestly, I think I was just too excited about The Ring to watch it again. Damn, this almost feels like a bad movie confession but The Ring is not a bad movie. It's just kind of there. I think that it and the Dark Water remake are the best of the Asian horror remakes that have come out thus far. Oh and I liked Mirrors despite its glaring problems ("Stay away from the water, it makes reflections."). I think the remake business got some of my money because when I'm in the mood to see horror in theaters and there's nothing good playing, I'm going to go anyway and see whatever is on the dang screen.

So for the first time in 8 years, I watched The Ring (1998) and oh yes, I had some observations. The first thing I noticed is that The Ring is beautifully shot. Yugoslavian-born cinematographer Bojan Bazelli casts the film in muted greens and grays giving it an undeniable atmosphere. There is an eerie tension between the big scares and some fantastically strange imagery on display. And it's scary. The film is aggressively terrifying and will not let up until the viewer is wrecked and shaky. One little thing that particularly impressed me was the lack of brand names in the movie. The only one I picked up on is when Rachel (Naomi Watts) pays for something with her American Express card.

So where does this remake falter? Before I compare this film to the original, there are a couple of little problems here. The filmmakers must have thought only morons were going to be watching this film. There are a plethora of things that could have been subtle nuances or cool little hidden things that are delivered with all the sensitivity of a pulled pin at a grenade factory retirement party. For instance, upon second viewing, the infamous tape that drastically shortens one's life expectancy is kind of lame. It has a few really dumb little faux-scary things in it like the box of wriggling severed fingers. So spooky! And speaking of not-so-subtle moments, Naomi Watts does get a little cheesy when, after her son views the tape, the phone rings, and she screams "Leave him alone!" It didn't hit me the first time but my eyes rolled so hard on re-watching it that I got a little disoriented.

Unlike The Ring, I've watched Ringu multiple times over the years. Right away, I can tell you that it's the better film. Boop boop boop boop boop! Did you hear that? It was an obvious revelation detector going off. First of all, Hideo Nakata's original masterpiece is just that: A MASTERPIECE! This is a scary ass movie with a whole mess of class, really cool ideas, and beauty packed into its 96 minutes; 9 minutes shorter than its American counterpart. The American version takes longer to tell a more convoluted story while the Japanese one is simpler and all the better for it. Ringu is also quite subtle and leaves a great deal to the imagination of the viewer.

The cursed videotape is much shorter and more direct than in the American version. However, when I add up the lists of what I like about the tape in the American version and what I like about the tape in Ringu, they come out pretty much equal. The tape in Ringu is more functional. It shows more clues to the story than the tape in The Ring does but the tape in The Ring has two or three little jabs in it that make it scarier. The goat with a less than standard number of limbs hopping along and the horses dying on the beach just really freaks me out. Somehow, the mixed up newspaper clipping in the Japanese version just doesn't send chills up my spine.

While I loved Brian Cox's short but amazing performance as Samara's suicidal father in The Ring, the backstory of Samara's parents leaves a lot to be desired. In fact, it doesn't make much sense. Samara's history is alluded to and it just kind of paints her as a little girl who may or may not have been adopted and who is just plain EVIL! Nice origin story… Not! In the Japanese version, we're treated to a family of psychics who produces Sadako, a young lady more powerful (and EVIL!) than any of them can imagine. You know, it sounds ridiculous but somehow the latter just works better in my mind.

One thing that my sweet wife LeEtta pointed out during my little comparative experiment was that she now finds Sadako much scarier than Samara. I have to agree. When I look at screenshots of Samara, I'm not really affected by it. However, the longer I look at Sadako, I just feel the hairs standing up on the back of my neck. Jeez! The final scare is certainly more effective in the Japanese version. When Sadako climbs out of that TV, damn it, I still get freaked. When Samara goes after what's-his-face, it doesn't really do anything for me now. It seems as though The Ring is a much better film when it is doing something different. Like that horsey scene on the ferry. Oh man, that still gets to me. When it tries to imitate that last awesome moment, it just doesn't fare well under scrutiny.

For the longest time, my biggest bone of contention against Ringu was that the corpses Sadako leaves in her wake weren't as scary as the ones in the American version. Gore Verbinski had Rick Baker doing the makeup and he went with the severely corpse-like look which is just plain hard to look at. That moment in theaters (and one that still gets me on the DVD) is when we see the first victim. So we see this putrid looking corpse and it moves. IT FUCKING MOVES! I think about the American aesthetic that Verbinski had to have thought about when remaking Ringu and frankly, its genius. Sure, it's more of a popcorn movie but it worked on American audiences and I know there are other people besides my wife and I who found The Ring to be quite traumatic, especially in the dark confines of a movie theater. When I first beheld the corpses in Ringu, I laughed out loud. They are just actors in a little bluish makeup holding very still. The funny thing is, now that I've watched Ringu several times, those pasty frozen faces are starting to get to me.

In the end, I have a very strong affection for both The Ring and Ringu. Hideo Nakata's film is simply stunning and it is worth a look or ten. Gore Verbinski's version is a superb translation with only a few flaws. Both films effectively show the horror of the curse of a little misunderstood psychic girl (or young woman in the case of Sadako). The curse's victims lose their identities -see how their faces blur when you try to take their picture- and then seven days later, they lose their lives. Two final things I must point out: 1) the musical score for Ringu is a million times more amazing than that of The Ring and 2) how the hell did Rachel survive the tumble down the well in The Ring? She even hits her head on the way down! Come on. That is some lame shit.

Okay, I'm not quite done yet. Aidan, the little kid in The Ring, is so much creepier than his Japanese counterpart. And what the hell was Abby from "NCIS" doing in the movie? Okay, I'm trying really hard not to go into a bunch of shit about the The Ring Two. Oh yeah, Margie (my mother-in-law), who joined us for the Ring Comparison Projection 2010, said that she liked the way the ending plays out in the Japanese version better. And LeEtta concurs. They both like the idea of -SPOILER ALERT- the kid's grandfather being the one sacrificed to the tape. Okay, enough rambling.

Arang (2006)

Min, a seasoned detective with a troubled past, returns from suspension to investigate the mysterious death of an ex-felon. She gets saddled with a green rookie named Lee to help her solve the case as more bodies start piling up; all of which died under similar yet inexplicable circumstances. All of the victims know one another and all of them were tormented by visions of two ghosts: a woman and a child both bleeding from their eyes. The mystery is connected to a salt storehouse in a small town where a rape and a murder took place ten years ago. Min and Lee begin to unravel the truth and it is even more bizarre and horrible than they could have guessed.

I'm keeping this plot description vague because I don't want to spoil anything, especially when Arang takes its unexpected turns. While the film does have some generic aspects (a long haired ghost and a cursed website), first time director Sang-hoon Ahn's lucks out with an engaging story, excellent pacing, and more than a few cool scenes and surprises. The cinematography is top notch and the film has a rich atmosphere of unease and beauty.

"Better to see a ghost than a pervert!"

I didn't find Arang all that terrifying but the haunting imagery and the tragic, well-told story kept me hooked until the end. This is anything but a half-assed horror flick. All of the performances from the cast are very good so I actually cared about what happened to these characters. This is just a beautiful film with some very dark and painful moments. And let me tell you future detectives out there that a dead dog's stomach is the first place you should look for clues during a murder investigation.

X-Cross (2007)

Two friends, Shiyori and Aiko (Nao Matsushita and Ami Suzuki), head up into the mountains to stay at a remote hot springs. Once there, Shiyori is besieged by a village full of insane woodsmen who cut off the left legs off of their women so they can't run away. At the same time, Aiko has her own problems as a maniacal gothic Lolita chick (Ayuko Iwane) with a giant pair of scissors is trying to cut her to pieces. The night gets longer and longer while the two friends try to stay alive.

One of the biggest surprises during my visits to Asian horror land has been the scrumptiously entertaining X-Cross. Not content to tell a story in linear form, director Kenta Fukasaku (son of the late great Kinji Fukasaku) cuts back and forth in time showing incidents from the two main characters' perspectives. The plot itself is so unbelievably simple that its cut and paste format helps keep this from being a half hour movie. I've seen some films try this style of storytelling and it blew up in the filmmakers' faces. It takes a brisk pace and a lot of creativity to pull this off and those are two things that X-Cross has up the wazoo.

The actresses involved are lovely and clearly got into the spirit of the project. They make it look like a good time. You know what? This damn film is really difficult to describe. There's the crazy melodrama and the just plain crazy. X-Cross is a bizarre flick that practically redefines pop horror because it's so much friggin' fun. Take the sweetest confection you can think of, put it in a hotdog bun, deep fry it, and then eat it while watching Battle Royale II on fast forward (something I recommend anyway) to get the same sensation. That's what X-Cross is like, only better. You need to see this. Seriously.

Spooky Encounters (1980)

Bold Cheung (Sammo Hung Kam-Bo) isn't exactly the brightest guy in the world. He makes foolish bets with his stupid friends and he happens to be married to a miserable battle-axe of a wife (Suet-Moi Leung). Worse still, Cheung's boss, Master Tam (Ha Huang), is sleeping with his wife behind his back. He nearly catches the two together one day but Tam escapes out the back window. Fearing Cheung's famous kung-fu skills, Tam decides to hire a wizard named Chin Hoi (Lung Chan) to kill the poor sap with black magic.

When Chin Hoi's colleague, Tsui (Fat Chung), learns of his plans to use his powers for financial gain (and evil), he decides to help out Bold Cheung. With the two sides playing against each other, Cheung becomes a pawn in a battle between the two former colleagues. To top it all off, when it looks like the black magic isn't going to be enough, Tam and his evil crony frame Cheung for his own wife's murder. Reanimated corpses, possession, zombification, a very determined police inspector (Ching-Ying Lam), and two really tall altars; that's what awaits you in this wacked out flick.

A friend at work lent me two movies on a Thursday before a long weekend. Those two movies were Spooky Encounters and Mr. Vampire (1985). The following Saturday, I watched both flicks and I've never been quite the same. My love of kung-fu films had gone into a coma since the 90s when I just got sick of the shitty quality of the VHS tapes available at my local Blockbuster video. Spooky Encounters was the shot of L-Dopa my kung-fu De Niro needed to come miraculously back to life! I recently replaced my gray market copy of Spooky Encounters with the awesome version from Fortune Star. A brilliant move on my part if I do say so myself. Hold on while I pat myself on the back... Okay, moving on.

Sammo Hung's Spooky Encounters is quite possibly the greatest kung-fu horror film of all time. If there is anything I can criticize this film for, it's the flimsy plot which is a series of setpieces only tenuously tied together from scene to scene. But really, what horror flick (or kung-fu flick for that matter) doesn't have that problem? Oh and women aren't exactly portrayed in the best light. The only female characters that have any dialogue are both adulteresses. The cinematography and the atmospheric lighting perfectly compliment the stunning fight choreography and incredible stunt work.

The first time I saw Sammo Hung in action, he immediately became my favorite kung-fu star. Hung is a big dude which makes his kung-fu all the more impressive to me. Other kung-fu legends featured in this film are Fat Chung, Lung Chan, and Ching-Ying Lam. Lam would go on to star in Mr. Vampire and many other lesser variations of the same story. Chung would also get bitten by the hopping vampire bug and appeared in several films of the same ilk.

So what's so special about all this insanity? It's friggin' energizing! Spooky Encounters has an undeniably infectious energy thanks to its perfect mix of fantasy, horror, action, and comedy; the presence of the charismatic and hilarious Sammo Hung and an excellent supporting cast help greatly too. Hung directed many films but this one is still my favorite with its boundless verve (verve?) and imagination. Other assets to this essential film are the dark humor and its downbeat yet riotously funny and abrupt ending that must be seen to be believed.

Midori - A First Taste of Midori (2009)

Folks who know me might notice that I like some pretty noisy ass music. And I can listen to it early in the morning or late at night. That's just how I roll. A while back, my wife sent me a YouTube video of a band, casually mentioning that it was something that she thought I would like. I forgot about the video until around 7:00am the next morning. I followed the link and it was Midori. Midori was a noise rock jazz band from Japan and the video was loud, fast paced, and features lots of footage of their lead singer running around and the band spazzing out in their practice space. To say that my mind was blown is an understatement.

I don't know what to compare this band's sound to exactly. Just imagine listening to every one of the Yeah Yeah Yeahs' songs at once. Only jazzier! Noisy they may be; Midori is immensely talented. The rhythm section's background is obviously jazz while Hajime's (the keyboardist) style seems as though it is rooted in classical music. The group also has a knack for making really abrasive music fun to listen to. So I guess this is punk noise jazz rock or something? One more thing: Keigo Iwami's bass playing is just unbelievably awesome.

I did some searching for the band which is not easy since Midori is a very common word in Japanese (it means "Green" and it is also a very popular name for girls) and I found that they had a concert DVD. Without a clue as to the quality of the DVD, the running time, or anything, I begged my wife to get it for me. She buys stuff from Amazon Japan once in a while so I made sure that she put this DVD on the list. When it arrived, I pooped- Woops. LOL! That was a typo. When it arrived, I popped the DVD into our region free player (essential), cranked up the speakers, and got punched in the face by one of my new favorite bands of all time.

When the film starts, the band is getting into the zone backstage and the crowd is gathering in front of the amphitheater. As the band members begin to emerge on the stage, I'm filled with anxiety. Somehow, Mariko Goto, the lead singer/guitarist, makes a huge impression when she steps up. How can a little Japanese woman in a schoolgirl uniform, armed only with a guitar and a Marshall stack, be so imposing? Then it starts and no, I was not ready for the full blown spaz rock insanity of Midori.

There are some theatrics involved – I mean, this footage was edited a whole lot. Microphone stands go flying, sound guys are scrambling around, guitar strings are broken, and everyone except the drummer runs around on stage like a bunch of crazy people. Hajime stuffs his microphone into his mouth so we can hear his guttural screams from… the inside? Whatever, it's all entertaining.

Mariko is the most unhinged of the band. She is all over the place. She climbs up on the speakers, walks off the front of the stage and into the crowd, she hits herself on the head with the microphone repeatedly, licking her lips, and even sobbing during one of her songs (something the editor really dances around - showing that much emotion in public is kind of a rare, awkward thing in Japan). Is it all planned? Who cares!?! She's wearing a short dress with a black thong underneath. I'm sure that just, you know, happened by accident.

There is a lot of banter with the crowd that is lost on me (no subtitles here) and obviously I have no idea what any of the lyrics mean. The only phrase I pick out is "Destroy Cutie Honey"… Very interesting. Hopefully, their lyrics aren't all like "Fuck you, gaijin, don't listen to our music, you white piece of shit!" I might take offense to that. Just kidding, I'd love that! Mariko does encourage the very polite and rather tame crowd to climb out of the back rows and come down towards the stage. They are slow to get pumped but once night falls, the audience is enslaved my Midori. I'm perfectly and wholly jealous of everyone there. Oh well, the DVD does do the band justice. This concert film is professionally shot, edited, and has spectacular sound.

The Great Horror Family (2004)

When the Imawano family moves into their new house, something just ain't right. Grandpa (Shunji Fujimura) knows that there is an evil presence lurking in that house. He calls a family meeting in order to make a big announcement but drops dead before he can warn them. That night, Kiyoshi (Issei Takahashi), the youngest male of the Imawanos meets up with Grandpa's spirit who informs him that he has inherited great psychic powers and that he must prepare himself to save his family from a great crisis. Grandpa doesn't know what the crisis is but he suspects that it has something to do with their extremely haunted house.

The Great Horror Family is still one of my favorite impulse buys of all time. I took one look at the cover (which tricked me into thinking this was animated) and the synopsis on the back and I knew I couldn't leave the store without this series. The show is equal parts wacky comedy, horror spoof, and heartfelt family drama. All manner of Japanese horror films, sci-fi, urban legends, and traditional ghost folklore are poked fun at here.

All of the characters are loveable in The Great Horror Family and the cast gets into their performances making it look like this show was a complete blast to work on. Grandpa and Grandma (Tomiko Ishii) are the cutest old people ever and their comic timing is awesome. Issei Takahashi (of Meatball Machine) is hilarious as the unlikely and reluctant hero, Kiyoshi. His mom, Yuko (Shigeru Muroi), is a childish woman who is a little on the slow side but she knows just what to do when things are looking grim.

Kiyoshi's sister, Kyoko (Asuka Shibuya), has great potential as a psychic but doesn't believe in the spiritual realm. Not yet, anyway. And finally, there's Osamu (Moro Morooka of Infection), Kiyoshi's father, who is obsessed with the world of the unknown and the unexplainable. However, he has no supernatural abilities whatsoever. Other great characters include a gothic Lolita shop owner who sells supernatural items that cause nothing but pain and suffering and a wandering monk (Shoichiro Masumoto) who gets run over by a truck before he can help the Imawano family.

While it helps to be familiar with Japanese pop and horror culture, it isn't a requirement to enjoy The Great Horror Family. The comedy is very broad and often quite slapstick so it translates quite well. Everything from the well written characters to the bizarrely hypnotic theme song to the family dog is totally perfect. I think I have fallen in love with this show but I'm not going to marry it or anything. Jeez, that would be weird.

The Cat AKA Lao Mao (1992)

A writer named Wisely (Waise Lee) introduces the film and we're off. A trio of benevolent aliens hides out on Earth in order to collect a space weapon that has crash-landed on Earth and is now on display in a museum. Among the good aliens are Errol (Siu-Ming Lau), a space princess (Gloria Yip), and "The General" who is a super space cat. Also after this space weapon is an evil alien who does not have humankind's best interests at heart. This evil alien has the ability to clone itself into any form and will go to any lengths to get what it wants.

Wisely, his girlfriend Pai So (Christine Ng), and their cop friend Wang Chieh-Mei (Philip Kwok) are drawn into the struggle after Wisely pursues the space princess and her space cat. Not knowing they are the good guys, Wisely borrows a super dog from an eccentric dog breeder in order to challenge "The General". That's right, you guessed it! A cat and dog fight of epic proportions takes place. Meanwhile, the evil alien kills and clones Wang Chieh-Mei and sends him with a cache of weapons to kill them all and retrieve the space weapon.

Sometimes you see yourself standing on the edge of crazy and sometimes your foot slips and down you go, plummeting downward into complete madness. The moment you decide to watch The Cat, you're already on your way down, duder. This gory, wacked out, and insanely entertaining flick is a mishmash of horror, sci-fi, and action that will not only make you a better person, it will also prolong your life. The Cat is a Hong Kong style mash-up of Turner and Hooch (1989), The Terminator (1984), The Thing (1982), and That Darn Cat (1965).

"Hong Kong people are lucky, we can eat anything. Who'd care to emigrate?"

Director Ngai Kai Lam is responsible for some really insane films including Riki-Oh: The Story of Ricky (1991), Peacock King (1988), and The Seventh Curse (1986). Sadly, The Cat is his last film to date. One would think that a director this bonkers would still be out there making flicks or planning his big comeback. I can't think of a better film to go out with though. The cheesy electro score and the weird echoed audio track only add to the beauty of this ridiculous live action cartoon.

The cast is awesome or at least, they were contractually obligated to show up to the set every day. Either way, they rock! Both Waise Lee of Bullet in the Head (1990) and Philip Kwok of Holy Flame of the Martial World (1983) are prolific action stars. When Kwok goes into Terminator mode, watch out! Siu-Ming Lau also has made the rounds in everything from the awesome A Chinese Ghost Story (1987) to the disappointing Forest of Death but he's always good.

The sexpot role of the movie is fulfilled by Christine Ng, who gets one of the more uncomfortable scenes in the movie where Wisely admires every sweaty inch of her body after a tennis match. I'm more of a Gloria Yip man myself. She is as cute as a button as the (to the best of my knowledge) unnamed space princess. The scene of her playing with "The General" by flying through the air and bouncing on a TV antenna is priceless. And stupid!

It's badass, it's bizarre, and it's fricking awesome. It's badizafrisome! The Cat is one of the true epics of psychotronic filmmaking. The only way this film could be any weirder is if it had been narrated by Rip Taylor or taken place 9,000 years in the future. When the giant flying lightning mushroom from space comes to town and is eating up all your friends, you better pray that the space princess and her space cat aren't too busy to take it out with their space weapon. You have to see this one for yourself.

Animal lovers beware! There is one thing about this movie that is kind of not so great. The infamous cat vs. dog showdown that most folks who have seen this film remember so well does have a few sketchy moments where the animals, especially the cat, don't look like they're having a very good time. Luckily, most of the animal scenes are ridiculously fake and the offending shots are brief. But it just ain't cool, man!

Detective Story (2007)

Detective Raita Kazama (Kazuya Nakayama) is neighbors with salaryman Raita Takashima (Kurodo Maki). These two dudes may share a first name but they couldn't be more different. Takashima is a boring pushover who doesn't know how to say no. He gets dragged along on Kazama's wild journey to solve a series of gruesome murders that someone is trying to frame him for. On the other hand, Kazama is completely bonkers. His detection methods are completely unorthodox and yet he always seems to come out on top. However, Kazama's luck seems to be running out on this case when a woman who comes to him for help winds up as another one of the killer's eviscerated victims.

I freely admit that I don't always understand director Takashi Miike. I've been a fan of his since I first watched both Audition and Visitor Q many years ago. He did turn me off to his films with the potentially amazing but ultimately repetitive and dismal Izo. Of course, after a little break, I was ready to see what the guy had been up to. Not too surprising, the dangerously prolific Miike has directed over a dozen films since then. One of those films is Detective Story, a gory, hilarious, and eccentric slap in the face to any doubters of the director's greatness.

This shot on video horror flick is no cheap throwaway. Detective Story is freaky, nasty, fun, and wildly original. The main characters are totally outrageous and over-the-top and the actors are all up to the challenge. Nakayama (who had the unfortunate task of playing the title role in Izo) is fifteen different varieties of awesome in this film. His portrayal of the odd, brutish, and yet somehow loveable Raita Kazama is probably the best thing about this film. Kurodo Maki plays the other Raita, the sheepish, perverted, and perpetual stick in the mud with gusto. It feels good to watch him suffer. My favorite, of course, is Kazama's secretary, Mika, who is played by the lovely Asae Oonishi. Mika somehow manages to be even more deranged than her employer.

So if you're like me and you loved Miike's MPD Psycho but you were left wanting more, then you will definitely get a kick out of Detective Story. He delivers the weirdness, the jazzy soundtrack, the disgusting gore (when it's not curiously pixilated), and the crazy characters. All of this is mixed together in a strangely delicious blend of splatter, film noir, and comedy. Check this out, y'all.

Jigoku (1960)

Shiro Shimizu (Shigeru Amachi) has got some real problems. One night, while hanging out with his "friend" Tamura (Yoichi Numata), he takes part in the hit and run of a gangster. This gangster's mother (Kiyoko Tsuji) witnesses the crime and vows her revenge on both Tamura and Shiro (even though he wasn't driving) with the aid of her son's girlfriend Yoko (Akiko Ono). As if this weren't bad enough, Shiro's fiancée, Yokiko (Utako Mitsuya), is killed in a taxi accident the night she was going to tell him something very important. While falling into Yoko and the gangster's mom's trap and shunned by his future in-laws, Shiro gets a letter from home that his mother is dying.

While his mother (Kimi Tokudaiji) lay dying in a cheap and corrupt rest home, Shiro's father (Hiroshi Hayashi) is living in the next room with his mistress. Shiro meets Sachiko (Akiko Ono again), a girl who reminds him an awful lot of his dead fiancée and who he immediately has a crush on. She lives at the rest home with her drunken artist father who sells his paintings of hell to get by. Tamura shows up in town to cause more trouble for Shiro as does Yoko and the gangster's mom. Someone serves some bad fish at the rest home's tenth anniversary (plus there's a bottle of poison sake going around) and next thing you know, pretty much every single character we've met up to this point goes straight to freakin' hell.

But wait, there's more! Now in hell, Shiro discovers some disturbing revelations about his family and is forced to face all of his earthly sins. Oh and Enma, the king of hell, is going to get his money's worth torturing him for all eternity. In the underworld, Yoko reveals to Shiro that she was going to tell him she was pregnant the night she died and that their unborn child is trapped somewhere in hell. Our whiny, miserable "hero" decides to get his shit together and go rescue their child so that she won't suffer along with all the lost souls who totally deserve to be there. But will this young man's will be enough to challenge the will of the king of hell? Wait, why is Sachiko in hell? She's a nice girl? Oh man, why is there a river of pus and excrement? That's just nasty! These questions and many more are answered in Jigoku!

What's the most fun you could ever have going to hell? With legendary wacko director Nobuo Nakagawa's 1960 film, Jigoku, you silly! The cacophonous and sensual opening credit sequence alone is enough to make this one of the strangest films about H-E-double hockey sticks ever made. Jigoku is as much about the tortures of hell as it is about guilt and what spectacular failures human beings are. There's also melodrama so overwrought and irony so ironic it's almost too ironic for me to even be talking about it. Either way, I bet you haven't seen anything quite like this before.

I've rarely enjoyed a movie that was this hard to sit through. Its two sections, the earthly plane and the world of hell, are both filled with agony and misery. The second half just has more screaming. The feeling of dread is excruciating as everything just keeps spinning out of control. Lives are wrecked and people just keep making stupid ass choices that land their butts on the griddle. The tortures awaiting them, though cheesily staged, are brutal. There's a demon whose job it is to smash yer dang teeth in. It's a living! The compositions by cinematographer Mamoru Morita are striking and the film's wild score by the prolific Michiaki Watanbe is simply mind-blowing.

All of the actors are totally devoted to this piece of insanity. You know you've got an excellent cast when the viewer is willing to die and go to hell with them. And it takes a great actor to make an unpleasant character into a fascinating portrait and that is just what Shigeru Amachi does with Shiro. The funniest aspect of this character is how he's a magnet for women. Yukiko, Yoko, Sachiko, and even his father's mistress, all go for this friggin' guy. I wonder what cologne he uses.

However, for me, the shining star of Jigoku is Yoichi Numata (Ringu). I think it was around the second time that Tamura materialized out of thin air that I realized this character had a little more up his sleeve than just a sleazy prankster. It's quite clear that this roguish gentleman is a catalyst for sin, a mad soul from hell on an unholy mission, a total dickweed trying to make everyone suffer as much as he, etc. Numata's performance is wildly over-the-top, spastic, and totally perfect.

Is Jigoku a classic film? Oh yeah. Is it also shrill as hell -ha ha, "shrill as hell", huh? I just made myself laugh- and intentionally exasperating during the bulk of its running time? Mm-hm. It's a fairly obvious art movie that is trying to hide behind its tawdry tapestry of misery and horror. I urge you to watch this film as soon as you can but I must warn you, you will go to hell and your screams of perpetual torment will go unnoticed in the chaotic din of eternity. So bring your sinner friends! Jigoku is a great date movie as well. But you're not getting laid after it's over.

Spotlight on Takashi Shimizu

When the American remake of Ju-on came out, I really wanted to like it for some reason. It could be my inexplicable love of Sarah Michelle Gellar (even though I'm not a fan of Buffy in the least). Whatever the reason, I was pretty freakin' pumped when I saw The Grudge the same night in 2004 that I saw the first Saw film. Looking back, it was not a good night for horror. If I'd had a blog back then or Doomed Moviethon had been born a year earlier, I would have given the Ju-on remake a positive review and skewered Saw for its glaring faults (which I'll probably talk about some other time). Now I can't even watch the American Grudge or its sequels without feeling embarrassed.

After re-revisiting the original 2002 film and its sequel, I have to say that there is no excuse for me ever liking the remakes. Granted, the Sam Raimi produced versions are not the worst remakes of Asian horror films by any means (I'm talking about you, Pulse) but the magic of the originals cannot be recaptured, even with the same director, Takashi Shimizu, on board. Now there are some good moments in The Grudge and The Grudge 2 (2006) and even some striking visuals but the films almost feel like parodies. Some of the scares are telegraphed and dumbed down for American audiences. That's bad, okay. I've never seen The Grudge 3 (2009) but the trailers are laughable.

What's interesting about the first theatrically released Ju-on film is that Takashi Shimizu either takes for granted that everyone has seen the original movies he made that went straight to video or he is simply experimenting with how to reveal the double murder (triple if you include the cat) and suicide that started the curse in the first place. In the 2002 film, the flashbacks are shown in such an abstract manner that you have to use your imagination to fill in the blanks but technically, it's all there. One of the best things about Ju-on and Ju-on 2 (2003) is their chapter-like structure. It is a lot of fun to put these things together like in your brain.

I've seen the original straight-to-video films (released in 2000) and they are amazing. The shot-on-video feel adds to the scares immensely. The films feel even more disturbing than their theatrical counterpart. Now that the whole found footage genre has exploded, it's getting harder to appreciate or explain what makes these little cheapies so special.

Shimizu is definitely more hit than miss. He directed what is probably the best (though not my favorite) of the Tomie series, Tomie: Re-birth (2001). It is one of those films that despite its formulaic origins, it goes off on even more disturbing and unique tangents. It features some of the most iconic scenes of the entire series like a mother and her son bonding while they are chopping up Tomie's body with a meat cleaver. It's bizarrely heart-warming and lovely in its gruesomeness.

I was not overwhelmed by Shimizu's 2005 film, Reincarnation, but I know that I need to give it a second look because it felt at the time I watched it like it would grow on me. Marebito (2004) is an excellent yet slowly paced film filled with dread and packed with more dark and freaky ideas than scares. It's definitely worth a look. As for his American remakes, they aren't terrible really, I just wish he'd had a chance to make something totally different for American audiences instead of adapting the older material. I need to check out 7500 (2015), a non-remake horror film he did with American and Japanese producers.

Though he's directed a few things outside of the genre (like a live action version of Kiki's Delivery Service (2014)!), Shimizu continues to work in the horror genre. He has made two 3D horror films, The Shock Labyrinth (2009) which I really liked though no one else did and Tormented (2014) which I haven't seen yet. There's also a film called A Rain Woman (2016) that has a very promising trailer. So anyway, I'm glad homie-bro is sticking with horror. As for the Ju-on series, I recommend watching the original home video movies if you can find them. I also recommend watching the theatrical films Ju-on and Ju-on 2 back to back. They work very well together even though the second film is a little weaker than the first.

Mystics in Bali (1981)

Cathy (Ilona Agathe Bastian) wants to learn Leak (pronounced "lee-ack") magic for her book on black magic. Her boyfriend Mahendra (Yos Santo) introduces Cathy to the Leak Queen (Sofia W.D.) who begins to teach Cathy the ways of Leak. Mahendra starts to worry about his girlfriend so he approaches his uncle Machesse (W.D. Mochtar), a white magic mystic who has the skillz to counteract the evil queen's powers. Once Cathy is well versed in Leak magic, the Leak Queen uses her to suck blood from unborn babies so that she can achieve immortality. Mahendra and Machesse step in to challenge the Leak Queen before Cathy becomes her slave forever.

First things first, don't watch Mystics in Bali alone. For the rough spots full of meandering and hilariously dubbed characters speaking outrageously stupid dialog, you'll need a friend or three to lend their heckling support. The other reason you're going to want someone else around while you're digging on this Indonesian freakout is that you will feel, with some intensity, an urge to show Mystics in Bali to somebody, anybody, just so you'll know that something this insane really exists. Did you eat a Buffalo chicken sandwich with sweet potato fries dipped in wasabi mayonnaise too soon before taking nap or did you actually just witness this film in real life? You will need confirmation, trust me.

Director H. Tjut Djalil is known for some pretty outlandish films like Lady Terminator and Dangerous Seductress. One of the things he's not known for is a cohesive story and interesting characters. Performance wise, most of the cast of Mystics in Bali are terrible but the dubbing is so bad that it hardly matters anyway. Take, for example, Ilona Agathe Bastian. She is not charismatic at all and is actually rather homely. Not that an attractive woman would have done any better in the role but jeez, there are some scenes that require at least a baseline level of sexiness. At least prolific actress Sofia W.D. shoots it out of the park with her insane portrayal of the blood-drinking and jewel-licking Leak Queen.

"Mm, delicious! This is good blood!"

Mystics in Bali is grotesque, macabre, wildly funny (thanks mostly to the script*), and just plain nuts. Oh and it's confusing too but the film is dumb that it will make you feel embarrassed for being confused. Any movie that feels a little slow at less than 90 minutes and also introduces new characters DURING THE CLIMAX has got some problems. And yet, it's all worth it if you like schlocky foreign cinema. The silly synth-driven music score, disturbing transformations sequences, flying heads with guts hanging from the neck-hole, talking fireballs, and dubious special video effects will warm your cold, lifeless heart. So make sure you and your drunken friends check out this mesmerizingly weird film. You will/won't be sorry/glad you did.

*My favorite moment in the movie happens right after Cathy pukes some green stuff and a couple of very confused and very much alive white mice. She talks about how she dreamed that she was at a banquet eating strange food. Mahendra suggests that perhaps she just ate something that upset her stomach! Trust me, every time I swallow live frickin' mice, I feel a little funny in my tummy too.

The Boy from Hell (2004)

Dr. Setsu Emma (Mirai Yamamoto) is a famous surgeon but all that really matters to her is her son, Daio (Shota Someya). In a tragic (read as: hilarious) traffic accident, Daio's head is severed by a passing truck while her servant (Baku Numata) is driving them home one day. Stricken by her grief, Setsu takes the advice of a madwoman and sacrifices a boy the same age as Daio over his grave in order to resurrect him. Daio (now played by Mitsuru Akaboshi) comes back possessed by the spirit of a creature from hell and immediately begins killing and devouring anyone unlucky enough to cross his path.

Meanwhile, a snooping detective, Hanamizu (Hanae Shoji), who has an impossibly huge nose, shows up to investigate the recent rash of cannibal murders. His nose can detect criminals and his sneezing leads him to believe this is all connected to Setsu and her family somehow. You see, his nose can smell a criminal and she's got him sneezing up a storm. Setsu comes up with a brilliant plan to fix her crazed son: give him a brain transplant! She takes to kidnapping neighborhood boys to find a suitable donor. Kooky hijinks ensue.

Adapting Hideshi Hino's magnificent horror manga to the screen isn't easy. For starters, his art is very stylized and everything from the characters to the gore is way, way over the top. Director Mari Asato attempts to give us a glimpse into Hino's mad world and is surprisingly successful. With a very small budget, The Boy from Hell's crew relies on their imaginations and a tongue-in-cheek attitude to bring this story to life. Having Daio played by a dwarf when he returns from hell is genius and the wildly plagiarized Deep Red soundtrack is also pretty darn awesome. The Boy from Hell is a lot of fun and its short running time and campy aesthetic help its watchability immensely. I now have a crush on Mirai Yamamoto. What a woman!

The Boy from Hell is one of the 6 films in the Theater of Horror boxset. So far, I have seen Death Train which is all right and Occult Detective Club: The Doll Cemetery which is boring and terrible. Let's hope the rest are as deliriously entertaining as The Boy from Hell. And by all means, check out Hideshi Hino's manga. It's good times!

Killer's Nocturne (1987)

Mr. Yin (Alex Man) is taking over all the nightclubs in town and oh yes, he is doing it hostilely! Mr. Yin wants revenge on Mr. Law (Yin Tse) for beating him at mahjong gambling. It's because of the shame of this defeat that forced Yin and his brother Hoi (Alex To) to live in exile in Japan for many years. Yin kills Law but makes it appear as though it was a suicide. Law's son Fung becomes obsessed with getting revenge on his father's murderer.

Fung does have some time for matters of the heart as the woman he has been chasing for many weeks is none other than nightclub singer, Miss Rachel (Pat Ha), who just happens to be Mr. Yin's main squeeze. After Fung is severely beaten by Yin's bodyguards, Rachel takes care of the guy and even falls for him which, of course, gets her killed. Fung then flees the country and gets into the boxing circuit, fighting dudes and sometimes kangaroos. When he returns, he heads straight for Mr. Yin's Endless Night nightclub to settle the score once and for all.

If you're familiar with the films of director Ngai Kai Lam such as Story of Ricky, The Cat, or Seventh Curse then the fact that he directed a gambling gangster drama action kung fu period piece shouldn't surprise you. In fact, I'm so used to this director's ability to raise my eyebrows and drop my jaw that my face is in a permanent state of surprise all day, every day. Killer's Nocturne is both melodramatic and intensely violent. It has some comic elements, romance elements, and even some fantastical elements all mixed together in one magical concoction. Many of Hong Kong's best directors blend multiple styles in one film but few are as satisfyingly cathartic, mind-blowingly kinetic, or emotionally confusing as Lam's.

My favorite character in Killer's Nocturne is Fung. Siu-hou Chin (of Mr. Vampire) plays a very likable and righteous duder who becomes so driven by his quest for vengeance that nothing in the world matters to him more than destroying Mr. Yin. I love how, while on the boxing circuit, he finds out that losing a fight earns him more money than winning. So he becomes a human punching bag to make mad cash and unintentionally trains his body to take all kinds of abuse. In fact, Fung becomes so tough that when he finally comes back to Endless Night, Yin's goons have a VERY DIFFICULT TIME trying to kick his ass. Trust me, you will be amazed by the finale of this one.

I strongly encourage adventurous viewers to seek out the films of Ngai Kai Lam. I have enjoyed every single flick of his that I have seen with the exception of Saga of the Phoenix, which is a little too kid friendly in an obnoxious and disturbing way. All of his flicks are entertaining and so damn weird. Killer's Nocturne has an especially depressing storyline but the action scenes are brilliantly staged and the characters are sympathetic. So in the end, you'll be left with a feeling of abstract ennui. Sounds good, right? An understanding of the rules of mahjong will help you out here as there are a couple of mahjong games that are part of the plot. If you, like me, don't know jack about the game, don't worry, the music queues and the actors' reactions to the outcome help immensely.

The X from Outer Space (1967)

Between the wildly wretched English dubbing for this film and its kooky theme song, I'm a very happy cult movie fan. Wait, there's a ridiculous monster too? Oh shit! So the plot goes like this: six crews of space explorers have traveled to a distant planet and all six have disappeared. Well, it turns out that the old saying, "the seventh time's the charm", is actually true as Captain Sano (Shun'ya Wazaki) and the crew of the Aabygamma (?) head out to make history (and hopefully not fucking die like all the rest).

The funniest thing during this journey is that Lisa (Peggy Neal of The Terror Beneath the Sea), the only female member of the crew, isn't allowed to touch any of the ship's controls. That's easily one of the most blatantly sexist things I've seen in a film and I have no idea if it's supposed to be intended as a joke or not. You see, Lisa needs all of her free time for a love triangle between herself, Sano, and his girlfriend Michiko (Itoko Harada), who is back at the space station, fuming with jealousy.

While they are out in space, a UFO that looks like a fried egg shows up and jams the crew's radio. Next the ship gets covered in weird glowing meteorites. They bring a sample inside and head back home to Earth. While they are busy celebrating at a very odd party, the meteor hatches like an egg. Then the giant monster known as Guilala comes out of fucking nowhere! What the heck? The editing on this film is wild.

Obviously, the monster -some reviewers call it a giant chicken but I call it "surprise LOL space-bird"- is headed toward Tokyo to do some damage. The goofy and clunky confusion continues as yet another mission to outer space is undertaken by our crew. What are they doing again? How will this last minute mission save the day? Guilala then turns into a ball and flies around, causing even more destruction. Somehow they stop it and- shit, I have no idea what to make of this baffling ending. You need to see this.

Total Destruction Anime Happy Time

Like a lot of folks my age (meaning very old), I got into anime through the little trickle of the genre that we got from TV in the 1980s. If you guessed that I'm talking about Voltron: Defender of the Universe and Robotech, then good for you! Both of those shows captured my imagination and left me wanting more.

The interesting thing about these two shows is that their American releases were fairly bastardized for our consumption. Voltron was made up of two shows: Beast King GoLion and the unrelated Armored Fleet Dairugger XV. Robotech was actually three shows cut together: Super Dimension Fortress Macross, Super Dimension Cavalry Southern Cross, and Genesis Climber MOSPEADA. Was that nerdy enough for you? I hope so.

Since I was 14 years old, anime has been almost as important to me as horror films thanks in no small part to Katsuhiro Otomo's film, Akira (1988). During a summer sleepover, one of my friends brought over a bootleg VHS of Akira. He had described this hyper-violent masterpiece to me that afternoon and I begged him to bring it over so we could watch it. Nothing I'd seen could have prepared me for the extremes of Akira.

This magnificent film transported me to a horrible world where teen angst meant comically macho freaks taking handfuls of pills, busting skulls in gang wars, wrecking motorcycles, and leaving a gaggle of pregnant girls (okay, maybe just one) in their wake. Throw in a crumbling society, government conspiracies, immoral medical experiments, and deadly telekinetic powers and I was moved. Writing about it now, I can still feel that hollow sickness in my stomach and my heart races just a little bit. I felt forever altered and the only thing that would satisfy me was more anime.

Come to think of it, during the late 90s and early 00s, anime was THE most important thing in my life. There's a lot of good stuff out there nowadays but back in the day, any newly discovered titles were sacred. Totally desperate, I would sit through all kinds of mediocre and sometimes terrible crap just to get a glimpse of some hyper kinetic Japanese drawings!

My friends, will you come with me on a little journey? I'm going to be delving into the world of anime. This is my big old belly flop into a very deep pool. I am focusing on stuff released in those dark times (the 80s/90s), the old school days of what we used to call "Japanimation".

I'm painfully aware of the fact that anime is not for everyone. Some people hate it because they've only seen the garbage (Dragonball Z, Sailor Moon (I can't lie, I love this show), Naruto, Yu-Gi-Oh!, etc.). Some people hate it because they have met one too many anime fans. Some people hate it because it's a huge industry with more genres and subgenres than you can shake a wooden sword at and they don't have a clue where to start. And

some people hate it because they just do. I'm definitely not going to convert anyone in this section of the book or even try. I'm just hoping that some of you will be entertained while I do my thang.

There are lots of cheesy horror anime titles out there and I assure you, those are high priority. However, there are so many more sci-fi, action, and sci-fi-horror-action hybrid titles in the anime abyss that I feel like I'd be missing out if I just tried to do horror exclusively. I'll be hitting up some serious giant robots too but avoiding the Robotech and the Gundam if I can. A lot of what I'll be talking about are TV series and not feature films but that's okay. Aren't TV shows just little movies? If you put them together, they make the biggest movie of all! So anyway, if you want to witness me breaking the nerd barrier or puncturing the nerd ovum wall or some other metaphor, then come on!

Ghost in the Shell (1995)

Hi there. I guess I should start with something overdone and over-analyzed to the point where it becomes generic. Ghost in the Shell is one of those titles that really is as friggin' good as everyone says it is. I first saw this film in a packed theater in Palm Beach back in 1996. It didn't matter to me that the place was a ratty dump with uncomfortable seats because I was seeing something totally new. This was an unprecedented moment in my life. It was the first time that I was seeing anime on the big screen*. If my being an anime nerd wasn't already carved in stone at that point then that night is the chisel and the mallet that made it happen. My best friend Scott was there and he told me later that the movie put him to sleep. How can two best buds be so totally different?!

There are masterpieces and there are masterpieces and then there is Ghost in the Shell. This ultra-violent spectacle has a Blade Runner boner and it doesn't skimp on the atmosphere at all. The animation is top notch with great attention lavished on lighting and shadows. Kenji Kawai's score is haunting. The guy scored Ringu and over a hundred other kickass films so yeah, you're in expert hands here. The only misstep I can find in this flick is the writing. There's a lot of cheese and techno-babble info-dumping in the dialog but you probably won't care. I know I don't!

One of the most astonishing things about this film is how it slows down and chills. When there is a moment where we can just pause and appreciate the beauty of a world overrun by technology, Ghost in the Shell never wastes it. In another film, these quiet moments might be filler or time-wasting animator showoff nonsense but this isn't over 2 hours; it's a lean 83 minutes. There are even long, philosophical conversations between cyborgs about what it means to be (formerly) human! Director Mamoru Oshii had already done a brilliant job with Patlabor 2, a gorgeous mecha movie that clocks in at 113 minutes. That 1993 effort is a fine film but it pales in comparison to this. Mad props to veteran editor Shuichi Kakesu for knowing where to trim and where to just let it ride.

Something that is a recurring phenomenon in anime of from this part of the decade is the daft English dubbing. Right now, I feel that voice actors who dub anime are a fairly respectable lot. Since anime is such a big industry, it seems to foster talented people and great performances. Well, Ghost in the Shell came out in 1995 which means the dubbing is going to be a crap shoot (emphasis on the crap). To be fair there are a few excellent voice actors in this movie and the rest are either directed to be hammy or are just overacting because no one told them to cut that shit out. How much of this is just corny dialog in the script and folks just trying to make the best of it? Honestly, I don't know.

I'm thinking that a lot of the technology and ideas expressed in this movie will seem trite or old fashioned one day (or maybe they feel that way now) but the care and artistic flourishes in every minute of this film will never go out of style. For folks who have trouble getting into anime, Ghost in the Shell is an excellent place to start. I also recommend the TV series Ghost in the Shell: Stand Alone Complex. It's a solid show and very entertaining.

As a final note, I just noticed that instead of making something new and awesome, director Mamoru Oshii decided to make Ghost in the Shell 2.0 with some CG moments and flourishes. This version is terrible and pretty much an abomination of the saddest variety. The CG is extremely invasive and the transitions between the original film and the new animation are jarring. Avoid it at all costs.

*Ah ha! I just caught myself falsely remembering Ghost in the Shell as the first anime I ever saw on the big screen but that isn't true. Technically, the first anime I saw on the big screen was Transformers: The Movie but that was an American-Korean-Japanese co-production so it kind of doesn't count. Anyway, the first real anime I ever saw (at that very same shithole theater) was Wicked City (1987) with a baffled and uncomfortable audience a few years earlier.

Locke the Superman (1984)

Locke is an ESPer (that's a person with telekinetic abilities). In fact, he's probably the most powerful ESPer in the known universe. He's famous for his hatred of war and his refusal to allow himself to age. He doesn't want to be become an adult because all adults think about is war. Adults are losers. Colonel Ryu Yamaki tries to employ Locke to help him stop Lady Kahn, an ESPer who is building an army of evil ESPers to take over the universe. This Lady Kahn character wants to create a kingdom with herself on the throne to rule for a thousand years.

At first, Locke is hesitant to join up with Yamaki because he doesn't like violence. Once he senses how dangerous Lady Kahn actually is, he signs right up! Meanwhile, Lady Kahn and her right hand lady, Cornelia Prim, plan to use Jessica (a purple-haired ESPer) as a tool to destroy Locke. They implant false memories (of Locke killing her parents) and violent suggestions in her head, give her a new personality named Amelia, and send her off to seduce Yamaki. The moment she lays eyes on Locke, all hell breaks loose as Jessica/Amelia attacks with all of her powers.

After this vicious assassination attempt fails, Jessica/Amelia is basically left a basketcase and Yamaki is injured but mostly in his heart (awww, you poor baby!). As Locke is leaving to go wreck some shit at Lady Kahn's space fortress, Yamaki insists on going with him. The two dudes teleport (oh yeah, Locke can do that) to the distant part of the galaxy where Kahn and her army are hiding out. An epic showdown takes place and you'll just have to check out the film to find out how it ends.

> *"This automatic gun will fire if you use your powers to snuff out any of those candles. Which means that man will die."*

This entertaining flick from Hiroshi Fukutomi, the director of Battle Angel (1993), really hit my sweet spot. All the blood, gratuitous nudity, melodrama, heavy-handed messages, and silliness I crave from 80s anime is all here. The animation is pretty good. There are some flubs and awkward transitions but the style is exactly the kind of old school look that I love. Did I mention the homosexual overtones between Locke and Yamaki? No? Oh well, maybe we'll have time for that if we all decide to never grow up. Locke the Superman is one heck of a good time.

Demon City Shinjuku (1988)

Ten years after a terrible disaster that left Shinjuku in ruins but the rest of Tokyo intact, a man named Levih Rah, who sold his soul to hell, is preparing to call forth demons from a rift in the sky to destroy humanity. A young man named Kyoya, who possesses great psychic powers, rises up against him after discovering that Rah killed his father. After the president is cursed by one of Rah's assassins, his daughter Sayaka approaches Kyoya to ask for help. She wants to get into Shinjuku and stop Rah before her father dies from the curse. Knowing that Sayaka will go in alone if he doesn't bring her along, Kyoya reluctantly agrees to help. Inside the cursed city, the two face many perils including demons, bandits, two-headed dogs, and Rah himself.

Silly me, I had Demon City Shinjuku mixed up with Doomed Megalopolis (1991) which I didn't like (but should probably revisit). So I didn't give this one a chance when I should have AKA a long ass time ago. Director Yoshiaki Kawajiri would go on to direct Ninja Scroll (1993) and Vampire Hunter D: Bloodlust (2000), both based on works by author Hideyuki Kekuchi, but I really like what he did here. My only complaints about this flick are the presence of kooky side characters with annoying character designs and some very dated music queues. But there are enough haunting moments and action-packed battles to compensate for these not-so-hot stylistic complaints.

> *"I've got more important things to do than saving the world's asshole."*

A word of warning: if you can avoid the English dub of this flick, then do it. It's good for a laugh but the subtitled version of the Japanese is much better thanks to a great cast. The dub is quite different with its total lack of logic and loads of very silly and pointless cursing. Younger anime fans have no idea what a crap shoot the English dubbing was back in the day. It wasn't that the voice actors of old were uniformly terrible or anything but most of the production companies couldn't always afford the best voice actors. It was quite rare to hear a good cast on a series or an animated feature film during the lean years of anime. Trust me, y'all got it good nowadays.

I speak from experience when I say that to find horror anime from the 80s that isn't embarrassing or totally lame is pretty special. There isn't even any tentacle rape in Demon City Shinjuku! (That might be a disappointment to some of you out there.) This is just the kind of thing that could have fueled my childhood imagination. And since I'm on my 8th childhood now, this is fitting in just fine. There are more cool characters than lame ones and there's also some gore on display. The story might be a little on the silly side but the short running time certainly keeps any potential meandering in check. All in all, I'm really glad I finally got around to Demon City Shinjuku.

Queen Millennia (1982)

The place: Tokyo. The time: 1999. You know what though? Tokyo 1999 looks like Pittsburgh 2076. Anyway, Yukino is just your average young lady who also happens to be a friggin' alien space queen (or whatever). She stays on the Earth to keep an eye on us stupid humans. Her one thousand year reign is up and it's time for one of her sisters (chick has a lot sisters) to take over. On Lar Metal, Yukino's planet, all of its people sleep during winter - which is a thousand years long- and they only wake up during the "momentary spring".

Well, these guardians are sick of the warlike, moronic humans who are always destroying the Earth and they want it for themselves so they can stay awake all throughout the millennium. They trick Yukino and the humans into thinking that Lar Metal is going to collide with Earth by throwing the entire planet into chaos with a wicked meteor shower. BUT IN REALITY, they are just going to get the planets close enough so that they can cross the "ephemeral bridge" (?) and take our planet for themselves. Bastards!

Yukino says, "Fuck you, fuckers!" (I'm paraphrasing) to her alien comrades and decides to rescue as many humans as she can and go to war against her own kind. With her student Hajime (one of those damn pygmy-sized male lead characters that you see over and over again in manga artist Leiji Matsumoto's work), her badass sister Selen, and a continent sized warship on her side, Yukino gives her all to stop the plot that her dumb dickhead alien shitface friends have concocted.

One of my favorite things about Queen Millennia is the score by Kitaro. It is electro-fabulousness of the highest order mixed with the most melodramatic orchestra in the universe. I fucking love it. For a 2 hour movie, I'd say the pacing is pretty good. Once you get through the first half hour or so, you'll probably get hooked. And when you've got all the gothic overtones and straight-faced, pretentious, and hokey dialog under your skin, it's hard to shake and that's a good thing. There's also some nice atmosphere, great animation, and some pretty spectacular disaster sequences.

The Curse of Kazuo Umezu (1990)

Horror manga master and general lunatic, Kazuo Umezu, introduces a pair of horror tales from the comfort of a swing in a park after midnight. The first story is about Masami, a young girl who thinks that Rima, the new and beautiful girl at school, is a vampire who is attacking her at night. Every morning she wakes up screaming from a nightmare with a small hole on her throat. A friend at school offers to let her use his video camera to record her bedroom while she is asleep to see what is really going on. Bad idea.

The second story involves two ditzy high school friends, Miko and Nanako. Nanako likes horror movies and being frightened while Miko is a bit of a scaredy cat. The two of them and a couple of their girlfriends from school decide to explore the supposedly haunted mansion. After some creepy weirdness happens, Nanako decides to taunt a ghost. Really, really bad idea.

One of the most frustrating things about horror manga artists like Kazuo Umezo is that it is almost impossible to adapt their work for film or TV. When it comes to anime however, there's a greater chance that something magical can happen. And that's just what happens here in The Curse of Kazuo Umezu. These two stories have a very corny yet dark ironic thing going on and there's lots of blood. It feels exactly like the artist's twisted manga and the animation style (though a little clunky and cheap) is perfect for the material. You need to track down this two story one-off wherever you can find it because it's just a silly, spooky, and gory good time. I was left wanting more!

Digital Devil Monogatari Megami Tensei (1987)

When Yumiko transfers to a new school, she is immediately drawn to antisocial computer geek Akemi Nakajima. She feels as though they have met somewhere before. She decides to stay after school and spy on this jerky loner. Akemi is obsessed with conjuring demons using his computer. He's using his hot teacher as a love offering to the demon Loki.

Unfortunately, Loki wants more and the "more" he wants is Yumiko. The demon breaks out of his computer chip prison, possesses the hot teacher, takes over the school, and tries to make Yumiko into a nice little snack. Akemi tries to fight back but he's kind of a wuss. Luckily, Yumiko is the reincarnation of a god and she might be able to help put Loki in his place.

When it comes to old school anime, I have a big old soft spot. So if the story is weak and the art is cheesy, I can be swayed if I get that nostalgic feeling of my youth spent tearing through Blockbuster Video's lame ass anime section looking for something, anything of value. Based on a popular role playing game (which itself is based on a novel), Digital Devil Monogatari Megami Tensei does indeed deliver the goods despite its faults. Another important factor is that my copy of this flick is a little under the weather. The grubbiness adds to the feeling that something just ain't right.

Digital Devil is bloody, horrific, a little trashy, and violent as hell. The story definitely does some meandering and goes down some convoluted paths. For instance, why did the demon need to infect that bank's computers and kill everyone there? Was the writer pissed off about those bounced check fees? Did the director have an ex-girlfriend who was a bank teller? I don't know, just enjoy the spurting blood, I guess. The music is also quite good in this one and the artists use some awesome colors to bring this odd story to life.

I've been waiting for this anime my whole life, I just hadn't found it yet. But it's not all roses, my friends. Before you go looking for this one, keep in mind that I did fall asleep at least once. I woke up, got confused by the plot, and tried to back track but it didn't really help. It's just not clear what's going on and it really doesn't matter. Digital Devil is a pretty great horror anime but story wise, it's got some serious issues that it makes up for with a dark atmosphere and some blood and guts.

X (1996)

The city of Tokyo is about to be ass raped. The final battle to determine the fate of the planet Earth is about to go down within the city limits and you know it's gonna get ugly. Kamui, who has mommy issues and looks really good in a cape, is coming to town even though his presence will bring about the apocalypse. He just can't resist meeting up with his childhood friends, brother and sister: Fuma and Kotari.

Some evil wizardy type folks with crazy powers are going to recruit Fuma to fight with Kamui over the city, the planet, and Kotari. Not surprisingly, Kamui is in love with Kotari so yeah, that's a thing too. Kamui is not alone in his fight since there are also good wizardy type folks with crazy powers who want to save the Earth. Blah blah blah, energy dragons, people with swords inside their hearts, cherry blossom petals, angel wings, etc. You get the idea.

Don't let my snarkiness fool you, I really dig X. The score is epic as are the battle scenes and prophetic visions. The animation is outstanding and I'm just guessing that this had a huge budget from the looks of things. Director Rintaro, who did Galaxy Express 999 (1979), really, really loves destroying Tokyo and it shows. This film makes me very curious about the 2001 animated series based on the same manga from Clamp.

My only complaints about this film are 1) it feels a little too long and 2) it also feels condensed at the same time. X has a lot of characters and many of them are barely introduced at all. At the risk of contradicting myself, I wish this film didn't feel longer but actually was longer. Fleshing out the characters, even just a little, would have helped things greatly. I would avoid the English dub on this one. The corny dialog is less painful when it's subtitled. For rivers of blood and lots of destruction, give this film a look. Just turn your brain off when it comes to the story.

Gamera, Super Monster (1980)

This film is about... Oh please don't make me think about it. Shit! Okay, fine. Space alien ladies come to Earth for some reason and a little dumbass kid named Keiichi does some stuff and there's an evil space lady and Gamera battles monsters and Keiichi thinks his pet turtle is Gamera or um- FAAAAART!!!! It really doesn't fucking matter.

My wife (because she's awesome) got me another Shout Factory double DVD set of Elvira's Movie Macabre. This time it was Gamera, Super Monster and They Came from Beyond Space. Until I put the disc in, I thought that I had never seen this Gamera film before. But after only a few minutes, the whole mess came flooding back into my brain. This less-than-half-assed garbage had kept me glued to the couch for 2 hours (with commercials) once upon a time. Before we go any further, I am NOT recommending this. Gamera, Super Monster fucking sucks. Got it? Good. I had to get that out of the way.

What's really interesting is how much I hate stock footage now, especially when a sequel or a film in a series reuses footage from previous entries. Obviously, flashbacks (within reason) are fine but when old footage is presented as new material I get pretty pissed off. However, I think 80 percent (or more) of this film is footage from other Gamera flicks (six according to IMDB). It's unbearably annoying seeing footage from 60s and 70s films cut into a film from 1980. That being said; how did this affect my enjoyment as a kid in the 80s? Not at all. This episode of Movie Macabre premiered in 1983 but God only knows when I caught it. Either way, my young mind just enjoyed the monster mayhem (and oh yeah, I had a huge crush on Kilara, one of the trio of super space chicks).

You might be wondering how the hell this film fits into anime. Well, speaking of stock footage, while crapping around in space, Gamera runs into two anime icons and it really blew my mind. First he runs into Space Cruiser Yamato during Keichii's dream and then later, he flies by Galaxy Express 999. Um, what the fuck? Bonus trivia: This film was so poorly received that it bankrupt the studio that produced it and there wasn't another Gamera movie for 15 years.

Leda: The Fantastical Adventures of Yohko (1985)

So this teenage girl named Yohko has a crush on a dude but he doesn't know she exists. She writes him a love song and chickens out when she's about to hand him the tape. Suddenly, Yohko gets whisked away to Ashanty, a magical land with fantastic beasts, bizarre creatures, and weird mecha. She makes friends with a talking dog named Ringhum, loses her Walkman with her precious love song, and falls into a plant that transforms her from boring plain ordinary Yohko into scantily-clad badass sword-wielding Yohko.

You see, her love song isn't just some ordinary pop jam. Hell no! In Ashanty, her dumb old song is the source of something called "Leda magic". And it is been prophesied that if the "Leda magic" falls into the wrong hands, a warrior will come to set things right. Obviously, Yohko is that warrior and those wrong hands belong to Zell, an androgynous duder who's looking for "Leda's heart". Zell wants to take advantage of the hole (tee hee) in space and time between Ashanty and Earth. Why? Brace yourself. He wants to conquer our planet!

So Zell has this army of robots or whatever. Sure Yohko is pretty cool and all with her newly discovered super sword-fighting abilities but she is only one person. How can she hopefully hope to defeat all this freakin' evil and get home to Earth so she can confess her love to that dude? Enter Yoni, a shrine maiden who pilots a giant mecha (that looks like the Tin Man), to help Yohko bring the pain to Zell and his weird cronies.

I like how the people behind this animated feature couldn't decide if they should go with the fantasy genre or the mecha genre or the whatever-the-fuck genre then they said, "Fuck it, let's do all three!" I expected this to be a lot more sleazy (don't worry, someone actually animated a porn version) and violent. There's no blood in the action sequences but they aren't hurt by its absence. This movie also features the least annoying talking dog in the history of animation. I like Leda despite the fact that the plot is embarrassingly stupid. The 80s cheese and accompanying soundtrack are big bonuses. Before he went all Pokemon on us, director Kunihiko Yuyama did one of my childhood favorites: Windaria (1986).

Boogiepop Phantom (2000)

One month ago, a beam of light shot into the sky and a surge of energy swept over the city giving people (especially teenagers) some special and terrible powers. As more and more people are disappearing, rumors spread about a mysterious figure named Boogiepop who will come and take you away. Is she a demon? An angel? What the damn hell is really going on? A girl named Nagi Kimira is trying to find out and she's out there, hunting Boogiepop. Can she handle the truth once she finds it? I know because I've watched this already. Ha ha! Now it's your turn.

A weird haze has settled over this strange and distorted world and nothing makes sense anymore. There are horrible, terrible things out there and they are hungry. Oh yes, I love me some Boogiepop Phantom. This anime series based on the novels by Kouhei Kadono is full of human misery and instilled with a dark, ironic beauty. There are several key characters to keep up with and the fractured timeline is intentionally told out of sequence to keep the mystery under wraps. This makes the pace quite erratic so sometimes the show will focus on something quiet for a long stretch but something creepy or just plain fucked up will come out of nowhere to keep things from getting boring.

Boogiepop Phantom has some briefly shown but crazy gore and an awesome electronic score. It is quite tempting to want to watch this entire hallucinatory series in one sitting but the show's atmosphere is perhaps too heady for that. You might want to try taking a break in the middle somewhere. Trust me. Telekinetic powers, electric ghosts, a secret organization, giant bugs that feed on grief, a drug that you take by pouring drops of it into a candle's flame (huh?), and a vicious serial killer all await you, dear friends, if you choose to hook up with Boogiepop. And I strongly suggest you do.

Megazone 23 - Part I (1985)

Shogo is a free-wheelin' hot rodder in early 1980s Japan. He cruises around with his buddy and chases chicks. One day, he nearly runs over a hottie named Yui Takanaka. While giving her a ride to an audition, Shogo finds out that she's a dancer looking for her big break. Sparks fly and he gets her number. But Shogo's life is about to change forever when his old pal Shinji turns up with a stolen mechanized prototype motorcycle called the Bahamut. Some evil government agents want the bike back and kill Shinji. Because he's such a skilled rider and such a radical dude, Shogo escapes on the Bahamut.

Shogo attempts to contact the MTV-like station to get the host and pop idol Eve Tokimatsuri to broadcast images of Bahamut and his story. But those tricky government agents block that shit and send even more agents after Shogo. On a crazy highway chase, the Bahamut transforms into a mecha! Whoa, I didn't see that coming! Yui and her roommates are drawn into the violence and we find out that the world that everyone knows is bullshit. SPOILER: The city is actually a spaceship floating around... in space. The military is preparing to fight aliens and for some reason, normal citizens are kept in this fantasy world of 1980s Japan. To be continued in Part II.

Oh Megazone 23, where have you been all my life? Director Noboru Ishigoru also directed one of my favorite animated films of all time: Macross: Do You Remember Love? (1984) so you know I am down with this shit. I love the character designs by Toshihiro Hirano. The story is pretty weak (that big revelation doesn't make a lick of sense) but this is some violent and bloody melodramatic entertainment. I am definitely looking forward (though somewhat terrified) of what Parts II and III may bring. I seriously wish I had seen this 25 years ago.

Megazone 23 - Part II (1986)

The humans aboard the spaceship Megazone 23 are still unaware that a) they're not on frickin' Earth and b) that they're at war with an alien race. Shogo (named Johnny Winters in the English version) is still a dang rebel rouser. He has been living underground since discovering the truth in the last movie. One day, he rides a motorcycle through a mall for some reason. Then he and his gang get into an all-out riot with some cops. He is reunited with Yui (AKA Suzy Sue in the English) and things are tense because they're dumb. Eve tries to contact Shogo so he goes off to try and meet her.

The military intercepts Eve's transmission and sets up a decoy to catch Shogo. He and his crew get ambushed by da gubbment but they escape on a Bahamut (a mecha-motorcycle thingie). Now Shogo's gang is arming themselves with machine guns and Molotov cocktails to go to war with the cops. Shit just got real. After some intense fighting, the alien enemy interrupts with their tentacle fury and the surviving members of Shogo's gang witness first hand that we ain't alone in da universe.

The military duder meets up with Shogo and explains to him what the heck is going on. There is an alien race called the Gorik and they are dicks. To combat them, the moon was built into some kind of weapon to destroy them. Of course, anything that gets in the way is also destroyed and Megazone 23 is now in danger. So yeah, the human race is up shit creek. Have I mentioned that I'm watching the Harmony Gold translated version? It's fucking obtuse. I'm not even sure I'm explaining this correctly.

Shogo and Yui finally get to meet Eve and it's just in time too. Yui got shot during the fight and of course a being like Eve (whatever she is) is able to heal her just in time. While that's going on, Eve and Shogo shoot the shit. He bitches about how grownups are jerks or whatever. She tells him that 500 years ago, the ship took the remaining humans into space and tricked them into thinking they were still on Earth. Then she enacts a program called ADAM which will take the ship back to Earth. Whether or not this will mean the extinction of the human race, well Eve doesn't know. This is a little damn confusing.

"Sorry Lightning, I'm just not in a party mood, I guess."

Well, Megazone 23 – Part II is pretty dang fun. The plot is a head-scratcher but there's lots of space and mecha action. The motorcycle gang scenes are ultra-violent and very reminiscent of the ones in Akira. Part II also has an intriguing atmosphere that I can't quite put my finger on. The animation is very nice though it is a different style from Part I. That being said, I really don't like the character designs. They're kind of ugly. Okay, they are really fucking ugly. Shogo even has a sexy mullet. Director Ichiro Itano would go on to direct the amazing Gantz anime series. The score is okay. It relies on too much heavy metal in the action sequences. For the record, I tried to watch Part III of this series but got about 2 minutes in and gave up.

Serial Experiments Lain (1998)

Lain Iwakura is totally not your average schoolgirl. She is a space cadet (not literally) and she knows nothing about computers. She is the charity case of some school chums. Alice, Reika, and Julie are always trying to get Lain out of her shell. Things get weird when another of her friends at school named Chisa sends Lain an email. I know what you're thinking: "Like OMG, Lain? How does she have friends? She's such a weirdo!" No, that's not the weird thing. The weird thing is that Chisa has been dead for a week (she took a header off a very tall building) and is claiming that her soul now resides on The Wired (AKA The Internet). Lain finds this intriguing and decides to look into this whole "computer thing".

Speaking of fucked up home lives, Lain's is a real doozy. Her father is a workaholic computer engineer who only pays attention to Lain when she starts showing interest in updating her Navi (AKA personal computer). Her mother is an emotional iceberg. Hell, they both might be robots. And lastly, Lain's sister Mika is a total beyatch so I guess she's the only normal one. Well, "normal" until she is replaced by a gibbering doppelganger but I'm getting ahead of myself.

Lain takes to The Wired like a middle aged pervert takes to a video camera at an anime convention. She immediately discovers her true self online, a totally badass hacker who doesn't take shit from anybody. The more time she spends on the computer, the stranger her world becomes. Some weird "Men in Black" type duders start following her around, someone on The Wired begins impersonating Lain for nefarious purposes, she meets a presence online that claims to be God, and she even witnesses a shooting at the local nightclub, Cyberia. Get it? Cyberia!

Back in 2000, when I first saw Serial Experiments Lain, this show was quite a game-changer. I had never seen anything this cerebral or unsettling in anime before. It takes techno-horror to a whole other level with huge doses of paranoia and depressing themes. Subjects like religion, drugs, video games, sex, aliens, the alienation of modern life, and people's fear of computers are done very well here in horrifying, surreal, and hallucinatory ways.

My only complaints about the show are that it is a little talky (more ideas than action), the technology in the plot is getting a little dated, and there were obviously some budgetary constraints since there are some reused and re-purposed shots throughout the later episodes. The English dub is kind of corny in spots but over the years, I've gotten so used to it that it doesn't bother me much. Flip it over the J-dub if it bugs ya. Either way, Serial Experiments Lain is definitely worth checking out.

Harmagedon (1983)

I was 16 years old when my mom sent me off to stay with our family friend in San Diego. I hit the local video store like a man possessed. I figured that video stores out in California would have huge selections of Japanese animation. Boy was I wrong (or maybe I was just at the wrong store). Anyway, they didn't have crap. The only tape that wasn't familiar to me was something called Harmagedon. It had Katsuhiro Otomo's name all over it so I figured "Hey, this has got to be as good as Akira, right?" Boy was I wrong again. I triple hated the shit out of Harmagedon and haven't watched it again... until now!

This fairly obnoxious doomsayer is running around Tokyo predicting terrible shit and then Princess Luna of Transylvania has a vision while flying in a big jumbo jet. A giant evil force named Genma is devouring the universe and it's got a big (metaphoric) hard-on for Earth for some reason. The plane is destroyed by an asteroid and Luna becomes Psionic Warrior Luna, defender of the Earth. She is commanded by Floy, a benevolent supernatural force, to take Vega, a 2200 year old combat android, to save the dang world.

Luna and Vega's first mission is to recruit Jo, an ordinary Japanese high school student (and jerkwad), and awaken his psionic powers. Jo freaks out and runs around misusing his powers. When he finally gets his shit together

Richard Glenn Schmidt

and faces his creepy sister-love complex, he agrees to join the fight against Genma. The slimy and weird looking monster generals that work for Genma go after Jo using the people he cares about like his bitchy girlfriend, his dorky friend, and of course, his sister Michiko. Ohhhh Michiko. Ohhhh, dear sweet, overprotective and smother MichikOH BABY BABY, OH BABY BABY!

So okay, whatever, Luna gathers together her multinational team of psionic warriors to train Jo on the fly and get ready to battle Genma. New York City is destroyed and Tokyo just kind of dies in a sandstorm or something. Jo finally stops being a pussy and rises to become the strongest of the psionic duders and well, you can kind of guess the rest of the movie from there.

I'm really glad I gave Harmagedon another chance. It didn't blow my mind or anything but it wasn't nearly as horrible as I remembered. Sure it is a little long in the tooth and there are a few cheese-stank maudlin moments (the scene where Jo leads the animals out of the burning forest like he was Animal Jesus!), but Harmagedon has some great scenes and even some dashes of horror that really worked for me. As for Katsuhiro Otomo's involvement, he did the character designs and some animation work. This really is Rinatro's beast.

Demon Prince Enma (2007)

Enma is a demon from Hell sent to retrieve escapees who are maligning and destroying humankind one soul at a time. Those who don't wish to follow him back to Hell are destroyed. To help him with his task (and to make sure he stays in line) is Yukihime, a sexy snow demon, and Kapaeru, a kappa who lives in Japan posing as a man in a costume promoting a hostess club. There's also Enma's talking hat but I won't go into that now. All you need to know is that there is some funky demonic shit going on and this ragtag group of private eyes are gonna rectify.

Demon Prince Enma (no, it's not ENEMA!) is a great though unfairly short horror anime series from director Mamoru Kanbe and writer Takao Yoshioka based on a manga/anime series from Gô Nagai. The animation is stunning though there is some computer generated business in the last two episodes. The interior of a haunted house has been created using 3D and it's pretty cheesy.

Apparently, the original Demon Prince Enma is a comedy series featuring monsters and demons. This OVA (meaning straight-to-video) drops all but a hint of the comedy in favor of amping up the mystery and horror aspects of the story. What little comedy is left has to do with Enma's lecherous personality and Kapaeru's goofy -though oddly charming- ways. The plot is pretty simple and you won't need to think too much when you watch Enma. My only complaint is that the third episode really drags. The characters spend too much time wandering around the CGI haunted house and it paralyzes the pacing. That being said, these four episodes are a bloody, eerie, and sexy (don't forget the sexy!) way to spend a couple of hours.

Odin: Photon Sailer Starlight (1986)

The year is 2099 and Earth is sending a new type of spaceship, the Starlight, out to explore the galaxy. The ship is a ship like with sails, a boatswain, a poop deck, a plank, I don't know, the works. This big laser sends a beam out through space and the Starlight follows it. When the crew is about to do their big warp drive test, they pick up a distress signal from a ship called the Alfred. Next thing you know, some asshole named Akira starts dive-bombing the Starlight with his little space fighter. The crew is amused and decide to let him on board. When they test the warp drive, Akira ends up piloting the fucking ship.

So they get to the wreckage of the Alfred and they find a lone survivor, a girl with white hair named Sarah Cyanbaker. The crew of the Starlight also encounter a dickish alien race who begin a series of relentless attacks on their ship. When the alien spacecraft self-destructs, it causes the Starlight to fly through a space buttcrack which transports them even farther away from home. The aliens are related to Odin or whatever. Sarah can read the ancient alien language or Norwegian and they are searching for Odin or whatever. I fell asleep a lot during this stuff. Long story short, the Starlight goes against the alien threat in a huge battle.

The first thing you need to know about this movie is the heavy metal songs in the soundtrack. The famous Japanese metal band Loudness provides the score for some pretty hilarious scenes of the crew running toward their posts on the ship. Be sure to stick around for the epilogue of the film when Loudness themselves actually make an appearance. The rest of the score is made up of pleasing synthy bleeps and bloops.

The second thing you need to know about this movie is its length. This movie is way, way too long for its own good. I actually recommend the American version over the Japanese. Its 50 minutes shorter and it keeps all the good stuff intact. If you choose to do the longer cut, just put it on mute, get high, and put on your Yes records or your Helloween records or whatever the fuck records. I tried to do the Japanese version and passed the hell out. I went back and saw that I had slept through the climactic battle. It's worth staying awake for, I guess. Or not.

Metal Skin Panic Madox-01 (1987)

This weapon designer lady named Ellie designs a weapon called the Madox-01. It's a mechanized suit that allows the person riding in it to blow shit up and fly and jump and shit. She pilots it and during a test run, she pisses off a tank driver named Shitballs. Shitballs vows revenge on Ellie but really he has no real plan of action. I mean, what can he do? This is the military, there's no room for personal vendettas. Do you understand what I'm saying? While the Madox-01 is being transported through the city, a drunk driver causes an accident and the unit falls into the hands of Daydreamer. Daydreamer is a putz who lives with Potato Head, the sexually frustrated freckle-faced jackoff bastard.

A couple years ago, Daydreamer broke up with his girlfriend because she wasn't paying enough attention to him or whatever. She's back in town and wants to meet up. Stuck inside the Madox-01, Daydreamer decides to keep their date at the top of the MacMillan Toy Company building. This fucking guy... Hilarity ensues when Ellie and Shitballs pursue Daydreamer so that they can reclaim the Madox-01.

Boy was I surprised when I started watching this garbage. Metal Skin Picnic is bafflingly shitty, totally generic, and boring to boot. There are good people behind this so maybe my expectations were a little high going into it. But holy shit, there is just no excuse for this. The action is okay-ish but the characters are very bland -they may be adults but they have teenage-sized problems- and the plot just isn't interesting. Don't waste your time.

Ariel (1989)

Dr. Kishida has developed a mecha named Ariel in order to combat aliens that are determined to take over the Earth. Unfortunately for Kishida, only his granddaughters can pilot Ariel and all three hate him. Well actually, only two. Aya is a brainy brat who just wants to finish college. Mia is a willful tomboy that refuses to be a mecha pilot. Kazumi is the youngest and least mature but she at least is willing to do whatever her grandpa asks of her. Hey, you pervert. It's not like that. Trust me, there's nothing like that going on here.

The aliens are led by Albert Houser, a droopy-eyed sort who is kind of a loser. He has grand scale plans for planet Earth but the accounting department is the biggest threat to a successful invasion. Houser is assisted by Simone, a real wet blanket who is more concerned with the bottom line than conquering the universe. Another alien, a badass named Ragnus takes over the invasion so that some shit will finally happen in this fucking anime. But he has to contend with not only Ariel but also a traitorous alien duder named Saber Starburst (I'm not making that up) who wants to stop his alien brethren for some dang reason.

I picked up Ariel real cheap on VHS and I'm glad it was cheap. Don't get me wrong, this isn't too bad. I dig the action (especially the giant monster designs) and the characters are okay. The score is abysmally generic and lame in the worst way. I love how the threat of an audit from the alien IRS is helping keep Earth safe. So yeah, this is a decent timewaster. I haven't gotten around to Ariel Deluxe yet so I don't know if that is an improvement or not.

Fly Me to the Moon

Speaking of game-changing anime titles, Neon Genesis Evangelion (1995) rocked my world when I first saw it back in 1999. Now don't get me wrong, it wasn't totally consensual. If you have a heart, this show (and the theatrical films) will emotionally rape you. I remember watching this with my girlfriend Kim at the time, being depressed for a week afterward, and loving every minute of it. This show made me a lifelong fan of its production company, Gainax. Whatever they have up their sleeves, you can be sure that I'll check it out.

A decade after mankind was nearly wiped out in a huge cataclysm, three teenagers, Shinji, Asuka, and Rei, are chosen to pilot the Evas, giant robots that have been built to protect the Earth from monsters (nicknamed Angels) that fall from the sky. For unknown reasons, these Angels are bent on destroying NERV, a corporation run by Shinji's father, Gendo Ikari. Battle after battle ensue as the Angels become smarter and more adept in their attacks. It's up to Captain Misato Katsuragi to train these kids to fight but at what cost? With the world on the brink at every turn, these questions remain: What are these creatures exactly and what are their intentions? Is the destruction of the human race really their only mission? What horrible secrets are lurking in the bowels of the NERV Corporation's giant underground fortress?

Sounds a little generic, right? Sounds like a thousand other giant robot shows? Well, let me tell you something, this ain't your ordinary mecha-melodrama. This show takes high octane, high stakes action and blends it (to be fair, not always seamlessly) with psychoanalysis and religion. Evangelion is really, really smart. It's also populated by well written characters that you actually care about. It's also a gory spectacle with lots of disturbing imagery and more than a few jaw-dropping surprises throughout its run.

Now when I recommend this one, I am not fucking around. You need to see all 26 episodes of the original series and both theatrical films: Death & Rebirth and The End of Evangelion. If you survive that then check out the newly revamped and retold Rebuild of Evangelion films which expands the story (but I feel like they don't really stand on their own; but I might be wrong, there are still 2 more full length films that haven't come out yet). So yeah, if you haven't seen this show, check it out. If you have and didn't like it, give it another go. Evangelion is a richly rewarding experience. They've also released a second series of films that expand on the original characters and stories. Essential viewing.

Richard Glenn Schmidt

4 FRANCO FRIDAY

One director that has always confused me is Jess Franco. Sometimes that confusion is a good thing and other times that confusion is more like a contusion on my brain. I think a lot of Eurohorror fans who've been down this road have had the similar disappointments and orgasmatic (that's orgasm plus cinematic) moments that I have had with this guy's often mind-blowing body of work. But MY PERSPECTIVE on his films is PRETTY AMAZING and TOTALLY UNIQUE. Just kidding, I have no idea what the fuck I'm doing traipsing around in this horny old man's profoundly mad universe.

In January of 2011, I attempted to review one of Franco's films every Friday for 52 weeks. I got through about 33 of them before I finally snapped and gave up. After a little time away from "Old Jess", I came back and managed to review around 20 more of his films. That leaves only 906 more films that Jess Franco directed left for me to watch. Here are all my Franco Fridays in the order that they happened. I hope you like them.

Kiss Me, Killer (1977)

A bunch of gangsters plan a drug heist that, of course, goes completely to shit and people start getting killed. Gangster Paul Radeck (Francisco Acosta) blames drug dealer Freddy Carter (Alberto Dalbes) for the screw-up and shoots him and his buddy. Believing that Freddy is dead, Paul then marries Linda (Alice Arno), his widow. Things are just hunky dory until one night, at a nightclub, Linda hears the band play a song that her dead husband wrote for her. Is Freddy alive? Let the intrigue begin! A stripper named Moira Ray (Lina Romay) comes along and seems to have some sort of agenda or something. Freddy, who is totally alive, hooks up with Moira and just keeps messing with Radeck's head until they meet up for a violent showdown.

The opening titles on the copy of this movie on Netflix looks like it was filmed on a roll of toilet paper. Luckily, as the film keeps playing, the quality continually improves. The soundtrack is drowsy and jazzy and the dubbing is totally outrageous. Is this just some slapped together moments of nonsense, pieces from other films, or what? The opening drug heist is filmed and dubbed so poorly that it is almost impossible to know what's going on. Who are these people? Why did that guy shoot that guy? Oh, there are drugs involved? Whaaaat? And that's just the first 7 or 8 minutes.

Kiss Me, Killer (a remake of Franco's own 1964 film, La Muerte Silba un Blues) is frustrating and yet it is definitely some interesting stuff, my friends. There are lots of confusing moments, seemingly random tangents, and parts that just kind of feel like Jess Franco's home movies. The funniest scene is when Alberto Dalbes runs into some street punks who try to shake him down and he kicks their asses. An Asian woman, who was watching the whole incident, runs up and shouts, "Ha ha! They got what they deserved!" And that's the last time she shows up in the movie. It's quite awesome.

Lina Romay is so great! Whether she's in the shower, doing a striptease, spray-painting a stripper's butt with gold paint, licking a statue of David, getting whipped with a belt, whatever! And hats off to her voice actress too for a perfect performance. I have fallen in love with Alice Arno. The reaction she gives when Linda finds out that the love of her life is still alive is fucking brilliant. It's like someone just told her that the air in her tire is low. The tire isn't flat, she just needs to put a little air in it.

Kiss Me, Killer is part softcore sex romp, part listless crime caper, and part jazzy jazz jazz movie that has some cool moments hidden away in its overly long running time. Much to my surprise, I couldn't help but get wrapped up in the characters. And speaking of softcore sex, I gotta warn you, this film has lots of it. I'm pretty meh about the whole constant zooming in on a lady's gooch and what not. So yeah, there's that. But it's worth slogging through if you can. The finale where every one of the voice actors reads a paragraph of very helpful exposition is a riot and the director himself plays a guru who raises his hands up in the air and proclaims that the end is near. Perfect.

The Bloody Judge (1970)

Some happy-go-lucky pagans are hassled by the cops and Alicia Gray (Margaret Lee) is arrested for consorting (read as "getting it on") with a man accused of witchcraft. Judge Jeffreys (Christopher Lee) asks for the executioner (Howard Vernon) to test her with some horrible tortures to see if she is a witch herself. Alicia's sister Mary comes to Judge Jeffreys to beg for his mercy. Since Mary is totally hot, Judge Jeffreys asks for her to give herself to him in order to spare Alicia. She refuses and Alicia is put to death. A blind witch named Mother Rosa (Maria Schell) prophesizes that Mary has some bad shit is coming her way.

Of course, Judge Jeffreys is paranoid, corrupt, and is using his power to stamp out enemies of the king. His spies report that a man named Barnaby (Pietro Martellanza) is behind a conspiracy against the king. The Judge finds out that Harry (Hans Hass Jr.), the son of his associate Lord Wessex, is friends with Barnaby and that he has taken up with Mary, the object of his desire. The judge takes Mary away to hide her from Harry. When Lord Wessex's lackey Satchel (Milo Quesada) tries to rape Mary, she shoves his face into a fireplace. Luckily, Harry shows up and takes her away.

While a bunch of armies are fighting over England, Barnaby is injured and Harry takes him to a hideout. Satchel, who is now deformed and working for Judge Jeffreys, discovers this and has all the rebel women rounded up to be tried and executed. Harry and Mary are arrested and put on trial. Harry is spared thanks to his father's connections but Mary gets into even more trouble when she tries to murder the judge. What will become of her and will someone finally hold the judge accountable for his actions?

I'm astonished by how lavish this production is and I still can't believe Franco made this. Now I'm not saying that the guy was a bad filmmaker but I definitely didn't see this one coming. The Bloody Judge is more than capably directed and has excellent sets and scenery. The superb music score comes from the amazing Bruno Nicholai. There is also a thick layer of sleaze that doesn't surprise me one bit. There's a particularly pointless scene where Mary is forced to pleasure one of her fellow female tortured souls for the amusement of the guards. Funny, I haven't seen any men being tortured yet. Why? Because men aren't as sexy as women when they're being tortured. Duh!

This is why British people aren't allowed to have laws or government anymore. They always abuse their power. That's why no Americans live in

England anymore. Back in the 1850s or whatever, we were all like "no demonic possession without representation". I find it very inspiring that Jess Franco wasn't afraid to tell this story of how Judge Jeffreys became the first King of the United States of America. If it wasn't for all the royalty and stuff, where would we be today?

Okay, enough gibberish. While I wouldn't call it a favorite or especially life changing, I really enjoyed The Bloody Judge. The film is well written, well-acted (Christopher Lee is frickin' awesome, as usual), and is certainly well-made. It's fascinating to see just how large of a production that Jess Franco could handle. The torture scenes are painful to behold and are mostly gratuitous. You know when the dubbing of the film suddenly switches to German, you're gonna see some twisted stuff. Oh yeah.

Venus in Furs (1969)

A man named Jimmy (James Darren) rushes out to the beach and digs his trumpet out of the sand. No really, that's how the movies starts. Moments later, the body of a dead woman washes up on the beach. Jimmy knows her but he can't quite remember how or from where. It all starts to come back to him. Her name was Wanda (Maria Rohm) and we see that she was this happening chick who was killed (maybe accidentally) by a gang of rich sexual deviants (played by Klaus Kinski, Dennis Price, and others) for their pleasure. Before you can say, "Hey, nice wig!", Wanda is back from the grave and is making Jimmy crazy. Jimmy's nightclub singer girlfriend Rita (Barbara McNair) is not too pleased about all this but she's pretty understanding. Next, Wanda starts hunting down the jerks who brought about her demise and is killing them with her obtuse yet sexy methods.

The moment it begins, you know that Venus in Furs is going to be a lush and sensual feast for the senses. There is something so magical about this film. Its slow motion, dreamy, sexy, and hallucinatory vibe is instantly hypnotic. This film will not let you go until it is done with you. Even the soundtrack is magic. There are several jazz numbers, brassy lounge pieces, and even some slinky freak-outs stashed all over the film.

Everyone in this movie is perfect in their role. I really like James Darren in this movie. He plays this totally hopeless schmuck who can't catch a break. His character is just someone for Wanda to leech off of and yet he's totally awesome. And speaking of Wanda, Maria Rohm (of The Bloody Judge) is simply amazing as the revenge-seeking undead sexy lady. Let's not forget good old Klaus Kinski playing a sheik of some sort, what more could you really ever want from a film? Or from life?

Also on hand to really class things up is Barbara McNair as Rita, a nightclub singer so popular that she can just lie on the floor and sing. No seriously, Rita, you're too good to stand. Did I say "class things up"? I did and of course, I was talking about veteran actor Dennis Price. His character's name is Percival Kapp. So awesome. I really appreciated the presence of Adolfo Lastretti from Umberto Lenzi's Spasmo as the detective hot on Wanda's cold heels.

"We escaped from the real world into a dream world that I never wanted to end."

Movies as sexy and as fun as Venus in Furs should be illegal but since they're not (well, they're not in the good ole US of A anyway), you gotta check this out. It's got some whipping, some sex, some stock footage, some none too subtle necrophilia, a cheesy theme song (VENUS IN FURS WILL BE SMILIN'), an untrustworthy narrator, and even a car chase. This is how I stopped worrying and learned to love the Franco. Hmm, that was pretty lame, wasn't it? This film has nothing to with Dr. Strangelove. Why would I even go there? Just watch this movie.

The Rites of Frankenstein (1972)

Shortly after he completes his monster, Dr. Frankenstein (Dennis Price) is murdered by Melisa (Anne Libert), a blind bird woman with a taste for human blood. The doctor's daughter Vera (Beatriz Savon) shows up, takes her father's body from the tomb, and revives his corpse long enough so she can find out who is behind this crime. The Frankenstein monster tries to kidnap a woman for his new master but Vera convinces him to take her instead.

It turns out that the evil magician, Cagliostro (Howard Vernon), wants to create a super being by mating the Frankenstein monster with his female counterpart, which he orders Vera to complete. After he hypnotizes and whips the heck out of her, she immediately goes to work on the she-monster. Meanwhile, Doctor Seward (Alberto Dalbes), a former colleague of Dr. Frankenstein, steps in to rescue Vera and stop all this madness.

Holy shit, Rites of Frankenstein is even more insane that I thought it would be. Hell, it's even better than I thought would be too. If you like pseudoscience, sacrifices, psychic powers, reanimated dead people, whippings, and other ghoulish delights, you need to see this film, duders. Jess Franco is firing on all cylinders with one crazy scene after another. And by all cylinders, I mean one cylinder is firing furiously and the rest are melting. This thing could explode at any second but the movie is only 85 minutes so disaster is averted. The soundtrack has got it all with everything from fuzzed out synthesizers to free jazz to stuffy library music.

The elephant in the room of course is that this is the clothed version. That's right folks, this is supposed to be The Erotic Rites of Frankenstein but since I'm not all about the porn, I couldn't care less. Oddly enough, I think Lina Romay (who plays a character so slight, so poorly realized that you could categorize her role as a cameo (but that might be too generous)) is hotter with clothes on. There was definitely a moment for a prolonged masturbation scene and it jumps to her readjusting her wardrobe. Did I feel cheated? Hell no, I didn't. I was relieved. Sorry you dang perverts, but I'm just here for the horror and the weirdness.

I love Rites of Frankenstein and you should love it too. This movie needs love. It's a hilariously childish and morbid horror fantasy with its head screwed on backwards and sideways. Seriously though, how the fuck can a film have striking cinematography and yet be slightly out of focus for nearly all of its running time? There's even a machine that looks an awful lot like an air conditioner that reanimates the dead and some acid that instantly melts a human head thrown in with all this tomfoolery. Damn it, you need to see this. Did I even mention the silver Frankenstein monster?

The Awful Dr. Orlof (1962)

The police are baffled as beautiful young women keep disappearing throughout the city. Witnesses claim to have seen a man with freaky eyes carrying a body through the streets while others claim a well-dressed man is wooing these young ladies away into the night. Both of these scenarios are correct! Dr. Orlof (Howard Vernon) and his blind assistant Morpho (Ricardo Valle) are capturing their gorgeous victims so that the doctor can restore his daughter's crunked up face with his experimental skin transplant techniques. Despite a lack of solid leads, Inspector Tanner (Conrado San Martin) refuses to give up.

The inspector's fiancé, Wanda (Diana Lorys), is doing better at cracking the case than he is and of course, no one believes her. Unfortunately, Wanda bears a striking resemblance to Dr. Orlof's daughter so he puts her at the top of list of victims for his experiments. When she goes undercover as a woman of loose morals, Wanda gets kidnapped by Dr. Orlof. Will her dumbass fiancé- I mean, the great Inspector Tanner- find her before it is too late?

The Awful Dr. Orlof is a fun slice of gothic horror that, despite its status as a Spanish version of Eyes without a Face, is way ahead of its time. Director Franco shows his skills here by making a film that is both beautiful and easy to sit back and just enjoy. There's lots of dark humor and a couple of silly cliffhanger moments that will instantly win over any fan of classic horror. And because this is Franco, there are even a few surprisingly bold sexy moments that are jarring to behold in black and white. The cinematography is stunning and the English dub is a dang riot.

This is where the whole Orlof cycle began, my friends. Franco would return to these characters time and time again throughout his career making several different versions of (and quasi-sequels to) this flick. And it's easy to see why. I'm sure anyone involved in this project would look back with fondness on this landmark in Spanish horror. I won't say The Awful Dr. Orlof is a good starting point for future Francophiles but you could definitely do worse.

Kiss Me, Monster (1969)

The Red Lips detective agency consists of Diana (Janine Reynaud) and Regina (Rosanna Yanni). These two wild ladies have taken on some pretty tough cases before but this one, oh boy, it's a real humdinger. This new case falls into their laps when a musician brings them a piece of music ("The Abilene Anthem") containing clues to a strange mystery. He is immediately knifed in the back. In fact, everyone that Diana and Regina try to get clues from die from a knife sticking out of their back. It turns out that an evil scientist is trying to create a race of supermen to take over the world. Diana and Regina track the scientist to his lair on a Caribbean Island. They steal the secret formula, Interpol gets involved, and- If I try to tell you any more about the plot of this movie, my head will explode.

Am I being punked?

After 20 minutes of Kiss Me Monster, I turned it off and begged my wife and mother-in-law to watch it with me just so I wouldn't have to watch it alone. Oh, it's not scary or anything, it's just that this film is so impossibly bizonkers that I had to watch it with someone so that I could make sure that I wasn't going insane. I mean it. Don't watch this movie alone. If you do, Ashton Kutcher shows up and beats you to death with a Nikon. Kiss Me Monster is the weirdest thing I've seen from Jess Franco (so far) but it's also a new favorite. The film is totally outlandish and obsessively obtuse while somehow managing to remain entertaining and hilarious.

Janine Reynaud (Franco's Succubus) and Rosanna Yanni (Count Dracula's Great Love) sure seem to be having a great time making this film. They never appear out of place playing dueling saxophones or stealing a "nutrition solution" from a wacky and (presumably) gay scientist. I like to pretend that this film is a documentary and that they just forced Miss Reynaud and Miss Yanni to change their names to Diana and Regina so that all the secrets of the secret society of men in black hoods would stay secret!

What you need to know is that Kiss Me Monster is a comedy but for us viewers of Euro-trash, the jokes will likely fly over our heads at first. The dubbing for this film is so bad and so strange that I immediately overthought what I was watching. I concentrated so hard on the story and the dialog to try and figure out what the intent was that I completely forgot that Franco might just be fucking with me. It honestly feels like the voice actors improvised the dialog. Yeah, it's like that, dawg.

And lastly, the story feels like it was written by a 5 year old. It is so convoluted and disastrously simple that it's oddly brilliant. Any gap is filled with pseudoscience or skipped over with coincidence. But it's all gobbledygook. Don't waste another precious second of your life, my dear friends, check out Kiss Me Monster. It's pretty fabulous and just about the nicest slap you can have right in the movie-face.

Nightmares Come at Night (1970)

Anna (Diana Lorys) is losing her mind. She is tormented by nightmares as well as her lover Cynthia (Collette Giacobine), a domineering and abusive beyatch. Cynthia calls in Dr. Paul Lucas (Paul Muller) to help Anna work her way through her problems. She resists at first but eventually Anna opens up to Dr. Paul and tells him of her nightmares, of her days as a strip tease artist, and how she suffers in her very not nice relationship with Cynthia. Meanwhile a young woman (Soledad Miranda) watches from a nearby house with her lover. She is waiting for something. Something is definitely going to happen. I hope.

I'm not going to lie to you, folks. I had a tough time getting through Nightmares Come at Night. The movie spends more time on the softcore bits and not nearly enough time on the nightmare bits. This was bound to happen. I hate to appear so prudish but after the initial "Oh awesome!" of a nude scene, I start looking at my watch pretty quickly. This film is definitely worth watching though even if you're a stuffy un-perv like me. The score by Bruno Nicolai is superb and the cinematography by frequent Franco collaborators Manuel Merino and Jose Climent makes even the most mundane moments of this film look gorgeous.

Diana Lorys, who was so awesome in Blue Eyes of the Broken Doll, is very good here (not to mention her voluptuous body is just mindboggling). It is easy to care about her character Anna and you really want to her just snap and take an axe to that Cynthia chick (she doesn't). Jack Taylor of Night of the Sorcerers and The Vampire's Night Orgy is in this one as some kind of a sex guru and also the subject of Anna's nightmares. If Paul Muller looks familiar it's because he's been in every dang movie ever. I know him best from Lady Frankenstein. IMDB lists Howard Vernon as being in this film but I can't remember him at all.

The only thing about this movie that really irks me is the freakin' DVD from Shriek Show. The cover art features Soledad Miranda as though she were the star of this flick. That just ain't the case here. Miranda's character is totally useless and we only see her a couple of times in the movie. Her best moment happens when she is sitting on a mattress, guzzling a bottle of wine, and wearing nothing but thigh high leather boots and a shawl.

Scrawled in red paint on the wall behind her are the words "Life is all SHIT". That's pretty impressive for sure but Diana Lorys should have been on the cover, damn it. She's the star of this freak fest.

> *"To escape a dream… Go through the long corridor to the past. And death… And pleasure… Begging me to join in. It attracts me irresistibly."*

Nightmares Come at Night really outdoes itself with the Euro-sleaze factor. This film is practically a comedic parody of every trashy arthouse piece of Euro-quackery from the seedy 70s. This is artsy, pretentious, and it's got extended lovemaking scenes that drag on for what seem like forever, and yet, it's also kind of great. This haunting flick definitely stays with you long after it's over. Hell, it's even got a little bit of a giallo feel to it and you know I dig that. Leave it to Franco to take a whole bunch of nothing and make it a soft focus daydream (not as nightmarish as the title would suggest) with moments of unbearable tension and brooding sexiness.

99 Women (1969)

The prisoners of the female jail nicknamed the "Castille de la Muerte" sure do got it rough. Their names are taken away and replaced with numbers. Their fancy clothes are replaced with drab and very short, gray dresses. Worst of all, their warden is Thelma Diaz (Mercedes McCambridge), a diminutive sociopath whose only real accomplishment is making her lady prisoners suffer. She also lets Governor Santos (Herbert Lom), warden of a nearby men's prison, have his pick of the most beautiful girls for his unwholesome desires.

Enter Leonie Caroll (Maria Schell). She has been sent by the government to inspect the prison which will likely lead to Thelma losing her vice-like grip on the prison. All hell breaks loose when three prisoners decide to make a break for it. Helga (Elisa Montes), Marie (Maria Rohm), and Rosalie (Valentina Godoy) take off through the jungle to freedom but run into a group of AWOL prisoners from the men's prison. Things do not end well, let me tells ya.

I'm not going to lie, I'm not really a huge fan of the Women-In-Prison genre. Rape, degradation, and limitless sorrow? I get enough of that from one episode of "Glee". I will say this, 99 Women sure as hell starts off with a bang. Some lovely lady prisoners being taken by boat to the "Castille de la Muerte" accompanied by a kickass theme song is a pretty fantastic opener. I asked myself, "Is this the one? Is this the WIP flick that's going to break me? Why is my heart beating so fast?" But then the film settles into what I consider pretty humdrum stuff for this type of film: lesbian rape and non-lesbian rape! RAPE RAPE RAPE! I really like the flashbacks showing how some of the girls ended up in the jail in the first place.

Anyway, what does make this film watchable for me is the phenomenal cast. Everyone is totally awesome here. Mercedes McCambridge is perfect as the insanely cruel warden. Herbert Lom is definitely not wasted as a sadistic piece of shit. These two actors chew up the scenery like it was something that you chew on a lot and they were the kind of people who chew on stuff a lot.

Maria Schell is very good as Leonie, a woman who genuinely wants to help the lady prisoners. Isn't that nice? Elisa Montes (who looks a little like Bjork) really stands out as the tough as nails Helga who keeps moving forward even when everything looks grim. My absolute favorite actress in the film is Rosalba Neri (Lady Frankenstein, Amuck!) as the conniving rapist bitch, Zoe. Was Neri ever not good in a movie? Seriously, the more evil and the more nasty she gets, the more I love her!

I both love and hate 99 Women, just like I both love and hate the ending. I was incredibly depressed after this film was over and I realized that I really cared about the prisoners. It also occurred to me that I wanted to jump into the TV and take a machine gun to their captors. The film is incredibly stylish with great camerawork and phenomenal locations and sets. This is definitely worth watching even if you're not really into this type of film and that vibe of hopelessness will stay with you days afterward. I will say that I found the middle portion of the film rather tedious and dreary because damn it, I like my women like I like my coffee: FREE! But with lots of cream and sugar.

Please note: I almost forgot. There is some animal abuse in this film so tread carefully. A snake gets his head bashed in by some idiot actor in this movie. Lame!

Count Dracula (1970)

Johnathan Harker (Fred Williams) has been hired by Count Dracula (Christopher Lee) to help him find residence in England. Harker ventures out to Transylvania to meet the Count and some spooky shit happens. Long story short, Harker ends up in a sanitarium to recover from nervous exhaustion and the Count has a new home in a big ass creepy house. Dr. Van Helsing (Herbert Lom) is treating Harker and tells his fiancé Mina (Maria Rohm) to chill while he recuperates. Ever since the Count's arrival in town, one of Van Helsing's patients, Renfield (Klaus Kinski), has been going apeshit in his cell.

Next thing you know, Mina's friend Lucy (Soledad Miranda) is attacked by the Count (cleverly disguised as a bat-like creature) and drained of some of her blood. While Lucy fades away, Mina begins to suspect that this mysterious Count is to blame. After Lucy "dies", Van Helsing, with the help of Harker and Lucy's beau, Quincy Morris (Jack Taylor), discovers the proof he needs to prove beyond a shadow of a doubt that Count Dracula is none other than Count Dracula himself, A VAMPIRE! The Count gets mad and summons a dragon with laser beams to shoot out Van Helsing's eyes. The end.

Jess Franco's and Christopher Lee's attempt to make a more traditional version of Bram Stoker's book is rather successful, I guess. I wish they had attempted to breathe a little life into the old story instead of trying (and failing) to take it all quite so... seriously. Jeez, Count Dracula just ain't cuttin' the mustard in the department that some people call "entertainment value". There is plenty of atmosphere in parts and some effective moments but this film runs out of steam (and money) way, way before the credits roll. Basically, this Count Dracula only comes to life when Christopher Lee delivers an awesome monologue and then again when Dracula goes after Lucy. As usual, there's just something magical about Soledad Miranda that just lights up the screen.

Cinematographers Luciano Trasatti and Manuel Merino and composer Bruno Nicolai do their jobs wonderfully and at least make this film easy on the eyes and ears. There is a pretty wild scene where some stuffed wild game come to life -like in Lucio Fulci's Manhattan Baby (1982)- but it's just not enough to save the day. A slightly larger budget may have helped this one a little (especially with how listless and cheap Dracula's demise plays out) but come on, this is Franco! When did he ever need a bigger budget? Seriously! It feels silly even typing that but something is just wrong here.

I don't know, I'm not sure what else to say. This movie has a few good scenes but overall it's just too drowsy and too stiff. Count Dracula got my hopes up once things finally got moving but then it settled back into the tedium. Franco fans and Dracula nuts will definitely find some good things about this movie with its moments of gothic beauty and hilarity (when Lucy faints, I swear Van Helsing uses the opportunity to cop a feel) but yeah, this nearly bloodless melodrama just didn't do it for me.

Bloody Moon (1981)

After donning a mask at a disco party and murdering a girl in her bed, the hideously scarred Miguel (Alexander Waechter), is put away in a mental institution. Years later, he gets out and is put in the care of his ever so slightly incestuous sister, Manuela (Nadja Gerganoff). Manuela runs a boarding school for language study students. She is constantly at odds with her mother, the Countess (Maria Rubio), who still has control of the finances and who constantly makes sure that Manuela knows her place (which is somewhere between shit and dirt).

But it's a new semester at the boarding school and new student, Angela

(Olivia Pascal), is ready to learn! Of course, she ends up in villa #13, where Miguel claimed the life of that girl, but who cares, right? She's got her eyes on Antonio (Peter Exacoustos), the super stud and master of tennis. Before you can say, "Hola, me gusto el sexy Antonio!", a crazed killer starts running around the school and murdering all the lovely ladies. Be careful, Angela, because everyone is a freakin' suspect, especially Paco, the very special groundskeeper.

Bloody Moon completely caught me off guard. I had heard from a few people that it was good and I had heard from many, many people that it was terrible. What I found is a beautifully shot, bloody, and wildly eccentric Euro-slasher. It instantly won me over with the great locations and wide-eyed craziness (especially of Olivia Pascal). I guess people don't like this flick because it doesn't feel like Jess Franco. His erotic wistfulness and jazzy spaced out vibes are not here but there's still lots of style, sleaze, and atmosphere. The fact that he could make a film that doesn't feel like one of his films amazes me.

The cinematography of Bloody Moon is sharp, colorful, and just plain gorgeous. The man on the camera this time around is Juan Soler, who worked with Franco on roughly 45 films during this period (1980-1987) of the director's career. If you like fuzz guitar and synthesizers that can peel the skin off your ears, then you'll dig the soundtrack from German composer Gerhard Heinz. He even incorporates freakin' flutes into the horror synth and strings and goes so far as to pair them with some disco fabulousness. It doesn't get much better than that.

As for the comedy, this flick has it all: ridonkulous dubbing, irrational character stupidity, a pointless incestuous subplot, and terrible fashions. Did I mention the subnormal groundskeeper, Paco? The guy's very presence in the film is just plain wrong. During one of the youthful gatherings in the movie, the teens are dancing to a bizarre 50s style rock song with a stern voice commanding you to "Shake your baby!" There is also a scene where Angela is nearly killed by a big fiberglass boulder.

This may be the first and last time that I approach a film by Jess Franco and instantly find my comfort zone. At risk of sounding close-minded and totally square, I really love just digging on this guy's more direct (and less "pornographic") films. I am constantly seeking out Euro-horror films to perpetuate "The Vibe" and Bloody Moon provided me with that feeling big time. The death scenes are great, the final girl is a friggin' trip (or seemingly on one in some scenes), there's plenty of nudity, and Bloody Moon also features the best use of a granite saw I've ever seen in a horror flick. Oh and as an added bonus for you giallo fans out there, the killer does don a pair of black gloves in this one. How could anyone not love this film?

"Dream about me, Angela. You'll sleep better."

Please note: There is some snake abuse in this one. An underpaid snake actor gives his life for a shock sequence. It's pointless, lame, but is over quickly. However, if any of you out there are sensitive to animal violence, you should steel yourselves for this one. But f you hate snakes then you'll love the garden-sheers-on-snake action!

Macumba Sexual (1983)

While taking a vacation in a resort on "Happy Bay", Alice Brooks (Lina Romay) is tormented by nightmares of Princess Obongo (Ajita Wilson) wherein she is beset upon by the princess's sexual slaves. At the end of the dream, Princess Obongo dies. Alice's boyfriend (Antonio Mayans) tries to comfort her as best he can (awwww yeah) but it is of no use. Alice gets a call from her boss with instructions to sell a house to a very real Princess Obongo. She travels to meet the princess, meets a creepy hotel clerk named Meme (Jess Franco), and gets friggin' seduced and stuff. It turns out that Princess Obongo wants Alice to take her place as the Goddess of Unspeakable Lust. Please note: "Unspeakable Lust" translates to sticking little statues in places that little statues do not belong.

If I had to review Macumba Sexual using only one word, I think that word would be… Demoralizing. This film takes the themes of sexual obsession, madness, sorcery, and more sexual obsession and makes them hard to look at and boring. Not to be completely dismissive, the film does sport some beautiful locations and plenty of foreboding. I was definitely into the characters and what was going to happen to them but after an hour of gratuitous gooch shots, I just wanted the film to fucking end. At this point, I feel like I've seen more of Lina Romay than any woman I've ever known in my life. I appreciate the scenes where Romay is roaming around the beach town in Daisy Dukes and a flimsy top more than the ones of her completely naked.

Sadly, the interview with Franco and Romay on Severin's DVD is more interesting than this damn film. I'm just not that interested in porno as entertainment and I don't really care how close to Franco's vision this boring crap is. The only reason this friggin' film ended up in my mailbox (thanks, Netflix) is because Franco directed it. I had absolute zero interest in seeing this but I knew I had better get it out of the way quickly. You gotta hand it to the guy, this movie is an enthusiastic little production and his cameo is priceless. Macumba Sexual feels like it's 10 feet tall, horny, and full of mescaline. Stay out of its way or get fucked.

Dr. Orloff's Monster (1964)

As he lays dying, Dr. Orloff reveals to his colleague Dr. Fisherman (Marcelo Arroita-Jauregui) his secret theory for resurrecting the dead. Fisherman puts the theory into action and reanimates the corpse of his brother Andros (Hugo Blanco), whom he murdered. With Andros's body, the evil doctor is able to satisfy his sick desires by commanding him to murder strippers. Just as he's getting started with his dastardly plans, Andros's daughter Melissa (Agnes Spaak) shows up to stay with her uncle and her drunk Aunt Ingrid (Luisa Sala). Melissa knows something hinky is going on in the castle and she enlists the help of her boyfriend Manuel (Pepe Rubio) to get to the bottom of things.

If you aren't convinced by the magic of Jess Franco just yet, then you need to check out Dr. Orloff's Monster. This film is easy on the eyes, full of ennui, fun to watch, comically dubbed (probably not on purpose), and it will even tug on the old heartstrings if you'll let it. Don't get me wrong, this flick is a thinly plotted sequel but its pop art sensibility combined with its gothic overtones make this a lovely if kitschy thing to behold. The music is equal parts dirge and upbeat jazz and the black and white camerawork by Alfonso Nieva is damn near perfect.

"If you'll permit a lack of taste, sergeant, I think I must express myself with a vulgar display of swearing... Gadzooks!"

This film is tragic magic. One might even say it is tragical. The melodrama is very strong, somewhere between 110-135%, so please, use only as directed. Do you like pseudoscience? Are you a pseudoscientist? Then step right up and rejoice. Stop being a square and watch Dr. Orloff's Monster, man. I can't promise you will be happy but I guarantee that this movie will tickle your melancholic fancy spot. For some reason, I like this even more than the original The Awful Dr. Orloff. What does that say about me? It says that I don't know when to say when.

Eugenie de Sade (1974)

The film opens with Eugenie (Soledad Miranda) undressing a woman. They are laughing. The woman lies down on the bed. This is a home movie. Eugenie's stepfather, Albert (Paul Muller), steps into frame and strangles the girl to death. This is a snuff film. Next time we see her, Eugenie has been beaten severely and is seemingly recuperating in a hospital bed. A writer named Attila Tanner (Jess Franco) comes to her bedside and asks that she tell her story. Eugenie agrees but only if Tanner agrees to put her out of her misery when her tale is finished. Tanner agrees.

Next, Eugenie tells of being raised by Albert after her mother died right after she was born. As she grew up, her stepfather, a writer of great talent but little recognition, became increasingly obsessed with erotic writing and literature. After she gets caught reading a particularly disturbing book from Albert's library, Eugenie discovers the true nature of her father. The man is a sadist who wants to take his psychosexual experiments to the next level and take a person's life. Eugenie agrees.

The two go out on the prowl for strippers, hookers, and hitchhikers. They pretend to be newlyweds, nice people, or maybe just a couple of perverts looking for kicks. Then they strike, murdering these people for their own sick desires, photographing or filming the event. With each of their evil little games, the stakes get higher and they become crueler. Albert suggests a game in which Eugenie take a lover and drive him to the brink of madness. He chooses Paul (Andres Monales), a sensitive jazz musician, for Eugenie to seduce and manipulate. But things do not go as planned and for the first time, Eugenie breaks the rules.

For me, Eugenie de Sade is the cinematic equivalent of getting hit by a bus. This erotic thriller is ice cold and -in terms of cold-blooded ruthlessness- it makes many giallo villains I've seen look like Captain Kangaroo. It's also a breathy, dizzy, and mesmerizing experience. Jess Franco directs this extremely well written piece of sex and violence like a man possessed. The colors are vibrant, the pacing is very good, and the story is intriguing. The score by the always brilliant Bruno Nicolai is achingly beautiful and menacing.

First and foremost, the performances of Soledad Miranda and Paul Muller are phenomenal. In the middle of this movie, I was like "Damn, these two have such a weird marriage. Oh shit, I forgot, that's her stepdad! AAAAAHHH!!!!" In the beginning, one gets a sense that Albert is just a normal guy raising his stepdaughter and you think that some trigger is going to be pulled and he's going to go off the deep end. Then as the story unfolds, it's pretty obvious that there is something terribly wrong with the man who would raise Eugenie in total isolation and fill her head with crazy ideas.

> *"I'll never forget the first time snow fell that winter. As if by some enchantment, everything became, white, neat, unreal, strange."*

I didn't really get Soledad Miranda until I saw her as Eugenie. Until then, I only knew her as the striptease vamp from Vampyros Lesbos and Lucy the juicebox from Franco's Count Dracula. She is a girl in love with her stepdad, a man who has always been her entire world. This is a person whose fate has been set since day one and the moment she strays and sees outside the little cozy cage she's been kept prison in, she comes to life and is willing to risk disappointing the one man who she has looked up to her entire life. She is the tragic heroine and also a demon capable of squeezing the life out of someone and having one wicked orgasm afterwards. Shit man, I can't even look at her now without wanting to cry.

Wait a second. There has to be a catch, right? This movie can't be a perfect masterpiece, can it? Okay, fine, I admit that the film is a little cheap. Some of the sets are a little more than slightly less than extravagant. I actually wrote in my notes: "How much of this film is going to take place in the library?" When someone is stabbed, a little bit of red paint is all the paltry effects budget would allow. And yes, that same red paint is used for bruising. Then there's the body hair. If you took Paul Muller's back and shoulder hair and Andres Monales' leg and butt hair and combined them, you'd have three Wookiees and half a Robin Williams. But seriously, folks...

This film is pure evil and yet it is a joy to behold. Innocence is shaped and molded into cruelty and horror by a madman. And then, during the awakening, when just for an instant, things are right and good; the darkness swoops in to crush the dream. Eugenie de Sade feels dangerous. Its subject matter is very dark and yet, once again, I connected with the characters emotionally. How does Franco keep doing that to me? Even when those characters are sick bastards toying with their prey to heighten their own satisfaction right before they take a human life, I'm still utterly fascinated. If you are curious about Jess Franco and want to know what the fuss is all about, check this one out.

Dracula, Prisoner of Frankenstein (1972)

Victor Frankenstein (Dennis Price) kills Count Dracula (Howard Vernon) and then takes him in bat-form back to his lab so that he can create an "Army of Shadows" to take over the world or the underworld or whatever. He then resurrects Dracula and has him drinking the blood of chicks and by "chicks" I mean ladies. Pretty soon, Dr. Frankenstein has a few too many vampires and they start running rampant around his castle and the nearby village. After his wife (Paca Gabaldon) is kidnapped by the Frankenstein's monster and he is beaten and left for dead, Dr. Jonathan Seward (Alberto de Dalbes) is nursed back to health by a gypsy woman (Genevieve Robert). She enlists him to help stop Frankenstein from spreading evil all over the world.

Director Jess Franco attempts to combine a full on monster mash-up with a subtly beautiful gothic horror poem. Is he successful? I can say, without a doubt, that he...is? Dracula, Prisoner of Frankenstein was shot, as far as I can tell, back to back with The Rites of Frankenstein making use of some great locations but this time the camera is in focus more often.

Yay! While not quite as in-your-face manic as Rites, this film is still the work of a kooky Spanish duder with an insane imagination and a mountain of determination.

At times, it seemed to me like the quieter and prettier moments of this film felt like something that Jean Rollin might cook up. And then, once the monsters start duking it out rather pathetically (notice I did not say "unenergetically"), Dracula, Prisoner of Frankenstein feels like something Al Adamson would have been proud to have directed. Like I said, the locations are great with the spooky old castle and the dilapidated village and stuff. Heck, there's buckets of atmosphere in this film, hampered only by the stuffy library music which gets way more time than contributions from composer Bruno Nicolai.

I hope that Dennis Price was instructed to act like a stupid and moronic dumbass idiot on camera because those are the results he gets. Every scene he's in, he has these little fits and starts that make me want to give up the ghost. On the opposite side of the spectrum is Howard Vernon. This duder is as stiff as a board as the Count. Best mannequin impression ever. Even the stone-faced Luis Barboo gets lively by comparison as Morpho, Frankenstein's assistant. Morpho? Hm... Where have I heard that name before? Gee, I wonder.

Alberto de Dalbes comes off very well in this film. His portrayal of Dr. Seward is sympathetic and pretty dang awesome. Dalbes is upstaged by Genevieve Robert as the gypsy woman. She is sexy as hell and very wise in the ways of magic. Other hot and sexy ladies in this flick include Britt Nichols, Paca Gabaldon, and Anne Libert. They keep their clothes on! Which makes me wonder if there is another cut of this film titled Dracula, Erotic Prisoner of Frankenstein out there somewhere.

I must warn you, animal lovers, there is some bat abuse in this one. Old cheapskate Franco splurged on this film and got a live bat. I know what you're thinking, "How many times have I seen a real bat in a European horror film? Oh yeah, NEVER!" (Well, almost never.) Anyway, Mr. Jess Moneybags decides to drown this poor little buddy in a beaker full of fake blood. This is supposed to represent Dr. Frankenstein resurrecting the Count. Well, it's fucking stupid and pointlessly cruel. I don't care if bats are vermin, they don't deserve a slow, agonizing death. Oh and there's another bat (hey why not waste two?) dangled in front of the camera by its wings. I thought I'd mention that if you were gonna keep score or something. Why do I watch this garbage?

How cheap is Dracula, Prisoner of Frankenstein? How's this? A group of villagers are seen storming the castle with recently extinguished torches! Hickory-smoked motherfuckers can't even afford matches. This movie is cheap beyond adjectives that describe cheapness but when has that ever stopped Franco? The gloomy atmosphere, minimal dialog, and (maybe intentional) comedy make up for lack of funding on this one. If only Franco's Count Dracula had been this deliriously fun.

So, damn it all to hell, I kind of like this movie and I feel very conflicted about it. This one is very daffy but combine that with how somber this one feels and you get a nice dichotomy of tones. Or just a rich, creamy lather of "What the fuck am I watching?" I only recommend this film to people who hate bats and those who have found out that they are desperate Franco addicts. Despite the glaring faults like bat abuse and a pubic hair werewolf, Dracula, Prisoner of Frankenstein lingers in the mind long after it is over.

X312 – Flight to Hell (1971)

A reporter named Tom Nilson (Thomas Hunter) sits down at his desk, presses record on his tape player, and begins to tell the story of how he survived a plane crash in the Amazonian jungle. The film flashes back to the fateful flight and its passengers. Aboard the plane is a bank tycoon (Siegfried Schuenberg) smuggling jewels out of the country. At the plane's last stop before leaving for Brazil, a man boards with the intention of hijacking the plane and forcing it to land where Pedro (Howard Vernon), an outlaw living in an old fort with his gang, can intercept and steal the jewels.

The plan goes afoul when the idiot pilot decides to fight with the hijacker in the cockpit. The survivors of the crash, led by Tom, start making their way through the jungle in the hopes of finding a village or some other form of life. Bill the steward (Fernando Sancho) decides to take the jewels for himself so he starts killing off anyone who gets in his way. And just when things can't get any worse, they do. Restless bow and arrow-wielding natives as well as Pedro and his gang start attacking the survivors.

The moment I saw the cover for X312 – Flight to Hell, I knew I was in for a treat. While nowhere near one of Franco's best, this film definitely has its charms. The stench of exploitation is very ripe but things never get out of hand. The ubiquitous rape scene takes place off camera and the sex scenes are brief. The action scenes, double crosses, triple crosses, and the sociological aspects (human beings are greedy!) of the story are played up much more than the sex. The soundtrack is kind of mediocre with occasional bursts of faux-pop pleasantness from the radio that somehow survived the plane crash. Camerawork by Manuel Merino is pretty good though there are focusing issues and the whole film looks really drab (which could just be the DVD I watched).

The sexy Euro-babes in the cast include the wildly voluptuous Espernaza Roy (A Candle for the Devil) as the snotty rich lady, Gila von Weitershausen as the childish teddy bear-toting goof, and the always lovely Ewa Stromberg (Vampyros Lesbos) as the slutty American. Howard Vernon is fifteen kinds of badass as Pedro. The duder is done up with some tan makeup and a bad mustache with glue so thick you can see it glistening underneath. American-born Thomas Hunter (The Hills Run Red) is excellent in the lead. Tom is a no nonsense kind of guy with a conscience that he should definitely stop listening to.

X312 – Flight to Hell almost feels like a throwaway flick for Franco but once again, I found myself engaged and I just had to know how it was all going to end. There were a few meandering bits, some laughably stupid moments (not surprising), and a terribly sped-up fight scene but overall, this is an enjoyably trashy though cheap adventure film. If you're looking for something sweaty, horny, blurry, just a little drowsy, and will leave you saying "Hey, this is kind of all right," then check this film out.

Women Without Innocence (1977)

A young woman named Margarita (Lina Romay) is found bloody and in a state of hysterics along with the bodies of a married couple. She is taken to a women's insane asylum where Dr. Antonio (Michael Maien) is using some experimental and bizarre techniques to treat his patients. But all is not as it seems in this house of deranged nekkid ladies. Nurse Irina (Muriel Montosse) and Dr. Whatshisface (no idea who this duder is) are actually trying to shock Margarita out of her mute psychosis so they can find out where her dead friends, who were freakin' diamond smugglers, kept their stash. To further complicate the situation, there is a killer running around stabbing the comely patients of the nursing facility with a butcher knife.

Other than Joe D'Amato and Jean Rollin, Jess Franco is the only director I go this far outside of my cinematic comfort zone for. I really knew absolutely nothing going into Women Without Innocence (great title!) but I was hardly surprised by all the softcore sex scenes. And there's a lot. There are sex scenes that segue into other sex scenes and I just want to curl up and die. But hey, it's Franco, there must be something good here, right? Begrudgingly, I say yes. Women Without Innocence, when it's good, is a lurid, woozy, and funny flick. The camerawork by Peter Baumgartner is excellent. Seriously, this movie looks way better than it should.

Lina Romay does it again. And by it, I mean, sneaks into my heart and makes me give a crap about another one of her characters. Margarita is in serious trouble and the more that is revealed about how she came to be a gibbering madwoman, the sadder and more interesting she becomes. There is a moment when Romay looks right into the camera. I don't know if it was intentional but her look just seemed to say, "I know I'm an actress playing a woman in a madhouse but seriously, get me the fuck out of here!" It is awesome and I have no idea if it was intentional or not. Another standout scene happens when Margarita wanders away from the institution at dusk. There is the rumble of an approaching thunderstorm and the whole bit borders on gothic horror.

"Make her stop, her moaning is giving me the creeps! She sounds like a dog."

I'm glad that Women Without Innocence has some redeeming qualities, many of Franco's bawdier titles do, but for me, watching and reviewing erotic cinema is still a chore. You'll never hear me say: "Wow, I love this! So happy there were some sex scenes to keep all that weird stuff and atmospheric crap from getting in the way!" Although this Franco flick has some points of interest (and definitely doesn't take itself very seriously), I can only recommend this one to only the most devout of his fans. File under "almost brilliant".

The Sadistic Baron von Klaus (1962)

Ludwig (Hugo Blanco) rushes home to find his mother on her deathbed. She reveals to him that his grandfather was a total sicko and she fears that the von Klaus family line is cursed. She also gives Ludwig a key to the Baron's private torture chamber below the castle so that he can see for himself how bad the duder was. Meanwhile, the raped and mutilated bodies of beautiful young ladies have been popping up around the nearby village and the people are convinced that it's the ghost of Baron von Klaus.

Okay, what happened? All the right pieces are here but none of them fit together. Jess Franco's The Sadistic Baron von Klaus is pretty disappointing. After the gothic gem that is The Awful Dr. Orloff, I was hoping for something much better than this. The black and white cinematography is stunning, the jazz music in the soundtrack is jazzy, and the ladies are sexy. Are these enough to make a great film? Nope. There are too many uninteresting, obnoxious, and flat characters. There isn't enough of a spooky atmosphere and, worst of all, the plot hits a major lull in the middle and never recovers.

The sets and scenery are both beautiful but it just doesn't matter when it's impossible to care what is going to happen next. Comedic moments and charming asides fail when I was constantly checking how much is left of the running time. The sexually sadistic content is shocking when one considers what year this film was released but I'm not impressed. I think The Sadistic Baron von Klaus was directed by an either overconfident or overwhelmed director. It almost feels too cool to bother being entertaining and not smart enough to make up the difference. This is a shame because the film starts off quite strong with an undeniable sense of foreboding and ends with a heart-wrenchingly tragic finale (even though I didn't give two shits about the characters).

I have a sneaking suspicion that I may have to revisit this film someday.

The more I bash it, the more I feel like I missed something important. I have been annoyed with Franco before but I've never been this violently bored. To be continued (maybe)...

Revenge in the House of Usher (1982)

Dr. Alan Hacker (Antonio Mayans) travels to the castle of his old professor, Dr. Usher (Howard Vernon). Hacker quickly learns that his old teacher has gone mad. Aside from claiming that he is 200 years old, Usher is obsessed with resurrecting his dead daughter by giving her blood transfusions from unwilling girls he's kidnapped. Usher has a bevy of servants at his disposal including the blind Morpho (Olivier Mathot), the portly Mathias (Jean Tolzac), and the lovely Helen the housekeeper (Lina Romay). None of these fools can help him with his craziness. Dr. Usher is haunted by the ghostly figures led by the spirit of his dead wife. And of course, in true Usher family fashion, the damn castle is gonna collapse.

I think Revenge in the House of Usher gets labeled as one of Jess Franco's worst because it has been out on home video (either in VHS or DVD) in the States for a long time. All of those people should have seen Eugenie de Sade and only like six people (myself included) should have even heard of this film. I have my problems with it but I enjoyed this inept romp probably more than I should have. This film's biggest offence: it uses footage from The Awful Dr. Orloff as flashbacks for Dr. Usher. Normally, I would consider this to be totally unforgivable but I figured out that if you were to remove (or fast forward through) the 15 minutes (!) of Orloff footage, you get this film down to a much more digestible 75 minutes. There are even the ubiquitous characters named Dr. Seward and Morpho.

One problem is that the film is obviously two different shoots, possibly two different sets of players, slapped together. The musical score for the film feels like it's been culled from the library. I doubt an original score would have done much to improve this film but hey, why not, right? The camerawork is excellent with lots of interesting angles. The same camerawork is also quite sloppy with out of focus bits and lots of annoying bouncing (this may have been the print I was watching but still). Luckily, this castle setting, that I've seen many Franco films take place in, is always very photogenic.

> *"Look Seward, I'm not very well versed in this new science of psychoanalysis. In any event, you don't start at the age of 200 which is how old he claims to be!"*

So what the hell? This sounds terrible! It is terrible but it's also the best kind of terrible. If viewed as a gothic comedy with occasional bits of horror and atmosphere, then Revenge in the House of Usher succeeds in every way. It's almost all the fault of the horrendous dubbing, something I am beginning to appreciate more and more from these Euro-cheapies. If this flick wasn't meant to be a comedy then no one informed the voice actors. The voice actor who dubs Howard Vernon is so outrageously bad in this film that he deserves some kind of an award or free pancakes for a year or something.

My soul asked for it and the gods have listened. I begged with my heart of hearts for Lina Romay to keep her damn clothes on and she finally listened. It's astonishing to me that Lina Romay fully clothed and acting seductive is 1000x sexier than her writhing around in ecstasy completely naked. She may have once been a contender for the title of Greatest Pair of Eurotrash-Bobbins ever but after film upon film of her undulating in her birthday suit, I needed a fucking break. And I love her character in this one too. Helen is the devoted servant who falls before the feet of Dr. Usher, begging him to love her. But hey, she's still a horny woman with needs, you know? She's gotta try to get some on the side.

I can see why people don't like this film. It's a hard pill to swallow what with how stupid and lazy it was made. The use of 15 minutes from another film is inexcusable. But damn it, Revenge in the House of Usher works especially when it doesn't. Alongside all of the goofy and utterly hilarious crap, there lingers a spooky mood and more than two heaping bucketfuls of weirdness. If you enjoyed either Rites of Frankenstein or Dracula, Prisoner of Frankenstein, there's no way you're not going to at least find this flick amusing. There's a game of Ring Around the Rosie, some ladies chained up in the dungeon, and enough slapdash confounding bullshit to make you crack a smile, all just waiting for you.

Two Undercover Angels (1969)

For the past 2 years, 8 beautiful women have disappeared and each case has too many coincidences not to be related. This looks like a job for Diana and Regina (Janine Reynaud and Rosanna Yanni), the Red Lips detective agency. In pursuit of the killer, the two run into all kinds of seedy and strange characters. Their chief suspect is an artist named Thiller whose paintings and sculptures resemble the victims. The closer the girls get to solving the case, the more people are trying to kill them with machine guns, hairy-handed henchmen, and exploding vases of flowers. Some people call it danger, Diana and Regina call it Tuesday.

The last thing in the world I expected from the horrifying and oversexed brain of Jess Franco is a flair for comedic films. Two Undercover Angels is very amusing on purpose and when the intentional laughs fail, the goofy and accidentally brilliant passages holding everything together just make the film even more delightful. The only complaint I have is that this film is so thinly plotted that when it ended, I realized that almost nothing had happened at all. But who cares? Personally, I got lost in the gags and the jiggling bobbins.

One thing that makes these European delights so entertaining is the way they are dubbed. There are scenes where the jokes and naughty double entendres are delivered with lots of attitude and perfect timing. Other times, the same actors have a huge paragraph to read and they robotically and speedily spout off completely trite and unnecessary bullshit further adding to the hilarity of the film. Throw in some swingin' jazz music and I couldn't be happier aurally.

"Oh such a dirty deal! And I was just at the hairdresser!"

There are times when I wish there had been 100 Red Lips detective movies but I also have a feeling that the two films might be more than enough. Janine Reynaud and Rosanna Yanni are just as vivacious, charming, and funny as they were in Kiss Me Monster (the better of the two films). As for how far out Franco gets, Rosanna Yanni even gets a scene when her character talks directly to the cameraman. Frickin' brilliant and totally bizarre! Though it is as far from the typical Jess Franco fare (does such a thing exist?), Two Undercover Angels is perfect for when you need some brainless and groovy Euro-fun and just a little kink.

Daughter of Dracula (1972)

Luisa Karlstein (Britt Nichols) returns to the Karlstein estate just in time to hear her mother's dying request. Her croakin' mom wants her to take a key, go to the family crypt, and have a look (there were no other instructions) at their undead ancestor, Count Karlstein AKA Dracula (Howard Vernon). Next thing you know someone is drinking the blood of local sexy ladies. Inspector Ptuschko (Alberto Dables) is trying to solve the murders and he enlists the help of Charlie the reporter (Fernando Bilbao) to do some extra snooping around the Karlstein place. Meanwhile, Luisa is behaving very strangely and starts up a relationship with her hot cousin Karine (Anne Libert). There is also a subplot. Maybe two. I don't know.

This is probably the closest thing to a parody of a Jess Franco film I've seen so far although I'm not sure Franco knew he was parodying himself. First, the plot mirrors his 1962 gothic flick, The Sadistic Baron von Klaus. Second, the cast is either misdirected, miserable, or underused but I'll get to that later. Third, the film is pathetically staged and choppily edited (which I like). And finally, The Daughter of Dracula feels like a half-hearted attempt at making a giallo. There are several scenes where the imagery on display feels very reminiscent of the Italian whodunits so popular at the time. I wish the film had gone more for the gothic feel or the giallo bit because it doesn't do both very well at all.

Let's talk about the cast. I feel bad about Howard Vernon even being in this movie but he does have the easiest job. He's all done up in the Dracula makeup and he sits up, flashes the fangs, and then lays down again. He does this two or three times in the film, gets a stake in the head (very original) and that's it. Britt Nichols kind of does the same thing except she gets to walk around. While she pulls some awesome faces and delivers one of the most ludicrous bitch-slaps I've ever seen, Nichols is still pretty out of it in this movie and just really dull.

Alberto Dalbes plays the inspector character very well, getting surly, sarcastic, and generally fed up with all the losers he has to put up with. Fernando Bilbao is rather annoying as Charlie, the goofy journalist. Oddly enough, Jess Franco is pretty decent in this as Cyril Jefferson, a side character that is actually pretty interesting. He's a well-read and tortured individual who believes wholeheartedly in the occult. He makes a potentially bland cameo into something memorable.

Of course, there is a show stealer in the bunch. Anne Libert! This chick friggin' rules The Daughter of Dracula. I'm not sure how to put it into words exactly. There is just something special about this actress. She is adorable and one of the only members of the cast who seems to be having a good time. There, I put it into words. Her character is the sad victim in all of this craziness and it's next to impossible not to pity her cruel fate.

While it fails on almost every level, I have to say that Daughter of Dracula was not a waste of my time at all. The melodrama and the inept silliness go together perfectly. The gothic overtones, creaky library music, cryptic dialog, and the beautiful locations also help save the day. My biggest complaint is about the overlong sex scenes. I know I complain about these all the time in Franco films but the awkward lovin' between Nichols and Libert are especially bad and they spend a lot of time going nowhere. It's not about my prudishness (for a change), there is just no chemistry between these two ladies. But like I was saying, I still enjoyed Daughter of Dracula, it is completely accidentally entertaining because Franco was just so unbelievably off his game. File under "moderately interesting/unessential". Ugh, I'm going to stop saying "File under..." from now on. Whose shtick is that anyway?

Jack the Ripper (1976)

In the magical city known as London, a serial murderer known as Jack the Ripper has been killing and mutilating prostitutes. The killer is Dr. Dennis Orloff (Klaus Kinski), a seemingly kind though completely mad physician who specializes in treating the poor. Inspector Selby (Andreas

Mannkopff) is on the case and is struggling with both a lack of evidence combined with moronic witnesses including a blind man (Hans Gaugler) with a great sense of smell. The inspector's girlfriend Cynthia (Josephine Chaplin) decides to help him catch "Saucy Jack" by going undercover as a prostitute.

In 1976, Jess Franco sought out to make the most historically accurate, dare I say it, factually perfect film on the Jack the Ripper case. Through tireless research, he- Naw, I'm just fucking with ya! In 1976, Jess Franco went to Switzerland and directed this sleazy and nasty film. Don't let the terrible English dubbing fool you, this is a competently made film with great lighting, camerawork, and set design. The sleaze factor is very high, especially with Jack the Ripper acting like Jack the Raper. I enjoyed the score for the film. It has a nightmarish carnival-esque quality to it.

Klaus Kinski is okay in this movie. His character is methodical, cold, and mostly emotionless. His best moments are when he smiles and acts charming with the ladies in order to ensnare them. I really liked his insane and yet completely devoted assistant/housekeeper (Nikola Weisse) who likes to play with the bodies of his victims. Josephine Chaplin is cute but doesn't get a whole lot to do. Andreas Mannkopff is pretty mediocre as the inspector but he gets very little in terms of characterization to work with. Lina Romay, who plays a singing call girl, meets a particularly brutal end but it's okay because she gets to lip sync a bawdy song. For your amusement, here are the lyrics (just imagine them with some very cheap, jaunty music and it'll be just like you're watching the film):

If you're feeling warm
Come and see my charm
If you're feeling hot
Don't talk a lot

Ba da buta buta buta buta bum
Ba da buta buta buta buta bum
We'll do
Be do bedo bedo bebo bedo bum bink
Exactly what you think

Come feel my ears
My love-ly tits
If you have the brass
I'll give you me ass

My skin is fine
My lips are for you

Look at my eye
I'm easy to lay

The only downsides to the film are a few shrill characters, weak writing, and some long dialog scenes while Selby goes over the facts of the case. And once again, Franco mines his previous works by borrowing most of this film's plot from his own classic, The Awful Dr. Orloff. Other than those meager gripes, I really dug the darkly entertaining Jack the Ripper. The material is not exactly what I would call uplifting but Euro-sleaze aficionados will find much to celebrate here.

"Yes, it gives me a bad bellyache, this filthy fog!"

There are some jokes in the film but comic relief comes from the English dub. It is splendidly piss poor with all kinds of faux-Cockney garbage (just wait until you hear the hilariously effeminate cop). The gore effects are cheap but are wet and stomach churning. And for you Franco-heads in the audience, there is a nice hallucinatory moment when we get to see inside the mind of Jack the Ripper.

The Diabolical Dr. Z (1966)

Lightning, the roar of thunder, and it begins. Hans Bergen (Guy Mairesse), a murderous fiend, escapes from prison the day before his execution. He manages to get as far as the home of Dr. Zimmer (Antonio Jiminez Escribano). Dr. Zimmer is ecstatic because he needs a human test subject for his mind control experiments and who better than a man the world would be better off without. The scientific community shuns Dr. Zimmer and he drops dead right there at the big science conference.

Dr. Zimmer's daughter Irma (Mabel Karr) vows revenge on the three scientists whom she believes are responsible for the death of her dear, beloved daddy. She carries on with his work (his dying request, of course) but not until after she fakes her own death, horribly burns her face, and practices plastic surgery on herself. Huh? Yeah, I know. Anyway, Irma uses Hans Bergen, her assistant Barbara (Ana Castor), and a beautiful exotic dancer Nadja (Estella Blain) to carry about her fiendish- no, DIABOLICAL plot.

Sometimes Franco is just Franco and sometimes Franco is on fire! I am kicking myself for not loving this movie the first time around. For some reason, it took watching 21 other Franco movies to make me appreciate The Diabolical Dr. Z which is silly because of how easy this film is to get into. Despite some corny plot holes and a bunch of nonsensical pseudoscience, this film has great pacing and cool characters. There is also razor sharp and energetic cinematography from Alejandro Ulloa, the man who shot some excellent titles like Horror Express, Companeros, and Paul Naschy's Night of the Werewolf.

The cast is excellent but I simply adore Mabel Karr. She truly gives her all in her role and is quite frightening with her tireless obsession to complete her mission of vengeance. Estella Blain is ten kinds of sexy and nails it as the reluctant (and insanely sexy) murder weapon. It's against her nature to kill but mad science makes it impossible for her to disobey. Another one of Franco's damned damsels? I love it!

I won't call this a favorite but The Diabolical Dr. Z has gone way, way up on my list of Jess Franco films that everyone should see (though I wouldn't call this a good starting point). Even with its clunkier moments (jump-cuts, continuity issues, etc.), the film is dynamic in writing and inventive in execution. One thing I greatly appreciate about Dr. Z is the pacing; it just flies by! In the shadow of Dr. Orloff, this films packs on the weirdness, the beauty, and the fun.

Blue Rita (1977)

Blue Rita (Martine Flety) is more than just a stripper, she's also a madam (you know, the boss of hookers kind) and an extortionist of money and secrets. With the help of her assistants, Gina (Pamela Stanford) and Franchesca (Sarah Strasberg), she lures men into her nightclub/brothel, captures, and tortures them for profit. The torture is the sexy kind because Franchesca has whipped up a green goo that makes men super horny. When duders are hard up, they talk; they always talk. There is a new girl among her evil team. Her name is Sam (Dagmar Burger) and she is hot stuff. She is instantly assigned only two tasks: seduce dudes and be Blue Rita's lover.

Pretty soon, Sam is given the task of catching the eye of boxing champ, Janusch Lassard (Eric Falk), and adding him to Blue Rita's collection. She does this easily but she can't seem to stay cold and calculating like she's supposed to. There's just something about this guy that Sam can't resist. But that's not all that's going wrong; things are spinning out of control in Blue Rita's organization. It seems that there is a traitor among her most trusted accomplices and Interpol is closing in.

What I love about Blue Rita is that the plot feels like it was written by a pervert (what, no way!) but one with the brain of an 11 year old (oh, I see). Though the budget is very small, it's obvious that the producers of this movie were very nurturing to Franco's needs as a director and (presumably) gave him complete freedom. It kind of reminds me of Jean Rollin's Bacchanales Sexuelles only way more stoned. Even if you have no interest in seeing Blue Rita, the LSD-addled opening credit sequence alone is worth watching. The lighting and the camerawork compete with one another to see who can outdo each other in the garishly tacky department.

The cast of this film is frickin' excellent. Everyone has a bizarre or goofily written part and they all go for the gold or at least the cheese. Martine Flety is great as the diabolical, often undulating, and sadistic Blue Rita. Her backstory is that she was tortured with a red hot poker in a very private place so she takes great pleasure in torturing men. Don't worry though, Franchesca is whipping up a pink potion to slowly rehabilitate Blue Rita's vajayjay. I really dig Sarah Strasberg too. Her wide-eyed surprise takes are friggin' genius.

"I'll take you to my friend Andre. He has lovely little piranhas in his pool."

My two favorite ladies in Blue Rita are Pamela Stanford and Dagmar Burger. Burger is very charming as Sam (her name in the German version is Sun, btw). I wasn't that sure about her at first. She seemed distant, not that into it, and she has this mannish body that just makes me feel strange inside. But of course, she totally rocks in her role and I love her to pieces! Stanford is outrageous as Gina, the -I don't know- vampish muscle behind the operation. She runs over a hooker with a car, wears a very revealing silver jumpsuit and gigantic sunglasses, and just exudes sexiness in every shot. Her character gets a raw deal in this movie. That's gratitude for ya.

I guarantee you will not believe your eyes when you see Blue Rita. This is Franco combining the experimental with both fun and intentional hilarity. Eric Falk gets a fight sequence that had me falling out of my chair with laughter. If you like drug inspired flights of fancy wrapped in a sickly sweet candy shell or you just have an inflatable furniture fetish, check this out immediately. Let me give you an idea how fucking ridiculous this is: with only 10 minutes left, I found myself saying, "Wait, this is a Cold War spy caper?" My only criticism of this film are some of the softcore sex scenes and stripping sequences are too long but nowhere near as bad or as interminable as the ones in some of this director's other works (Macumba Sexual, in particular). Blue Rita is very close to essential Franco.

Lorna the Exorcist (1974)

19 years ago, Patrick Mariel sold his unborn daughter to Lorna (Pamela Stanford) for wealth and unimaginable sexual pleasure. It's like that old saying: A man who sells his daughter to a witch is a son of a bitch. What? You don't know that one? It's pretty famous. Well, his daughter Linda (Lina Romay) is all grown up and Lorna is coming to collect. She gives Linda all of her mystical sex powers or something. Crabs crawling out of vaginas!

The score for Lina the Exorcist is incredible. The slinky, sexy, fuzzed out, and sad guitar makes me feel more than a little anxious. The dubbing is awful (so of course, I love it) and this movie is too long. There are some long-winded gambling scenes and dull disco dancing scenes but what I'm really tired of is all the endless softcore porn on display. Sorry folks, it's just boring. The plot is darkly ironic and breathtakingly cruel and the damned characters are fascinating. But these things don't stand a chance when the movie just keeps going back to the sex over and over and over again.

"Good evening, Patrick. I want your daughter."

Pamela Stanford again! Yay! I just saw and loved her in Blue Rita but now I never want to see her again. In this film her eye shadow looks like it was applied with Homer Simpson's makeup shotgun. She looks like a Ziggy Stardust disco demon. She looks like something Abba threw up. And her character's full name is Lorna Green. Seriously? Is this a veiled reference to Lorne Greene of TV's "Bonanza"? Man, I am freaking out! My favorite character other than Lorna is Marianne (Jacqueline Laurent), Patrick's poor schmuck of a wife who gets a really bum deal in this deal with the devil.

Atmosphere? It's got it. Weirdness? It's got it. Slow motion bizarreness? Yeah, it's got that too. But who cares? I don't. I have to warn you: don't listen to me and don't trust this review. I am not myself right now but that's my fault. This director and I are going through a rough patch. Lorna the Exorcist is nothing but endless shots of vaginas and bush. Oh and there's a bloody dildo. This might be a good and challenging movie but I can't help but wish this was the clothed version. So now I like censorship? That's Jess Franco's (and Lina Romay's vagina's) fault. This is one extreme and depressing piece of cinematic insanity. And although the ending is awesome, I can't recommend this to anyone but the most dedicated Franco fans. I guess I'm not a Jess Franco fan because watching this film made me want to kick someone's face in.

The Girl from Rio (1969)

After stealing 10 million dollars in stolen money, Jeff Sutton (Richard Wyler) finds himself on the run in Rio de Janeiro. First he is pursued by Sir Masius (George Sanders), a gangster with as much style and class as he has henchmen and trust me, he has a lot of henchmen. Next, Jeff runs afoul of the mysterious Sumuru (Shriley Eaton), a mysterious woman who has managed to acquire enough wealth and female followers to form Femina, a country of deadly women with very strict laws and extremely skimpy outfits. But don't you worry, men of the world, the insatiable and irresistible Jeff has a few tricks up his sleeve.

And so it begins: a woman in a mesh dress writhing around in the mist of a smoke machine. Could this be the one? No. There are two problems with The Girl from Rio: 1. the leading man is wretchedly awful and 2. there is a major lull in action in the middle of the film. I'll get to both of those things in a moment. Obviously, this film is not meant to be taken seriously. It's kooky, silly, campy, and cheap in all the right places but I wouldn't go so far as to call it likable. I'm afraid The Girl from Rio is just too off to be classic Franco. Not even the excellent score by Daniel White can save the day. The music is a combination of sultry pop (the theme song is to die for), jazz, and lush orchestral goodness. That and the fine cinematography are the best parts of this darn movie.

"What kind of a space age sorceress are you?"

Almost everyone in this movie is pretty amazing. Almost. Shirley Eaton (Goldfinger) attacks her insane role with lots of gusto. George Sanders of All About Eve (!) is slumming it but seems to be having a great time, reading Popeye comics and clowning around. Maria Rohm, Elisa Montes, and Marta Reves are all vivacious and just wonderful to watch on screen. So what the fuck is up with Richard Wyler? He's going for a James Bond/Lee Marvin kind of a thing but fails at both. If this guy had stopped trying to be tough or too cool for school and actually squeezed some charm into his performance, he might have actually worked out. But no, his character is a smarmy dick and he literally has one good moment in the entire film.

Like I was saying before, The Girl from Rio has a major boring bit in the middle. Even the musical score just kind of stops for a while. This occurs while Jeff is being held prisoner in Femina. When the film should have been more hallucinogenic, comedic, or just over-the-top, it just slows down to a crawl. All the crazy costumes and naked lady flesh on display don't make up for how I bored I was during this part. This part segues into some Carnival footage taken in Rio that would show up again in Venus in Furs. Yeah, it's not interesting here either.

All complaints aside, I still enjoyed the beginning, the end, and the afterglow of The Girl from Rio. This film is very uneven but the enjoyable bits are very, very rewarding. And if you happen to dig on Richard Wyler's douchebagel performance then you might even like this even more than I did. Any time that Elisa Montes is on camera, I am happy. She is the bright shining star of this movie and steals every scene she's in. So yeah, Franco made a cheesy comedy S&M crime/spy caper but managed to make it boring. Go figure.

Night of the Skull (1976)

After Lord Archibald Marian (Angel Menendez), the patriarch of a large and affluent family, is murdered by a mysterious killer in a skull-like mask, his family gathers on the family estate for the reading of his will. Inspector Bore (Vicente Roca) and Major Oliver Brooks (Alberto Dalbes) are called in to investigate the murder and get more than they bargained for as the bodies of Lord Archibald's descendants keep popping up. Things get even more nuts when a second will is discovered and it turns out that someone isn't who they claim to be.

In Night of the Skull, Franco mixes an Edgar Allen Poe (actually Edgar Wallace) story with elements from the krimi and giallo genres with fairly successful results. On a clunky scale of 1-10, 1 being not very clunky and 10 being very clunky, Night of the Skull rates around 11. The killer's mask is a dime store rubber cheapie and many of the scenes feel like rushed first takes. Surprisingly, instead of patching over the holes with weirdness and sex*, Franco charges forward, delivering a very different film from his usual fare. It's almost as if this wacked out director decided to just cool it and do a normal movie for a change.

The film's score by Carlo Savina (Fangs of the Living Dead) is superb and really gives the film a special vibe. The camerawork by Javier Perez Zofio is decent enough. There are some out of focus bits (standard Franco) and it's a little dark at times (which may just be the substandard Image DVD) but he does make the most of the old architecture and decent sets. Now don't get me wrong, this movie looks cheap as shit most of the time and hastily thrown together for the rest but I'm not complaining.

What this movie needs is more characters! It seems like every time a scene where a character's introduction ends, another one begins. I don't mind so much since I dig this cast and everyone is pretty distinct in their respective roles. Alberto Dalbes is especially spirited in this film and gleefully jumps into his role of the energetic and slightly naughty Major Brooks. In one scene, he talks to a woman on the phone while spying on her through a keyhole, even commenting on how good she looks in her nightgown. And this guy is supposed to solve a crime? It's also nice to see Yelena Samarina (Werewolf Shadow) as intense as ever. She plays Deborah, the stern and very suspicious maid, and she's just awesome.

Lina Romay is the only one who gets screwed on this one (zing!). Her character Rita, the illegitimate daughter of Lord Archibald, is cold, somber, and damaged almost beyond repair and she does a great job. But then in a couple of scenes, she suddenly starts sobbing and it's really awkward and terrible. This is the first time I've been disappointed with a performance from Romay. Hell, she even stays mostly clothed in this one! I can't help but think that some better direction would have helped her but yeah, she is pretty bad in this. There's no way around it.

While it does take some (read as: a lot of) patience and a good attitude (I happen to have a great attitude!), I really like Night of the Skull a whole,

whole lot. The murders aren't bloody but they are quite sadistic. Even with all of the characters, I enjoyed the twisty story and there's even a very odd séance sequence which always improves a film in my estimation. The atmosphere is that of an old-fashioned gothic chiller and you know, it's gonna get dicey when there's an inheritance involved. Some will call this a slapdash mess but Franco won me over once again.

*I'm going to go out on a limb here and guess that this is the Spanish clothed version of Night of the Skull. I wouldn't be surprised in the least if a naughtier version of this film exists somewhere. I really don't care because all the sex would just fuck up this film's perfect running time.

Marquis de Sade: Justine (1969)

In a prison cell, the Marquis de Sade (Klaus Kinski) is tormented by visions and thus writes the story of Justine. Two girls, Juliette and Justine (Maria Rohm and Romina Power), find out that their father has fled the country in shame with creditors nipping at his heels, leaving them alone in the world. They get kicked out of the convent and sent along their way. Juliette takes up living a life of crime that includes but is not limited to working in a brothel and drowning people. Justine attempts to stay virtuous, ends up losing what little money she has, and goes on all kinds of terrible adventures.

Jess Franco knocks another one out of the park with Justine. This film is full of ribaldry, silliness, beauty, and tragedy. It is also a visual spectacle. The lighting is very colorful and the camerawork by Manuel Merino is fantastic. The musical score by the always brilliant Bruno Nicolai is sometimes bombastic, always lush, simply amazing. Yes, my friends, this is very, very classy smut. And it's not all poisoned puppies and thorny roses either because the world is populated by lecherous creeps, whores, crooks, and murderers.

Horst Frank! Sylvia Koscina! Jack Palance! Rosalba Neri! Howard Vernon! (I don't know why I put an exclamation point after Howard Vernon's name.) This is a star-studded affair and everyone is good. Mercedes McCambridge is awesome as Madame Dubois, an escaped convict and leader of a pack of ruffians. Klaus Kinski is like a caged animal, tormented by visions of women in chains and specters. Romina Power is very good as the virtuous and tragic Justine even though, according to trivia, Franco was forced to cast her in the role and hated her performance. Maria Rohm is perfectly devilish as her naughty sister who is more than willing to follow her own wicked excesses to the bitter end. Palance is particularly unhinged in this movie. He gives me the fuckin' creeps, man. Jeez!

"Now remember what I told you, virtue must be avoided. It is sure disaster. And poverty must be avoided at all costs."

My only complaint about this sumptuous production is the running time is 124 minutes! I'm sorry but all the fish eye lenses in the world can't help a film like this stay interesting for that long. I thought Justine was supposed to be 90 minutes so when that came and went, I was kind of let down that this thing just kept going. Even with its bloated running time and meandering plot, I still think that Jess Franco fans will find plenty to enjoy here. According to IMDB, this was Franco's most expensive film and it really shows with its lavish sets, huge cast, and decadent... um... everything.

Faceless (1987)

After his sister's face is melted off by an unsatisfied customer, plastic surgeon Dr. Flamand (Helmut Berger) conducts illegal experiments in order to restore her beauty. He and his assistant (Brigitte Lahaie) pick up models, hookers, and actresses so that Dr. Moser (Anton Diffring), a former Nazi surgeon, can cut their faces off and use them for possible transplant candidates. When they kidnap a model (Caroline Munro) with a rich father (Telly Savalas), they draw the attention of private eye Sam Morgan (Christopher Mitchum). Faces and other human parts are gonna fly!

If you take all the elements of Faceless separately, nothing adds up. Let's start with the music. While I admit that it is very catchy, the songs are some putrid sub-basement level pop garbage. The score during the horror scenes peps up a bit. The acting is all over the place and the actors are either dubbed or should have been dubbed. But I'll talk more about that in a moment. The editing gets real impatient during the dialog scenes but that is totally forgivable with this script. The sleazy elements of this movie are very awkward. You can almost feel the pent up frustration of horny old Franco as his actors paw at each other like teenagers in a darkened theater while Jaws: The Revenge plays unwatched up on the screen.

I've got to hand it to Jacques Gastineau, the guy can make some splatter happen. His gore effects are quite satisfying here. Maybe his faux heads look a little weak but most of the other parts are solid. Or squishy. Thanks to Gastineau, Faceless has eye violence, severed hands, a nasty rotting head, and, as promised in the title, facelessness. If you're not at least a little shocked by a certain scene where a face transplant goes awry and some wicked face shredding takes place then my friend, you need to take a break from horror for a while. Go watch some "Murder She Wrote" until gore means something to you again.

"You dirty bitch! When I get outta here, I'll tear your heart out!"

The more I think about this cast, the more my brain aches. Brigitte Lahaie (Grapes of Death), who has never disappointed me EVER, is great as the loyal, evil, and insanely greedy Nathalie. Helmut frickin' Berger (The Bloodstained Butterfly) is in this one and the only way his character could have been any more awesome is if his name had been Dr. Fromage. The great Anton Diffring is totally awesome as the hilariously evil Dr. Moser. Keep your face peeled for a sweet cameo from Lina Romay as the wife of Dr. Orloff. Oh that's right, there is a Dr. Orloff in this movie and he is played by Howard Vernon. I think I will call him HoVern from now on. You like that?

I will admit that these are some very stiff performances but who cares? This is Euro horror, my friends. Deal with it. Telly Savalas probably wasn't the only person who didn't give a shit on the set of Faceless but he's the only one letting it show. And just for the record, I am softening on the issue of Christopher Mitchum. I used to really dislike this guy but then it dawned on me: He is a B movie actor, so I gots to chill, dawg! Those are words from my actual brain. To be fair, he's actually okay in Faceless. His fight scenes are good and when he meets up face to face with a very dark twist in the plot, the guy gets it together. I wanted to see more of him and Caroline Munro. Their brief scenes together are pretty promising but whaddayagonnado?

I don't know why but I dig Faceless as much as I do. It might have something to do with the fact that Howard Vernon has more makeup on than Brigitte Lahaie and Caroline Munro combined. It might be the garish lighting and the French cinematographers. Heck, it might even be the presence of one of the worst gay stereotypes ever in the form of the bitchy fashion photographer. I think someone actually told this guy to out-sass the dude in The Case of the Bloody Iris. So anyway, there is just something irresistible about Franco's adventures in splatter. This and Bloody Moon are good time films and are sure to garner him some fans that will be totally confused when they get to something like Women Without Innocence. Yeah right, I'm the only one dumb enough to watch that!

A Virgin Among the Living Dead (1973)

Christina Benson (Christina von Blanc) travels to her family estate to hear the reading of her father's will. The moment Christina arrives, she senses that all is not right with her bizarre family. More and more she begins to suspect that these aren't just a bunch of greedy douchebagels but undead servants of "The Queen of the Night" (Anne Libert).

This film is odd even by Jess Franco standards. This is a super simple idea with painfully obvious metaphors laid out in confusing layers. The whole film relies completely on the ultra-freaky performances of its actors. A Virgin Among the Living Dead is told with beauty, the sexy bodies of its female leads, bizarre menace, and dark comedy. If you revel in the absurd and the painfully sad then this film is for you.

Bruno Nicolai, you magical son of a bitch! Hot fucking damn! Whenever Franco and Nicolai get together, the results are always astounding. This score starts off super weird with a tricked out synthesizer and bass guitar making some unsettling and yet funky sounds. Then the music gets jagged and even more dangerous in a fuzzed out and crazy way. And what would a Bruno Nicolai score be without those lovely vocal pieces? It just wouldn't!

Jess Franco pulls double duty on this picture by stepping in front of the camera to do some of his finest acting. Sure Basilio is an idiotic, murderous, and mute manservant/freak but Franco is actually rather lively in this role. He's just one of the kooks in this flick. One of my favorites, Anne Libert, plays "The Queen of the Night". Nuff said. Rosa Palomar and Howard Vernon play Christina's bonkers aunt and uncle and they do so with a fiendish delight that I want to bottle and deal out on the streets.

So Christina rejects the phallus, thus condemning herself to death? Really, Franco? That is like Sleazy Cinema Symbolism 101, duder. I think I'm going to call you Jeff from now on. Jeff Frakno. That is your new name. Yo readers, don't let any of the DVD covers or posters for this film fool you, this ain't no zombie fest. I'm sure all the Franco fanatics have already seen this one. It's pretty much classic Franco with some excellent moments that demonstrate the guy was ahead of his time back in the day. As usual, he is so sex-obsessed that he looks like a fucking buffoon even when he's getting everything else right. A Virgin Among the Living Dead is definitely worth a look.

She Killed in Ecstasy (1971)

When Dr. Johnson (Fred Williams) reveals to the medical council that he has been using human embryos for his experiments in genetic research, he gets ousted from the medical community and all of his research is destroyed. The medical council takes things just a wee bit too far and drive the poor guy to madness and suicide. Mrs. Johnson (Soledad Miranda) decides to target the four doctors who are the head of the medical council and make them pay for what they did to her hubby. She seduces and kills them one by one while an ineffectual cop (Horst Tappert) manages to stay one step behind her vicious acts of vengeance.

This eroti-tragedy (I just made that term up) by Jess Franco could very well be the director's best film. This isn't my own personal favorite but I was stunned by just how much this film gets under my skin and stays there, happily festering away. This just goes to show you that whenever Franco and Soledad Miranda got together, the results were phenomenal. And like every other person who appreciates their collaborations, I can't help but feel fucked up about her untimely death in August of 1970, over a year before this film was even released.

I gotta say that the score for She Killed in Ecstasy is very, very good. It is also very dynamic with its freaky funky jazzy bits, tense experimental bits, and moody bittersweet bits. That's a lot of bits. Composers Manfred Hubler and Sigi Schwab (holy friggin' wow, what a great name!) give this film a dynamic and bold soundtrack that could have only happened (and worked) in the early 70s.

Two more amazing things about this film are the locations and the cinematography. Some of the ultra-modern buildings where key scenes of this film are shot look like the future. Well, the future according to people in 1971 anyway. It's all stark and rather appealing if you like things that look like spaceships or alien civilizations (which I know for a fact that you do). The camerawork is credited to the always reliable Manuel Merino. Sure, there are some out of focus and shaky moments but I bet you big money that Franco yelled 'action' while the poor guy was still setting up a shot. Reshoots? Ha! Franco laughs in the face of the poor SOB who asks about reshoots. Merino will make you weep with his framing, that much I promise you.

The cast does not disappoint with the alluring Soledad Miranda, not too surprisingly, giving her all and stealing the entire movie. She gives an excellent performance that is painfully sad and insanely raging in equal measure. Mrs. Johnson is also a well written character with her obsession with revenge, potentially supernatural powers, and predilection for cutting off dudes' wangs. When she is in the arms of her enemies, she dreams of making love to her man. Now that's a real woman!

Like I said before, this isn't my favorite Franco film of all time (Eugenie de Sade is) but She Killed in Ecstasy would be a great starting point for folks looking to see what Jess Franco is all about. It's a little repetitive and slow at the beginning but fear not, this film gets to the dreamy goodness and wacky weirdness before you know it. If nothing else, see this for Soledad. She is so hot in this movie that it hurts me in my pants area. Also, this film contains the best suffocation-by-inflatable-zebra-pillow ever!

Vampyros Lesbos (1971)

An indiscernible voice prattling through a megaphone over some toxic jazz segues into a relentless blast of organ music. The first images we see? A striptease. A brunette in a red scarf takes off what little lingerie she is wearing and dresses a living mannequin on the stage with her. The finale of the act comes when the mannequin suddenly comes to life. A blond woman in the audience is particularly affected by this display. This is Vampyros Lesbos, dear reader. Fasten your ill-fitting braziers, it's gonna be a funky night (day, actually).

Linda Westinghouse (Ewa Stromberg) has been haunted by dreams of a woman she has never met. This woman beckons to her. While she and her boyfriend are staying in Istanbul, Linda is called in to draw up the estate of the Countess Carody AKA Nadine (Soledad Miranda). I think she's a lawyer or whatever. It should be no surprise to anyone watching this film, the Countess is the woman from her dreams. Much like the title promises, the Countess is a lesbian vampire and she wants to drain Linda dry.

Linda's boyfriend Omar (Andres Monales) is very concerned for his lady who seems to be fading away before his eyes. He contacts Dr. Seward (Dennis Price) who is convinced that vampires are real and that Linda is in grave danger. Locked up in his hospital is Agra (Heidrun Kussin), one of the Countess's previous victims/girlfriends, who has completely lost her mind. She spends her days writhing around in her bed with a very phallic-looking rubber clown and prophesying the Countess's imminent return. Agra is the Renfield of this movie. Nice work if you can get it.

Of course, Dr. Seward is an unethical motherfucker who wants the vampire's power of immortality. He tries to trap the Countess in some lame scheme but he doesn't count on her manservant Morpho (Jose Martinez Blanco) showing up and wrecking shit. Did I mention that Linda is being held hostage by a madman named Memmet (Jess Franco)? No? Oh well. I probably forgot to talk about how Linda is special (she's strong willed?) and that the Countess has decided to bestow all the powers of the vampire upon her. Yeah, sorry I forgot all that stuff. Omar and Linda's therapist (Paul Muller) show up to save the day. But will they be too late?!?!

Director Jess Franco delivers a pervasively moody, if uneven film with Vampyros Lesbos. The adventurous cinematographer Manuel Merino does not disappoint delivering a lush and very pretty film full of vibrance in even the most washed out sets located in Istanbul, Germany, and Spain. Merino also makes great use of lots of colored gels and inexplicably bizarre lighting setups, giving the film even more spice. The soundtrack by Manfred Hubler, Sigi Schwab, and Franco himself is overwhelming and should just about melt your ears off.

"My friend is the Queen of the Night."

Even after all the Jess Franco films I've seen, Vampyros Lesbos is still pretty damn weird. Vampires that go sunbathing in the nude, mysterious blood dripping down a window, a scorpion drowning* in a swimming pool, and candles burning in broad daylight are just a few bafflements in store for adventurous viewers. The only major complaint I have is the striptease at the beginning of the film is repeated pretty much in its entirety late in the running time. I can't help but wish this had been abbreviated. It's a poignant scene in its own way but the Countess's act is so elaborate that it's a little dull the second time around. Here I am, complaining about naked women again! Maybe Franco just ain't for me.

I love this silly, silly movie but I suspect that without Soledad Miranda's super-cool performance, I doubt this would be as highly revered (or perhaps just remembered thanks to Synapse's 2000 DVD) as it is. I think this is certainly better than Daughter of Dracula, released the following year. This film does have some laughably outrageous overacting (Kussin) and forehead slapping underacting (Monales) but Miranda and Stromberg help you forget about all that. As far as starting points for Jess Franco, Vampyros Lesbos is an excellent place to begin. Just don't tell a newbie that this is his greatest film. That just wouldn't be true.

*Scorpions can't fucking swim, Franco!

Succubus (1968)

Lorna Green (Janine Reynaud) is an S&M dominatrix in a nightclub owned by her boyfriend William (Jack Taylor). When she's not whipping the crap out of people, she's out partying, dropping acid, and getting all sexually frustrated and stuff because William is usually too drunk to fuck (like the Dead Kennedys song). Next thing ya know, Lorna descends into a dream world where all kinds of freaky shit happens. Everything goes all soft focus and she goes to a castle. She also stabs a guy (Howard Vernon) in the eye with a needle and kills some people. Oh, and her collection of mannequins come to life. Are these only fantasies? Or is this mysterious stranger (Michel Lemoine) have some devious plan for Lorna?

Mr. Jess Franco drops us into his dream world of soft focus sexual perversion and fantasies bathed in diffused light. This film is bizarre, silly, practically plotless, and mannequins do come to life but this film is crippled by its artsy-fartsiness. Awkward stripteases, murder, J&B sightings, and LSD trips abound but I am still bored. I need to stop making these friggin' list sentences. Sorry.

One thing I am thankful for is Franco introducing me to Janine Reynaud. Before this film and Kiss Me Monster, I just thought that Miss Reynaud was just that weird looking lady from The Case of the Scorpion's Tail. Now I know she's that weird looking lady from all kinds of movies! But seriously, Reynaud is always a welcome sight to behold and her performances just warm my dang heart. Other great faces in this movie are Howard Vernon (who looks awfully comfortable in that bar that employs hot naked dudes), Oregon's own Jack Taylor (who is becoming one of my faves), Adrian Hoven (and his rakish good looks), and actor/director Michel Lemoine (who is totally creepy).

"Will you always stay?"
"I will stay until the end."

So where does this film go wrong? The writing! I have sat through Franco's unique brand of improvised saxophone solo filmmaking many times before but rarely has pretentious dialog turned it into an almost unbearably embarrassing experience for me. From the blatantly obvious themes hammered into the viewer's brain to a super snooty word association/name-dropping game (that just about made me vomit), this film has its head way, way up its own ass. That being said, all of this pretentious shit is very funny so if Franco meant it as a joke... GOOD!

I do enjoy the visual aspects and the score of Succubus. Because of those aspects, this is a lovely and enjoyable cinematic poem. In his introduction to Obsession: The Films of Jess Franco, Tim Lucas refers to this film as the beginning of Franco's peak years and the first film where he was given complete freedom. So I'm not surprised this would be both great and slightly full of shit. Succubus is incredibly dated and a bit of chore to sit through but fans of Jess Franco will dig it. It's like John Coltrane. You know you're supposed to dig Giant Steps for what it is but you've already moved on to A Love Supreme. There! I'm like Franco now.

The Obscene Mirror (1973)

Annette (Emma Cohen) is about to marry her fiancée, Arthur, when her sister Marie (Lina Romay) kills herself with a sword. Annette calls off the wedding, abandons her needy father (Howard Vernon), and runs off to make a life for herself in the world. Unfortunately, Annette and her sister had some kind of an incestuous thing going on, so she is now plagued by visions of her dead sister HAVING GRAPHIC SEXUAL RELATIONS. To support herself, Annette plays piano and smokes dope in a jazz bar. She is being romanced by a creepo trumpeter named Bill (Robert Woods).

Marie (from the grave and/or evil mirror) commands Annette to kill or play with vaginas. I'm confused on that point. During a performance at the bar, Annette has a vision where she kills Bill (funny, right?). In an indescribably hilarious moment, Annette comes to and the band asks her to play something upbeat. She flops and flails around at the piano, laughing while everyone smiles and snaps their fingers. Brilliant.

Next, Annette starts dating Michel (Simon Andreau) AKA Mr. Corny Car Horn, a director who finds her inspiring or something. She has another vision of her sister's body double fucking someone and then she stabs Michel to death in the theater —which is actually a surprisingly creepy scene (the stabbing not the fucking). After losing (and possibly murdering) two lovers, Annette decides to kill herself. Right after she slits her wrists, her good friend Clara (Alice Arno) shows up and calls 911 (according to the dodgy subtitles).

After she recovers from the suicide attempt, Annette and Clara go off to the seaside. It is there that she meets Pipo (Phillippe Lemaire), who is a Class 5 Midlife Crisis. Despite the fact that his wife(?) Tina (Francoise Brion) is like right there, Pipo starts putting the moves on Annette. Even though Pipo is disgusting, Annette is totally into him. WTF? They get it on and, of course, Marie is screwing someone in a vision and telling her to kill. And she totally stabs the shit out of Pipo. When she comes out of her murderous reverie, Annette flips out and takes off in a little yellow car. So here it is, the climax of the movie, and it is genitals. Big genitals on the screen.

"Life is strange. One tries to fly but ends up falling back in the same shit."

Jess Franco, you fucking sellout. No wonder I quit reviewing this shit. I almost feel bad for Old Jess but the presence of Lina Romay makes me think that the alternate cut is at least partially his fault. As for the XXX inserts, they are just from some random porno flick. There is a good movie buried in all this mess but any chance of atmosphere, subtlety, and beauty is squashed out by droopy vagina lips and a big old dick. Not even the lovely and excellent Emma Cohen can save this one. Hopefully, this film will one day appear in its original form: The Other Side of the Mirror. As for The Obscene Mirror, avoid at all costs.

Erotikill (1973)

The Countess Irina Karlstein (Lina Romay) walks out of the mist, eyes sunken, breasts not sunken, wearing only a belt and a cape. The camera zooms to her PUBIC REGION then back up to her face. Then the Countess proceeds to walk into the camera lens. Poetry? Comedy? All I know is that an actress couldn't ask for a better entrance than that. She goes to a farm in this getup, seduces a simpleton, and bites his neck. His strangely guttural cry can be heard miles away by Baron von Rathony (played by the brooding mustache of Jack Taylor). Suddenly, the Countess flaps her cape and flies away. Scree! Scree! Woosh!

We are briefly introduced to Inspector Idiot and Dr. Robertson (Jess Franco). He tells the inspector that the murder victim was killed during orgasm and was drained of blood and semen. Gee, I thought the Countess only bit that dude's neck. She's amazing! It's almost like this version of the film is missing something. Meanwhile, back at the hotel, we see that this lady vampire likes to sunbathe, in the nude? No, actually fully clothed. Haven't you read your vampire lore?

So my favorite scene of this entire movie happens when Anna (Anna Watican), an intrepid reporter, approaches the Countess for an interview. Of course, she agrees and they go sit in a hotel room to talk (one-sided, of course). For what feels like hours (oh God, I wish!), Anna interviews the mute vampire. This is seriously the best interview of a mute character ever filmed. Next, the Countess writhes around on a bed while her mute servant (good old Luis Barboo) smiles, appreciating every moment. The Countess decides to kill the hotel masseuse and she hypnotizes him by flashing her vagina at him over and over and over and over and over.

Frustrated by trying to convince Inspector Idiot that vampires exist, Dr. Roberts meets up with Dr. Orloff. He's the blind son of an old colleague, eh? Very interesting. The Countess shows up in Anna's hotel room and licks her lips and touches herself (while fully clothed) for a while, driving Anna mad with desire. Then she leaves Anna horny, totally unfulfilled, and crying in torment. Ha ha! She comes back after a costume change and then kills Anna. That makes everything all better, doesn't it?

The Baron finally meets the Countess. He asks her if she will one day take him with her behind the mist. I drop my pen (what did you think I was holding?) and just stare at the screen, entranced. This movie just got to me. Next, Alice Arno and Monica Swinn magically appear in the film, playing Yahtzee, and waiting for The Countess to appear. She does and the two of them show her just how they treat their guests. Nakedness, shackles, and a very thick, sharp switch are utilized in their games. After some bloody whipping, the Countess calls bullshit, hypnotizes Arno, and then drinks Swinn dry. All the while, the soundtrack drops out, making the whole scene very uncomfortable; like it was totally unplanned.

The Baron admits that he has a mega-crush on the Countess. They kiss and she's like "No! Go away! You're too vanilla. And I'll drink your mustache!" Look, she's mute, I have to ad lib. They kiss again, they screw, and she kills him. She gets a little bummed out and tells Dr. Orloff that she wants all vampires to go away forever or something. Then she takes a bath in some bloody bathwater, writhes around, and then arches her back in order to shove her PUBIC REGION into the air repeatedly. Dr. Robertson shows up, kills her manservant, and then watches her drown in the bloody bathwater. Maybe. They show her walking around in the mist some more so who the fuck knows?

> *"You can well listen: I am quite sane. And I state that this murder is surrounded by a mystery that is not easy to elucidate."*

I don't know what cracks me up more, the barely competent as well as successfully hilarious dubbing or the Peanuts-like jazz that plays through some of these scenes. The rest of the score is snippets of haunting melodies and classical yearnings. As for the dubbing, everyone involved is reading off the most banal claptrap ever written without missing a beat. The dude who dubbed Jack Taylor is the worst though. His accent is almost impenetrable. Lina Romay is lucky that her character is mute but not even she can escape the cheesed out voice-acting. Her internal monologues are delivered by a melodramatic robot.

I'm not going to lie to you, I love Erotikill. It has a few slow spots but I fell deeply for this very flawed gem. All of the shit that is wrong with this version just works perfectly for me. Lina Romay was very amateurish as an actress at this point in her career but she was also a mesmerizing weirdo (as always) so this film is perfect for her with the muteness and the nudeness. Her breasts almost steal the movie. I can wholeheartedly recommend Erotikill to anyone who likes watching Jess Franco movies with all of the boning cut out and presented in a pitifully cropped full frame transfer. One day, if I ever give a double damn, I might sit down and give the Female Vampire cut another go.

The Sinister Eyes of Dr. Orloff (1973)

Man, where do I start? Wheelchair-bound Melissa Comfort (Montserrat Prous) has a recurring dream of her father (Jess Franco) standing (rather lasciviously) over her younger self. The dream becomes even more disturbing when blood pours out of his mouth and onto her. He dies right in front of her and she's awakened by her super sexy half-sister, Martha Comfort (Loreta Tovar). Martha informs Melissa that their uncle Henry has called in a specialist to examine her. His name is Dr. Orloff (William Berger). Dun dun duhhhhhhhhh!

Of course, no one in the Comfort family wants Melissa to get better because they are money-grubbing pigs. Her aunt Flora (Kali Hansa) is the worst of the bunch and would rather see Melissa committed to an asylum than show any improvement. After her first treatment with Dr. Orloff, Melissa has a nightmare in which she kills her uncle. A nightmare? Yeah right! Of course, there's no body and uncle's hunting gear and car are gone, so everyone just keeps thinking Melissa is a crazy.

But not all hope is lost. The Comfort family's manservant, Matthews (Jose Manuel Martin) is on Melissa's side. In fact, I think he's in love with her which makes it even sadder when she has a "dream" of beating him to death with a tire iron. Okay, send in the hippie! Living next door to the Comforts is a dang hippie named (and I'm not making this up) Davey Procop Robert Eugene Hutchinson AKA Davey Sweet Brown (Robert Woods). This fucking guy has a crush on Melissa and believes that her family and Dr. Orloff are up to no good. He tries to convince the police inspector (played by Gay Dracula himself, Edmund Purdom) to investigate. Maybe there is no hope after all.

To no surprise to anyone -except the characters in this movie- Dr. Orloff and his sexy assistant (uncredited) are up to no good. Orloff was in love with Melissa's mother back in the day but her dad wooed her away from him. Now he is using all of his Orloffian powers to use Melissa as his tool of revenge. Between Melissa's hypno-murder spree and Aunt Flora's scheming, there's not going to be anyone left to collect on the Comfort estate.

First things first, the score for this film really knocked me out. It seems like someone is just absentmindedly sitting on the keyboard of an old Hammond but then the insanity comes pouring out and I'm loving every second of it. However, the less said about Davey Sweet Brown's folk shenanigans the better. I love the camerawork on this film. There's lots of close-ups, fish eye lens weirdness, and a penchant for perfectly capturing the garishness of the early 1970s. Intervision's DVD may be full frame and sourced from an old VHS but I ain't complainin'. There's probably a nicer looking porn version of this movie that I never want to watch.

There are more than a few familiar faces in this film. William Berger's wild eyes have so much Euro-cult goodness that I don't even know where to begin. Montserrat Prous was in Franco's Diary of a Nymphomaniac which I haven't mustered up the courage to watch. Edmund Perdom... 'Nuff said. Both Loreta Tovar and Kali Hansa can be found in Amando de Ossario's Night of the Sorcerers and other Spanish horror treasures. Jose Manuel Martin was in tons of stuff like Curse of the Devil and Death Walks on High Heels. There's an actress in this that keeps her clothes on so I didn't recognize her. It's Lina Romay!

> *"I plan to have thousands of adventures with the hottest men of the Earth."*

I'm completely sober and in my right mind when I say this: The Sinister Eyes of Dr. Orloff delivers. I judged a book by its cover and came out a winner. This particular Orloff film has one of the most talky, convoluted, and generic thriller plots ever but processed through the Jess Franco machine. The result is ineptly vivacious and one of my new favorite Franco titles. There's just something fabulously droll and off kilter about Sinister Eyes so that it plays out like it was made by a crazy person (or Al Adamson).

Richard Glenn Schmidt

The Devil Came from Akasava (1971)

When an ancient, mysterious, strange, and also deadly stone is discovered in a cave in Akasava, all heck breaks loose. The stone is stolen and Dr. Forrester (Angel Menendez), a world-famous mineralogist, has disappeared (and is presumed dead). Sir Philip (Siegfried Schurenberg) contacts Miss Jane Morgan (Soledad Miranda), a secret agent posing as a stripper and/or hooker. He informs Jane that aside from its evil death rays, the magical stone is also said to be able to turn lead into gold or whatever. Knowing what would happen if this precious item got into the wrong hands, Jane takes the case.

On her way to Akasava, Jane meets Rex Forrester (Fred Williams), the son of the missing Dr. Forrester. He is traveling to Akasava with his friend (?) Tino (Jess Franco) to find out what happened to his dad. At the hotel, Jane teams up with Irving Lambert (Alberto Dalbes), another secret agent. They pose as husband and wife but Jane also does a striptease at a local nightclub. You know, just to keep a low profile and stuff.

Jane and Irving's main suspects are Dr. Thorrsen (Horst Tappert) and his wife Ingrid (Ewa Stromberg), who run a clinic in Akasava treating an outbreak of narcolepsy affecting the local indigenous population. This part was really confusing. Anyway, Irving is killed and Jane ends up in the arms of Rex Forrester. Honestly, I could go on all day with this freakin' plot. All you need to know is that there are double crosses and nonsensical reveals as Jane and Rex find out who is really behind the stone snatching and what really happened to Dr. Forrester.

"I hate hair gel."

While not quite as fun as Kiss Me, Monster, this film comes pretty damn close. You really can't go wrong when there's a Philosopher's Stone thingie that looks like weapons-grade quartz in your plot. It's more of a McMuffin than a MacGuffin. Just when you think things are flying by too fast and the dialog is all balderdash, the plot takes a bong hit and everything just downshifts into super-chill mode for a few minutes, and then it picks back up again. Good times!

I did one of those "Common Cast/Crew Between Two Titles" searches on IMDB. I know, I'm a cheat! Deal with it. Eleven names were in common between this film and Vampyros Lesbos. Then I plugged in the same search comparing this with She Killed in Ecstasy and thirteen names came up! You know what I should do? Research! It's called "Franco Friday", okay? Not "Respect Filmmakers Friday"! Seriously though, this is a Who's Who of Franco regulars like Ewa Stromberg, Paul Muller, and Howard Vernon (who has a scene where he jumps out a third story window like it was stepping over a curb). Just FYI, I think this is the first film where I actually liked Fred Williams. Sigi Schwab provides the swingin' score full of sitars and jangly guitars to keep your toes tapping.

The Devil Came from Akasava is prime Jess Franco, folks. This is a wild spy caper with way more imagination than budget. The script is often childlike and utterly ludicrous. The story was apparently adapted from Edgar Wallace but after the second "But I'm a secret agent too!" revelation, all I could do was stare in wonder at the screen. My only complaint, after a fairly satisfying wrap-up, the film has a final coda that is utter nonsense. It's just a baffling and unnecessary moment that makes me feel like there's footage missing.

My friend Brad made a good point about this movie when he mentioned to me that he thought this was one of Soledad Miranda's best roles. Sure, she has a couple of ubiquitous strip numbers (non-dancing in a shredded garbage bag this time) but she plays an actual character here. She has a chance to show real range in Akasava despite how silly this movie is. I too noticed just how many expressions she pulls in this film and I saw sides to her acting ability that a film like Vampyros Lesbos just didn't give her the opportunity to show off. Despite the bewildering plot elements of this bizarre little romp, Miranda just kills it.

Attack of the Robots (1966)

A series of assassinations of ambassadors from all over the world are committed by some very strange, dark-skinned men (and women!). The police manage to capture one of the assailants and try to question him but he is unresponsive. The suspect tries to flee and the cops gun him down. As he dies, his skin changes from black to white. As more and more of these assassins are caught, the police discover that the only thing these random men (and women!) have in common is an abnormality in their blood called "Rhesus zero". Is your pseudoscience alarm going off yet?

Interpol decides to pick one of their agents with "Rhesus zero" and send them out into the field as bait. They get former secret agent, Al Peterson (Eddie Constantine), to go down to Spain to try and lure the baddies out. Down in Spain, under the pseudonym Frank Froiba (?), Peterson meets the lovely Cynthia Lews (Sophia Hardy), a striptease artist, but every time he makes a little time for her, some Mexican ruffian cock-blocks him by insisting that they duke it out. Meanwhile, an evil Chinese syndicate led by Lee Wee (Vincente Roca) is out to kill Peterson because he refused to be their double agent.

Finally, Peterson catches Lady Cecilia Addington Courtney (Francoise Brion), the mastermind behind the assassinations, snooping around his hotel room. She is kidnapping people with "Rhesus zero" and turning them into robots. Evil organizations from all over the world pay her to send these automatons out to commit assassinations so that they can keep their hands from getting dirty. Can Peterson get to the bottom of this crazy plot without becoming a robot slave to Lady Cecilia himself?

"There's a corpse in the bathtub. He's preventing me from taking a shower."

You know what? You should just get naked now because this movie is about to charm your pants off. All the bad women in this wear vinyl, what's not to like? If you enjoyed such films as Kiss Me, Monster or (to a lesser extent) The Girl from Rio, then you will love Attack of the Robots. Every cheesy gag, no matter how droll or eye roll-inducing, is thrown into the mix but this flick is never lazy or cynical. This is a fairly innocent romp (even the striptease is tasteful!) with lots of action and laughs.

You know what I don't like about this movie? Eddie fucking Constantine! His bloated visage just rubs me the wrong way. Lucky for this guy, the movie is so fun that I kind of just got used to him so as not to spoil my enjoyment. He is described by his colleagues as being "full of vinegar" -I just assume this is some kind of urinary problem he has- and is always somewhere in the world with a sexy blond on his arm. A blond what?

You know wha- Oops, I can't start every paragraph with that. Um... The other thing I can complain about is the whole black-face bit. As to why the killer robots are made to look dark-skinned is baffling and fairly offensive. But it's just so damn weird, I have a feeling it may have actually been a statement against racism. But then again, the way Chinese are portrayed in this film kind of sucks too. And Mexicans. Shit, I got nothing. This is insanely politically incorrect, what can you do?

The print I'm watching is on YouTube and compressed all to fuck so let's hope that someday this film will resurface on DVD in a more watchable version. Even with the cruddy presentation, Attack of the Robots looks pretty damn good thanks to the camerawork of Antonio Macasoli (Grand Slam (you know, that one Blue Underground title that you'll never watch)). Despite my complaints above, I highly recommend this one. Fun stuff.

Un Silencio de Tumba (1972)

A bunch of socialite and movie industry jerks just wrapped up production on a shitty spaghetti western and are on a boat headed for a remote island to have a little vacay. Valerie (Montserrat Prous) hates them all. You see, Valerie is the sister of Annette (Glenda Allen) and she can't stand the vacuous bitch. She has watched her sister throw herself at various men and destroy their lives. Not even the birth of her son (that Valerie raises like it was her own) has slowed Annette down. While everyone is partying like idiots, the child is kidnapped. Soon, the threatening notes and ransom demands turn into acts of murder. With every possible route of escape from the island cut off, Valerie turns to Juan (Alberto Dalbes) the only man she believes she can trust.

Well, color me surprised. This is a side of Franco I didn't expect to see. This is Franco working as close to the giallo genre as I've ever seen. I don't think Franco ever did anything as obvious as having a killer don a pair of black gloves and go around slashing with a straight razor but this does the trick, for sure. The opening song is haunting, beautiful, and downright depressing. The rest of the score is discordant and brooding and serves the material well. Even though my copy is a tad muddy, I can see the cinematography of Javier Perez Zofio shining through.

I love this cast save for one: The little kid actor isn't really what you might call... an actor. He looked like an unnaturally happy and blond kid-sized mannequin. Luckily, his screen time is very brief. I really dig Montserrat Prous. She is able to play these haunted characters very well. Her big eyes look so sad. Aww, poor baby! Alberto Dalbes is great as always. He is our go-to European stud with way more charisma than good looks.

"Poor, innocent Valerie, the only decent person in this shit-hole. I have to kill you as well."

Kali Hansa is very intriguing as Laura, the- um, housekeeper, I guess. She looks less mannish and more exotic than she did in The Sinister Eyes of Dr. Orloff. Her suspicious glances are the stuff that dreams are made of. Suspicious dreams! One actress that can't help but stick out is Yelena Samarina. She plays Vera, the photographer chick, and I wish she had a bigger part. You can see her suicide jaw in other Franco flicks like Daughter of Dracula and Night of the Skull but I know her best from Francisco Lara Polop's Murder Mansion.

If you ever doubted Franco's abilities as a filmmaker, look at the nail-biting climax of this film and you'll see a capable and confident duder at work. The guy could make a solid thriller and he really makes the most of a measly budget, a beautiful location, and a handful of capable actors in Un Silencio de Tumba. There is lots of dread in the air and a quiet menace throughout this flick. I can't help but recommend that you go for it, you crazy Francophiles.

Demoniac (1975)

Jess Franco plays Mathis Vogel, a defrocked priest and madman who believes that it is his duty to help sexy young women repent for their sins. Not too surprisingly, thanks to the release date of this film and the idiocy of the audience (myself included), the only way to do this is at the end of his switchblade. Some stupid cops are on his trail but they are stupid dumb idiots and stupids who are too stupid and too dumb to stop him. Vogel writes about his crimes and has them published by an erotic magazine published by some guy named Pierre (Pierre Taylou). He falls for Pierre's secretary, a swingin' happy-go-lucky gal named Anne (Lina Romay), and decides that he must save her soul as well.

My plan has backfired. You see, when I decided to watch the Erotikill version of Female Vampire, I found enough accidental magic to have myself a gay old time (that means "a happy time", by the way). I was hoping the same thing would happen with Demoniac, a bastardized version of Exorcism. In a (presumably) shrewd move, Franco filmed a couple more murder scenes and some shots of his character attempting to repent for his sins six years after Exorcism was released and cut them in to make this into a body count flick. Well, it worked! That's why this version is so famous and moviegoers the world over always have a fondness or -dare I say it- an orgiastic love of Demoniac.

"Nothing's wrong! NOTHING'S WRONG! Take off your pants!"

Of course, I'm lying. No one gives a triple tiger shit or a sweet tin fuck about this boring ass garbage. It took me over three hours to sit through this 79 minute bullshit. I took a nap and a lunch break just to get through this nightmare. So what did I like about it? Well, as you probably have figured out by now, I can sit through most any Euro-garbage. All of the scenes with the cops in this movie are great semi-intentionally funny droll comedy gold. The scene wherein a poor, innocent (and insanely sexy) hooker comes on to Vogel was pretty good. It ends with him calling her a "hussy" and stabbing her to death but hey, that's life in the big city. Finally, the best thing about this movie is that the continuity goes right out the window whenever they cut between the 1975 footage and the 1981 footage because Franco not only looks older but also has a terrific mullet (hair extensions?) in the new footage versus his long hair in the older. This movie could have been saved by more nightclub dancing sequences.

La Venganza del Doctor Mabuse (1972)

A mad scientist (and devotee of the infamous Dr. Mabuse) named Farkas (Jack Taylor) is using some mad science to steal stuff, kidnap foxy ladies, and program them to do his bidding. Oh and get revenge, etc. With the help of his assistant Leslie (Beni Cardoso) and his mute and monstrous manservant Andros (Moises Augusta Rocha), he intends to build an army and take over the world, maybe. A fast-talking striptease artist named Jenny Paganini (Ewa Strömberg) witnesses Andros kidnapping a woman and reports it to Inspector Thomas (Fred Williams), who dresses like a cowboy. Farkas sends his minions out to capture Jenny.

At the same time, Inspector Thomas uses Jenny as bait to capture the criminals but he loses her when his partner's shitty car breaks down. Leslie and Andros bring Jenny to Farkas's hideout in an abandoned lighthouse. Aww, Andros is sweet on Jenny. His one good eye likes what it sees. A drunken fisherman (Roberto Camardiel) catches a pair of panties in the river and takes them to the inspector. He has had his suspicions about the place and those panties confirm them!

Farkas hypnotizes Jenny and sends her out after Professor Parkinson (Ángel Menéndez). He uses her to hypnotize Parkinson so that he will cease research on some radioactive moon rocks. Then Farkas sends Andros and a safe-cracker out to steal the moon rocks for his evil plan. He also orders Andros to murder Dr. Orloff (Siegfried Lowitz), Parkinson's colleague. When Inspector Thomas's lady friend -who also happens to be Dr. Orloff's daughter- discovers Orloff's body, Andros kidnaps her. When Farkas finds out, he's more than happy to use her in his dastardly vague plan as well.

Dr. Mabuse? Yeah, right! This is a Dr. Orloff film through and through with some nice spaghetti western sets mixed in for some dang reason. Andros is such a Morpho! Here's another one of those crazy Franco flicks aimed at the easy-to-please "Saturday afternoon timewasters" demographic, filmed and thrown together very quickly. You know I can dig that! As usual, Manuel Merino's camerawork provides lots of fun camera angles that give this film some style with no budget at all. The score is bright and jazzy but it sounds like it was taken from other, older films.

La Venganza del Doctor Mabuse moves along at a great clip thanks in part to the short running time but really, this is just meant to be a silly sci-fi potboiler for kids with short attention spans. Ewa Strömberg is insanely cute in this one and seems to be having a blast portraying Jenny, a hyper airhead. She's rocking a brunette wig, hot-pants, and fringe go-go boots like it was nobody's business. The rest of the cast also seem to be having a pretty good time on this one. I would love to see La Venganza on DVD sometime as it is an easy watch. This is an international incident of weirdness!

Dolls for Sale (1972)

Al Pereira (Howard Vernon) is an unscrupulous private detective who gets in way over his head when he's paid by the lovely Lina (Doris Thomas) to sneak into a dude's apartment and steal an envelope with her name on it from a dresser and bring it back to her. The dude (Manuel Pereiro) wakes up and pulls a gun but Al beats him up and leaves, his mission accomplished. Unbeknownst to Al, someone sneaks in and kills the dude and frames him for the crime.

Now totally desperate, Al turns to his special lady friend and striptease artist, Valentina (Montserrat Prous), for help. She uncovers that Lina works with a psycho named Leona (Kali Hansa) at a strip joint called the Flamingo, owned by a suspicious woman named Benny (Anne Libert). All of these ladies -including a sadistic beyatch named Bertha- are somehow involved in a secret sexual society that exists in a place called "The House of Vice".

Al sends Valentina to the Flamingo to get information from (AKA have lesbian sex with) Benny. His plan both works and backfires when Leona recognizes Valentina as Al's girlfriend and kidnaps her. Leona takes Valentina to the "little red room" and tortures her with a long sword while that sadistic beyatch Bertha, Benny, and some random chick cream their jeans over the whole scene. Will Al get there in time to save Valentina and can he trust Lina to have his back?

I can't believe what I just saw. Montserrat Prous just slapped Howard Vernon's bare ass! I'm serious. This really just happened. Then they had a love scene. Also, Howard Vernon in bed with a woman? I used to understand the world but now I feel like my blood just turned to LSD and someone handed me a meth lollipop. BTW, this movie is pretty amazing.

All joking aside, I love Dolls for Sale. This movie opens with Kali Hansa's naked groin gyrating on the screen and I was all like "Well, this is going to be a fucking chore. At least I finally know that she's not a dude." But then this movie just kept getting more and more weird. Vernon playing the sexy and tough noir-ish detective that only diehard lesbians can resist and no man, no matter how poorly choreographed, can defeat? I'm telling you, this shit is out there, way, way out. It's your standard sexed up thriller (missing about a dozen pages of script) but it plays out so obtusely, it's like everyone in the cast and crew was on Quaaludes.

One thing that stands out is the soundtrack. For once, nobody was dipping into the library music and Daniel Janin's score is consistently cool and always dead on. Cinematographer Gérard Brisseau knows how to keep everything visually interesting when shit get sleazy and cheap which is pretty much this entire film. The sequence where Valentina is taken to the "little red room" and tortured plays out like a horror scene as the set is bathed in red light and it all feels super naughty and dangerous.

Two more observations before I leave crazy town. One thing that struck me as totally genius is that in the midst of all this lipstick lesbian craziness and macho bullshit fantasy overload, a male stripper hits the dance floor and owns it. I mean, this duder OWNS IT! And the funny part is, Howard

Vernon can't keep his eyes off of him. Intentional? I think so. Fuck it, I know so. And the other thing that just made me leap out of my skin is this: a character is found dead and Al closes their staring, lifeless eyes with his hand. As he did, the tape rolled and VCR static covered the screen. Whatever French VHS this was sourced from was communicating to me in that moment. I think it wanted to say, "This is what happens when you die. Your tracking goes all funky."

Eugenie... The Story of Her Journey into Perversion (1970)

Very few of Jess Franco's films open as ostentatiously as Eugenie: The Story etc. A young woman in a see-through nightie is reading a book and we see in her mind's eye, a sexy and blasphemous ceremony based on the works of Marquis De Sade. She closes the book and goes back to the real world. Her name is Maria (Maria Rohm) and she's a perv. Eugenie (Marie Liljedahl) is Maria's young friend. She is an angry teenager living at home with her parents who... just don't understand. What Eugenie doesn't know is that her father (Paul Muller) is having an affair with Maria.

Maria demands payment for her sexual favors from Eugenie's father. Her price: Eugenie. She wants Eugenie to come and spend the weekend at her island. Of course, he says yes! Next thing you know, Eugenie is on her way out to the island where God knows what awaits her. Maria's partner in crime is another terrible perv and super creep named Mirvel (Jack Taylor). He is Maria's stepbrother and I don't trust this fucking guy at all.

Maria is going to teach Eugenie how to be a woman (with Mirvel watching them with his filthy eyes) but in reality, they are going to sacrifice her to some crazy cult. Oh boy, this is going to be sleazy. To get this party started, they drug her. The only people on the island with souls are the mute servant girl Therese (Uta Dahlberg) and Augustin (Anney Kablan) who used to be one of Maria's playthings. He is now her gardener, boat driver, and guitar player. Mirvel can't wait for the sacrifice, he just has to rape Eugenie now while she's under the influence of the drugs they slipped her. Maria convinces Eugenie that her rape was just a dream. Thanks, bitch!

Some freaks, led by Christopher Lee, come to the island dressed like the Ren-Fest got out early. After a nice meal, Maria and Mirvel get Eugenie to smoke some funny cigarettes. She gets wasted and things start getting freaky. And I mean freaky like whips, chains, and tools a blacksmith would use! This time when Eugenie wakes up, she is haunted by the horrors of what happened to her. But where are the marks? Was it a dream? What sexy horrors are in store for Eugenie now that she is completely at the mercy of these nasty weirdos? Will someone please save this naive chick before she descends into a sadomasochistic hell?!?!

I have found yet another intoxicating and naughty gem in the Jess

Franco canon. Eugenie... The Story of Her Journey into Perversion (not to be confused with Eugenie De Sade) was right in front of my face the whole time but I just kept putting it off, until now. This is some well-made, high class trash, my friends. Maria Rohm and Marie Liljedahl are so unbelievably hot that my glasses fogged up. As usual with Franco, the camera lingers on their bodies to the point of abstraction. This over-the-top film is painfully stylish and seems like it's filled with horny ghosts.

"No modern home is complete without the works of the Marquis."

The musical score by Hans Gunther Leonhardt and the always reliable, Bruno Nicolai, is awesome! The pacing is great too and I was never bored. This film is also lushly and lasciviously lensed by Manuel Merino. But as beautiful as the scenery and the cinematography are, they can't hide the undercurrent of dread running through the beginning of this film. They also set up the viewer for a fall when acts of sadism at Eugenie's expense explode on the screen. This film is pure cruelty mixed with style and feverish desire. Highly recommended.

Oasis of the Zombies (1982)

Two silly girls go driving through the desert in a jeep and their Daisy Duke-esque shorts. They stop at an oasis and start wandering around and talking about finding dates. Pretty soon they discover old rusted guns and cannons, the remnants of a battle fought there many years ago. But this oasis has another secret and that secret is undead Nazis! Meanwhile, former Nazi soldier Kurt (Henri Lambert) and some dead-meat named Blabert (Javier Maiza) have heard rumors of some Nazi gold hidden in that darn oasis. After Blabert shows him the map, Kurt kills him and takes the map so that he can go after the gold himself.

University student Robert Blabert hears about his father's death and while going through his journals, he finds information about the Nazi convoy and the gold. Roll out the stock footage! It seems as though the Nazis in this particular convoy murder everyone they come into contact with be they military or civilian. Okay, keep that stock footage coming. After an epic battle (from another movie), Blabert tells of how he was the only survivor and the Sheik (Antonio Mayans) and some kindly nomads rescued him from dying alone in the desert.

Blabert falls in love with Aisha, The Sheik's daughter (Doris Regina). She shows him her boobies on a sand dune and they make love (implied). After that he returns to the stock footage war. Two years later, he returns to the Sheik's house to find out that Aisha bore him a son but she died during the boring. Boring? Bearing? Baby-shitting-out? Whatever! Robert decides to go after the gold himself, first stop: the Sheik's house. But he's not alone in this quest because he's bringing his stupid idiot college friends: Sylvia, Ronald, and Ahmed.

Kurt, his wife Ingrid (legendary actress: Myriam Landson), and a two man crew arrive at the oasis to search for the gold. What do they find? Undead Nazis! Everyone is killed except for Kurt who escapes with nothing but a zombie bite for his troubles. Robert and his friends show up in a nearby village just in time to see Kurt die from him wounds. They meet the lovely Erika (France Lomay), assistant to Professor Zaniken (Albino Graziani), and Ronald, that crazy kid, falls for her. They swim without their shirts on and kiss. Does that mean she's going to bore a child too? Bear a child? Exitus baby-stew?

Robert and his friends go and meet the Sheik who has grown a beautiful mustache and colored his temples gray. He gives them directions to the oasis but also warns them that it's dangerous. The fools proceed anyway. They get to their destination only to find Dr. Zaniken and most of his crew dead. I didn't even realize they were going to the oasis too but hey, that helps the plot! The only ones left alive are Erika and some random duder. He's in shock and rambles about undead Nazis. For some reason, Erika is totally fine, just a bruise or two. Hey, that helps the plot too! They all decide to stay and keep looking for the gold. This little desert adventure does not end well for these treasure-seeking goofballs.

"Let's get some bottles and make Molotov cocktails, like at school!"

The stock footage from an Italian war film used for the flashbacks is pretty effective even though it's dull as shit. Look, those guys in tan are shooting those other guys in tan! Good thing there's some tan scenery to make all of this exciting. It is hilarious seeing Javier Maiza edited to look like he is fighting alongside his tan bros to defeat the tan Nazis. Luckily for us, cinematographer Max Monteillet is here to make the most of the locations and sexy ladies in the footage that was actually shot for this film. Monteillet shot Rollin's The Living Dead Girl and Rollin's Zombie Lake (but don't hold that against him). The music score by Daniel White is beyond minimal. Shit man, it's paper-thin but it does the trick.

I have to say that a decent looking print does wonders for this film in my book. Skip the grubby full frame version if you can and give the widescreen a whirl. Oasis of the Zombies is still silly, stupid, slowly paced, and cheap but I found it entertaining. My initial impression for the longest time was how drab and boring this film is but I was just watching the wrong version. This is not going to be for all tastes (in fact, most reviews of this film are very negative) but Oasis of the Zombies delivers the Eurocine cheese (bad dubbing and bad gore effects), big time. As for why the zombies sound like the washboard player in a jug band, I have no idea.

Devil's Island Lovers (1974)

Love is blossoming between Beatriz and Raymond (Genevieve Robert and Andres Resino). Isn't that sweet? Well, it would be if they weren't about to get totally shit on by a mercilessly cruel and unfair world. You see, Raymond was having an affair with Emilia (Danielle Godet), his godmother (eww, I know, right?), and decided to break it off. Big mistake. Emilia is an evil beyatch. She plans to marry Colonel Carlos Mendoza (Jean Guedes), who has the clout to frame Raymond and put him in jail. But the evil plotting doesn't end there. Mendoza is totally in love with Beatriz so hey fuck it, let's put them both in jail on Devil's Island for a murder they didn't commit. A lawyer named Lindsay (Dennis Price) finds out about all of this and is determined to see that Beatriz and Raymond are set free.

This film's cast is quite spectacular. I really like Genevieve Robert. She's simply stunning to look at, is instantly likeable the moment she's on screen, and I actually gave a damn about her character. It's nice to see Anne Libert (of Rites of Frankenstein) again. I am really, really head over heels for this actress. Rosa Palomar is incredibly intimidating as Senora Cardel, the warden (or is that wardeness?). Of course, no Franco film would be complete without Howard Vernon. He plays Colonel Ford, the warden of the men's prison, but unfortunately, he plays it straight. Missed opportunity! Dennis Price looks terrible in this one but I did like his character.

Well kids, I will keep this short and sweet cuz there ain't no need when you revue a film as uncomplexicated as Devil's Island Lovers. This has all the usual content of a women-in-prison movie: lesbian overtones, revealing uniforms, ridiculous torture sequences, and catfights. Yet surprisingly, there is no nudity or long shower sequences. Whoa, really? Granted, I didn't need the nudity or the shower scenes, but this film really needed something to spice it up. There was some Franco weirdness from a bizarre torture device that I'm guessing was supposed to be some kind of sonic cannon but it was too little, too late.

In the end, I guess I mostly enjoyed this movie but it has more than a few loose ends that don't get resolved at all. I can't believe I'm going to say this: This movie should have been longer! According to IMDB, this movie is supposed to be 97 minutes but the DVD, and all the other reviews I've seen have this clocking in at 81 minutes. That don't seem right! Despite feeling like it has a chunk missing, Devil's Island Lovers does have some good going for it. The atmosphere is full of doom and gloom to go along with its bleak (though unsatisfying) outcome. And lastly, the score by Bruno Nicolai is great (as if he ever did a shitty score).

Lucky the Inscrutable (1967)

World class super spy/super hero/master of disguise Lucky the Inscrutable (Ray Danton) is hired by a secret society called Archangel to follow the trail of some counterfeit money in order to save the world's economy. Lucky teams up with a spy named Michele (Dante Posani) and off they go from England to France to Rome to Albania to wherever! Along the way they battle a vast array of double agents and soldiers armed with only their wits -oh, and guns and crazy spy gadgets.

If you're looking for a pop art-filled film with a ludicrous plot to make a great double feature with Mario Bava's Danger Diabolik or Franco's Kiss Me, Monster, then stop because your search is over. The spy spoof sub-genre is a tough sell for most viewers but this is easily one of the best I've ever seen. The first reel of this film is perfect for the short attention span crowd. It's filled with murderous thugs, spies, go-go dancing, people in crazy costumes, comic book panels and word balloons, and lots and lots of color everywhere.

Lucky the Inscrutable has not one but two cameos from Franco himself. One as an understandably speechless man with a knife in his back and then later as a tramp riding a train. Ray Danton is definitely having a blast. I like Dante Posani as Lucky's sidekick but I can't find any info on him. Rosalba Neri is so very young in this and is even more radiant than usual. The lovely Teresa Gimpera of Feast of Satan and Spirit of the Beehive is here too and the world is a better place because of that.

My one criticism is that this film loses a little steam before it's over. It never becomes a slog or anything (trust me, the mile-a-minute jokes never stop) but the barrage of color and attention-grabbing visuals fall away about two-thirds of the way in and Lucky the Inscrutable suffers for it a bit. That being said, the cinematography by Fulvio Testi is always good and the score by Bruno Nicholai never fails to keep your foot tapping. He even gives Lucky his own theme song! So yeah, definitely give this film a watch sometime.

How to Seduce a Virgin (1974)

Alice Arno plays Martine Bressac, a woman who just got out of the loony bin. For the record, she should have turned right around and walked right back in. In terms of sanity, Martine is an undercooked blueberry muffin. Although it's never made entirely clear if it the reason she was locked up or not: Martine has a vision (or a memory) of slashing a naked man in his genital region (implied) with a straight razor. One thing is for sure, Martine is a sexual predator/serial killer of the highest order. She has a museum of statues made out of beautiful women in her basement.

Since good things come in threes, Martine has two accomplices. The first is her husband Charles (Robert Woods). He helps Martine select her victims with his camera and a slideshow! The second is her mute little friend Adele (Lina Romay) whose skills include: moaning like an animal, running interference, and performing various somnambulistic sex slave tasks. These evil weirdos set their sights on Cecile (Tania Busselier), the teenage daughter of their neighbors. While the girl's parents are away, Martine and her cronies take care of Cecile by getting her drunk and taking her to sex parties. Predictably, things take an even darker turn when Martine becomes jealous of the attention that Charles is lavishing on Cecile.

"Oh Charles, that little slut really looks like a lecherous bitch!"

I really dig the score for this flick. It has all the funky bass lines, kooky keyboards, fuzz guitars, sorrowful flutes, and jaunty xylophones that you could ever ask for. Is it the only thing I like about How to Seduce a Virgin? Fuckin' almost! The biggest problem are the sex scenes. I know, I know, I sound like a broken record. But seriously, these aren't even good sex scenes. Either Franco was bored, his cast unwilling to play along, or he had some weird producers' criteria of what not to show. There is a threesome where we only see Alice Arno's bare butt and the rest is gyrating and moaning in the darkness for around 3 minutes. I feel humiliolated. That's humiliated AND violated. I will admit that Alice Arno is 110% gorgeous in this. Woo! So hot.

This isn't the worst of Franco but it is frustrating because it does have some style and the feeling of dread is palpable. I just wish that the duder had kicked this one into second gear a few more times. The best character is Malou, played by the unusual and diminutive actor, Alfred Baillou of Girl Slaves of Morgana Le Fey (1971). He is Martine's gardener and he's rather demented. Supposedly, he saw a bishop fall to his death and the memory of that moment drove him insane. It's a weird little detail that adds to the quirkiness of this rather dull skin flick but I'm afraid that it's too little, too late. There are some twists (okay, maybe one) and some kink (yawn!) but there are much better Franco flicks out there.

The Blood of Fu Manchu (1968)

Holy racial stereotypes, this plot is complicated! The evil Fu Manchu (Christopher Lee) has kidnapped a group of lovely ladies in order to carry out his plan. What is his plan? To master the world, of course! Fu Manchu and his daughter, Lin Tang (Tsai Chin), use the bodies of these fine ass bitches to be vessels for a terrible poison, delivered upon his enemies with their kisses.

Meanwhile, an archeologist named Carl Jansen (Gotz George) is determined to find the lost city of Whateverthefuck where Fu Manchu now calls his secret hideout. He and fellow archeologist Dr. Wagner are attacked by Fu Manchu's minions and the doctor is killed. When Jansen attempts to meet up with Ursula Wagner (Maria Rohm), the niece of the dead doc, he gets arrested for his partner's murder.

Double meanwhile, in London, Nayland Smith (Richard Greene) is one of Fu Manchu's intended victims. One of his women, Celeste (Loni von Friedl), kisses poor Nayland but he doesn't immediately drop dead as intended, he just goes blind. Knowing he only has a short time left before the poison kills him, Nayland intends to find Fu Manchu and stop his evil plan.

Making things even more difficult for poor old Fu Manchu is a bandit named Sancho Lopez (Ricardo Palacios) who likes to steal his supplies. One of Fu Manchu's ladies shows up to the town where Lopez is raping and pillaging. She begins to dance in a "sensuous manner". Her target is Lopez but before she can deliver the death kiss, the bandito psycho shoots her. Since that plan was a magnificent failure, Lin Tang and a small gang of Fu's soldiers raid the town and kill everyone except Lopez. Wha? They torture Lopez until he agrees to work for Fu Manchu.

Because he's such a good chess player, the charges against Jansen are dropped. He meets up with Ursula and tells her about her uncle. They decide to travel back to where they were ambushed and they meet up with Nayland on the road. Now it's a race against time or something because when the moon is full, Nayland will die and Fu Manchu's plan will be complete. You see, he intends to kill millions with an airborne version of the poison if the world does not bow to him. Holy shit, I still have half an hour of movie left.

"They tell me you can dance. Tonight, you will dance for the last time."

Did the world really need more Fu Manchu in 1968? Did Maria Rohm really have to dress like a dang Boy Scout? I have absolutely zero interest in the Fu Manchu character but I thought I'd give this flick a go. Christopher Lee's voice (as usual) is amazing. Every line he speaks is friggin' quote worthy: "The moon is full, the moon of life, let her taste the kiss... of death." The only person in the cast who even comes close to stealing his fire is Tsai Chin. She is awesomely evil and I'm actually more afraid of her than Fu. It's because she's a woman and women are scary!

The cinematography and editing are both great plus there some decent action (let me emphasize the word "decent"), half-naked beautiful women in chains, and gong-banging! The plot definitely starts to meander after the first hour. The writers just keep throwing more and more confusing shit at the viewer but they eventually run out of steam. The film has a decent score from Daniel White, there's lots of Jess Franco-isms that you might dig, and the rest of the cast is pretty fun. In the end, The Blood of Fu Manchu is kind of drab but pretty okay and I'm sort of glad I watched it.

The Castle of Fu Manchu (1969)

Fu Manchu (Christopher Lee once again) and his crazy daughter Lin Tang (Tsai Chin) are back to take over the world. This time, they're using a machine that can control the temperature of water anywhere on the planet. They manage to sink a huge ship sailing in the Caribbean by generating an iceberg in its path. He contacts the leaders of the world and threatens them with obliteration unless they bow down to him. Nayland Smith (Richard Greene) is once again called in to deal with this situation.

Lin Tang makes a deal with some drug dealers, led by Omar Pashu (Jose Manuel Martin) and his deadly cross-dresser named Lisa (Rosalba Neri), to help her steal a huge supply of opium. They break into the castle of the governor of Anatolia where there is enough opium to control half the world's supply. Once they take control of the castle, Fu Manchu shows up, double crosses Omar, and kidnaps Lisa. He takes the castle as his hideout and all that delicious opium for himself. Then Fu Manchu gets high, so high. I mean like totally wasted.

Next, Fu Manchu captures Dr. Curt Kessler (Gunther Stoll) and fellow physician, Dr. Ingrid Kauff (Maria Perschy), in order to force them to save the life of Professor Heracles (Gustavo Re) with an experimental heart transplant procedure because they need him to make crystals or whatever. In order to show the doctors that he means business, Fu Manchu destroys a dam and causes a great flood. They agree to the operation to save Heracles and it is boooooooring. Nayland Smith finally shows up to stop Fu Manchu's broadly evil and insidiously vague plan.

The cast and the skill of the filmmakers save this mess of a film. I love the lighting; there are purples, reds, and greens all over the place. The always reliable Manuel Merino did the cinematography. It's good to see Gunther Stoll from What Have You Done to Solange? and The Bloodstained Butterfly again. The guy had an incredible screen presence. He's almost completely wasted here. Jess Franco himself is on hand as a fez-wearing inspector who provides Nayland Smith with some important information. Maria Perschy of The Blue Eyes of the Broken Doll and Hunchback of the Morgue is here too. Yay!

"Send a warning to the phosphorus!"

What can I say, the first few minutes of The Castle of Fu Manchu are just... explosively bad. By using footage from other films, Franco manages to just embarrass himself and make the viewer feel stupid. Fu Manchu sank the Titanic? Really? Give me a fucking break, duder. I suppose one could interpret this as funny but yeah, no. If you can get past the opening 6 minutes or so (and I doubt many people have), what's left? A very unusual film, that's what. Castle becomes a ponderous travelogue mixed with tepid intrigue but I mean that as a compliment. There is also so much pseudoscience and mechanical mumbo jumbo thrown at you from the script that it's just baffling.

The Castle of Fu Manchu wasn't as bad as I'd read from other reviewers but that's not saying much. If it weren't for the uneven pacing, I could give this film a recommendation with lots of conditions. Unfortunately, this just feels like a bunch of leftover bullshit padded with stock footage and bland dialog. I won't say the film is a complete waste of time (NO NUDITY!?) but yeah, this is definitely non-essential Franco viewing. Eh, where else can you see Rosalba Neri wearing a fez or mowing down pajama-wearing motherfuckers with a Tommy gun?

The Corpse Packs His Bags (1972)

There is a knife-throwing killer on the loose in Soho (that's right, just like the one in that Rancid song). This killer has a peculiar habit of packing a person's belongings into a suitcase shortly before dispatching them. Frankly, it's brilliant! Well, it's pretty cool. Inspector Rupert Redford (Fred Williams) of Scotland Yard and his friend Charles Barton (Horst Tappert) are on the case. Are there drugs involved? Hell yeah, there are! Everyone is all wound up about a drug called Mescadrin. Never tried the stuff myself but they say it packs a hell of a wallop.

The first on the list of suspects is Dr. Bladmore (Siegfried Schürenberg), a physician who attended to one of the deceased shortly before he ceased. He is prone to giving out doses of a certain painkilling drug to people who ask him to. Is he the pusher, man? Let's hope that his lovely assistant, Helen Bennett (Elisa Montés), isn't mixed up in this dangerous business. All clues seem to be pointing to a mysterious man named Charlie Bennett, Helen's dead husband!

More red herrings -oops, I mean totally probable suspects- infect the plot of this film like something you would only whisper about to your local pharmacist to help you get rid of. I'm talking about THE VD! Come on, you prude. This is the 70s, we can talk openly now about such things. Anyway, there's a seriously bad ass chick (Barbara Rütting) with a henchman, a blind organ grinder (Andrés Monales) who always seems to just happen to be present at every crime scene, a stripper who doesn't know how to strip (Mara Laso), and a sleazy guy that my wife says looks like a

Persian cat with mange.

"You should see a neurologist. Did you crap you pants again, my dear?"

One of the things that never occurred to me until I was armpits-deep in Franco Lake is that Jess Franco made comedies. Before, I thought of him as totally serious. Or maybe he meant Vampyros Lesbos to be a side-splitting farce. Fucked if I know! The Corpse Packs His Bags is a krimi with a comedy streak so wide you'd have to be a blind organ grinder to miss it. You will laugh, I promise. Or maybe you'll just chuckle. Fine, I promise that you will see the always fucking great cinematographer, Manuel Merino, take this two dollar film and make it look like it was a fourteen hundred dollar film. And the locations don't hurt either. There's nothing like a well-written mystery film to make you appreciate the architecture of the buildings it was shot in. Did I say "well-written"?

I do love how the knife makes a "boing" sound when it hits its target in the back and that's funny because everyone knows that's the sound of an unexpected boner. Krimi fans who don't take themselves too seriously will probably get a kick out of this one. Franco fans who always take themselves too seriously will no doubt be pleased to see Franco wasting good German money again in the vein of La Venganza del Doctor Mabuse (though not nearly as baffling this time around). Determined to make you blink but not miss him, Franco has not one but two cameos in this film: one as a bystander at the first crime scene and another as Mr. Gonzalez, a Spanish expert on throwing knives. I like that.

Countess Perverse (1974)

Count Rabor Zaroff (Howard Vernon) and Countess Ivanna Zaroff (Alice Arno) are two eccentric psychos who live on an island in the middle of nowhere. Ivanna likes to hunt but her prey is people. Rabor enjoys cooking but his main ingredient is people. The two employ a couple, Bob (Robert Woods) and Moira (Tania Busselier), to help keep them well stocked with sexy lady victims. Things go awry when Bob falls for Sylvia (Lina Romay), their most lovely and innocent prey so far.

This film is beautiful thanks in no small part to cinematographer Gérard Brisseau who knows how to take minimal sets and grandiose architecture and make them flow together seamlessly. He also knows how to capture the simplicity of nature and bring out its inherit dread. The whole wide world never felt so claustrophobic.

I am digging on this cast like there's no tomorrow. Alice Arno and Howard Vernon just nail it as the two most evil freaks in the universe. They are a dark joy to watch on screen while they toy with their prey. Arno is so damn sexy in this movie that I can barely even stand it. I hope that she hunts me in my dreams. Lina Romay is really good as Sylvia, the innocent. When she walks in on the Count and the Countess preparing a meal, the terror on her face is believable. Her painfully drama school dropout fainting spell is 100 times less believable and it makes me love her performance even more.

> *"That's it, I'm off. I want no part in your vile orgies."*

I wasn't too hot on Kali Hansa in the first few films I saw her in. But now I'm really digging her. She is striking, Amazon-like, and thanks to Jess Franco, I've seen her vagina. I know I've seen Tania Busselier before but she didn't really stand out until this movie. The real star of the movie is Robert Woods' penis. Or maybe it's Howard Vernon's sack. I don't really want to go back and compare. Please, I beg you, don't make me go back.

Let me get up on my soapbox here for a couple of paragraphs.

If you've been following along with my little Jess Franco journey here, you probably noticed that I don't make excuses for the guy. When something pisses me off, you'll be the first to know. What really grinds my gears and makes me really turn on a film is a gratuitous rape scene. If it's a prolonged rape scene, one that doesn't serve the plot in any way, or -and this really is the worst of them all- the victim of the violation ends up enjoying the experience then I end up despising said film. Countess Perverse contains the latter kind and it just makes me friggin' disgusted. It's a thoughtless, throwaway moment but it really turned me against this film. Why did Kali Hansa's character submit to her attackers? What fucking purpose did it serve to the film? I'm all about irresponsible entertainment but any film that demonstrates to a would-be rapist that his/her victim secretly "wants it" makes my blood boil.

Another problem I have with this film (and this is just nitpicking, really) is the misuse of Alice Arno and Lina Romay. Now don't get me wrong, I have seen A LOT of these two actresses along the way and they are both great. What doesn't work in this film is Arno and Romay's sex scene together. It was one of the most awkward in Franco's films that I've seen so far. Chalk it up to the lack of cinematic sexual chemistry between the two actresses, poor direction, or whatever, it's just bad. There's more sexual tension and inherent eroticism when Arno's character is flirting with Romay's before their ruinous lovemaking even starts so I don't blame the actresses. Their sex scene together should have been cut.

These complaints I have make my viewing experience of Countess Perverse even more frustrating and make my review even less trustworthy than my usual shtick. I want you to know that I want to love this film. There are scenes in this film that are some of Franco's best. He takes The

Most Dangerous Game and makes it his own. This film is tense, gorgeous, and horrifying with victims that you actually care about and delightfully evil villains that are fascinating to behold. But there's some stupid crap packed in here too. Shackled by his own artistic needs or his producer's insistence or both, Jess Franco mixes bad softcore porn into yet another film that didn't deserve it.

Sinner: Diary of a Nymphomaniac (1973)

A beautiful young stripper (Montserrat Prous) picks up a man in a bar and proceeds to get him very drunk. She takes him back to his hotel room where he promptly passes out. Then she frames him for a murder. Her own! The man is Mr. Ortiz (Manule Pereiro) and he is quickly arrested and put in jail. Ortiz pleads with his estranged wife Rosa (Jacqueline Laurent) to help him prove his innocence. Rosa discovers that the dead girl is Linda Vargas, a troubled young woman with a sad story to tell (from beyond the grave (but not in a zombified way)).

First, Rosa meets up with the Countess Anna de Monterey (Anne Libert), a former lover and friend of Linda's. She tells the story of how being raped by Mr. Ortiz when she was very young changed her into a nymphomaniac. Next Rosa goes to another very special friend of Linda's named Maria (Kali Hansa), a stripper and smoker of the drugs. She lets Rosa read Linda's sexy diary and it tells the wildly depressing story of her downfall.

Once again, Franco paints another portrait for us of innocence lost and once again, it's another heartbreaking venture. Sinner: Diary of a Nymphomaniac is also incredibly silly with soap opera plot machinations and narration that sounds like it was ripped from the pages of a seedy romance novel. And what film from 1973 would be complete without the demonization of marijuana and disco dancing sequences?

Of course, the intentions of the writing and direction are heartfelt and meaningful. Unlike my previous complaint about Countess Perverse, rape is not just a throwaway and pointless act; nor is it sexy. In Sinner, rape and its consequences are deadly serious. Linda is an innocent whose mental stability and outlook on life is destroyed by the cruelty of a single incident. She runs from lover to lover trying to fix something that is beyond repair.

Maybe this film should have been called Surrounded by Nymphomaniacs! Although, I think Howard Vernon may be the biggest nympho of them all! I have to tip my hat to this cast. Many of the usual suspects from Franco's early 70s stuff are here and even Yelena Samarina (of Night of the Assassins and Murder Mansion) has a small part! I get the feeling that this film was meant to star Soledad Miranda but due to her untimely death, Montserrat Prous was cast in her place. Was she to be Franco's next muse?

If so, what happened? Did she get cockblocked -or would that be cuntblocked- by Lina Romay?

The musical score for Sinner is a lot of fun. It's got all the discordant jazz and acid rock that one expects from films of this era. The camerawork by Gérard Brisseau is quite good but not quite as eye catching as I'd expect from a film as lurid as this. Keep an eye out for an impossible-to-miss-cameo from Franco himself as a police detective. He looks into the camera for a split second as if he's not sure if they're still rolling or not. Priceless.

"When I'm buried, they can write on the stone: 'One who wanted too much'."

One thing I couldn't help but notice is how similar Sinner felt to another Franco film I've seen in terms of cast and locations. Lo and behold, Dolls for Sale and this film have not one, not two, but TEN common cast and crew between the two films (thank you, IMDB) which makes me have to assume they were filmed back to back.

Ópalo de Fuego: Mercaderes del Sexo (1980)

The movies opens to some sexy saxophone music (or would that be sexophone?) and some sweaty faces. What more do you need to know? Okay, I guess there's more. Cecile and Brigitte (played by Lina Romay and Nadine Pascal, respectively) are a pair of strippers (though they call themselves "perverse lesbians") that have traveled to somewhere vaguely European in order to perform at Club Flamingo. I think their act is supposed to be a striptease but really, it's more like performance art. Luckily, Cecile's talents extend beyond her choreography skills because she is actually working for a US Senator (Oliver Mathot) who sent her there to expose a ring of human traffickers or dope dealers or assassins or whatever.

It turns out that Irina Forbes (Joëlle Le Quément) and her husband (Claude Boisson) are a pair of sicko criminals who have a helicopter and some sexy henchwomen. They have hypnotized some chick named Estrella (Doris Regina) who may or may not be Irina's daughter to make her fall in love with Aristobolous Fargas (whoever the fuck that is). Worst of all, Irina does a strip number of her own as Salome and uses what might be a real severed head in her "sexy" act.

When Cecile gets too close to the truth, she is chased by some bad guys but is saved by a parrot. Later, someone leaves a corpse hanging in the wardrobe of her hotel room. But everything works out because Milton (Mel Rodrigo), the gay taxi driver/fixer calls housekeeping to come and take care of it. Cecile is captured by Irina and her gang but she manages to escape. Milton hides her with some hippies and- You know what? Screw this. Some more stuff happens.

"You know what women are like. They come for the discos and hamburgers with terrible sauces and they're happy. Goodbye, precious."

Sometimes washed out, forgotten Franco can have hidden magic. It can also be perilous if you don't like grubby porno movies. In this instance, I am happy to report that even though my porno sensors were going off the whole time, it turns out that Ópalo de Fuego is not, in fact, a porno film. I really dig the playful and fun vibe this movie gives off. Nothing is taken very seriously so any chance of an atmosphere of mystery is crushed by all the trashy crap going on that makes no sense.

If you like cheap ball-sweat jazz, cigarettes extinguished on boobies, and out of focus camera, then you'll love Ópalo de Fuego. Sadly, the phrase "severed head cunnilingus" is one I don't get to type very often but I'll be damned if it doesn't apply to this film. There could have been more care put into the writing of this film but the producers put all of the money into a surprisingly elaborate helicopter chase scene and a bottle of J&B that gets a lot of screen time.

This movie is freakin' crazy and the plot is beyond convoluted. And that's where the problem lies. With only about 15 minutes to go, this film slows down to explain what is going on. That was a dumb move. Ópalo de Fuego does recover in time for the ending but it's frustrating because Franco almost nailed this one. That being said, this goofy and super trashy film isn't a waste of your time. Standout scenes include Cecile and Brigitte practicing their mesmerizingly awful stripper act and Brigitte seducing (with the promise of French Champagne) and then raping gay Milton.

Ilsa the Wicked Warden (1977)

The movie starts in the jungle and we hear the sounds of a whip cracking and a woman screaming and moaning. A sexy female voice says "Wicked Warden" lasciviously and it's on. Before the two minute mark, we have women showering, complaining, and cooing nakedly at each at the Las Palomas women's prison (oops, I mean "clinic"). In her own private bath, Greta the "wicked" warden (Dyanne Thorne) is having a soak, washing herself luxuriously. I kind of want this movie to be over already.

A girl screams and starts flopping around while the guards try to control the situation. Oh snap, this was just a distraction so another inmate, Rosa (Angela Ritschard), can make a run for it. She barely escapes with her life. Dr. Arcos (Jess Franco) manages to save her but he is forced to return Rosa to Greta and the "clinic". Later, he finds out that Rosa died shortly thereafter and her body was cremated.

Horrified by the incident, Dr. Arcos pleads to the worldwide community to shut down Las Palomas but with no evidence, they tell him to get stuffed. Arcos is approached by Abbie (Tania Busselier), Rosa's sister and a total badass, who volunteers to go undercover in Las Palomas to find out what's really going on there. Abbie gets in and is given a number: 41. She is told that if she ever tells anyone her real name, they will burn the number into her breast.

Abbie meets the other lost souls including Juana (Lina Romay), the lead inmate who is in good with Greta. Abbie finds out very quickly that this "clinic" is a sick and evil place where no one escapes. Let's hope that all the prescribed sexual humiliation, genital mutilation, and shock treatments won't keep Abbie from carrying out her plan. Wait, what was her plan again?

Of course, Greta gets word that Abbie has been asking too many questions about what goes on in the "clinic". In a bizarre twist, we discover that Abbie's sister Rosa is alive, hidden in some dark place in Las Palomas. She has been tortured nearly to the brink of death. Rosa gives up Abbie almost immediately and, on top of that, she names Dr. Arcos as a leader of a terrorist group. Arcos is immediately murdered by the corrupt police. Now the shit had really hit the fan.

How does Greta keep getting away with all of this shit? The "clinic" practically pays for itself. The lead guard (Eric Falk) sells films of the torture and sex to a local rich weirdo. Mo' money! Mo' money Mo' money! Of course, it helps that Greta is in bed (literally) with the Governor (Howard Maurer). This sleazebag motherfucker is banging Greta and using her "clinic" to eliminate his female political prisoners. I just got to the gang-rape scene. Ugh, just kill me. After Abbie is turned into a gibbering madwoman, the inmates revolt and tear Greta to shreds (literally). The end.

Good news, everyone! I guess I'm not jaded yet. The sleaze is so fucking thick on this film that I need a shower now. Seriously, every couple of minutes, I just felt totally demoralized by what I was watching. Not surprisingly, there is an insane amount of female flesh on display and so many trashy situations that it's impossible to take this crap seriously. That being said, Isla the Wicked Warden is a pretty darn good film for old Jess. The cinematography, editing, and the score are all very good. Ruedi Küttel, who shot Blue Rita, delivers some of the best experimental camerawork I've seen in a Jess Franco flick in a while.

> *"Ah, piss off, you blonde bitch! And you can take your brother,*
> *jack him off, and stick him up your singing ass!"*

I can't recommend this movie to anyone who is even remotely sensitive in nature. The torture scenes, while not overly explicit, are pretty powerful even by suggestion alone. I'm not gonna lie though, seeing Lina Romay give

Dyanne Thorne a nudie massage is well, pretty awesome. Of course it degrades immediately into the naughty kind of acupuncture. And that's part of what makes this film so insane. Every "pleasure" is tempered with something horrible.

My favorite character is Number 9 (Dagmar Burger offran Blue Rita), the lady who used to be a man. She was into dudes when she was a man and now that she is a woman, she is all lesbian, baby! She tries to help Abbie out and I don't know, she's just likeable. I needed something to grasp onto to keep my happy thoughts during all of this garbage. Good thing this Ilsa movie had a very satisfying ending or else I would have probably flipped out, changed my sex, and checked myself into Las Palomas. This move also contains boot licking.

Killer Barbys (1996)

While out on tour, a band called The Killer Barbys [sic] run into some trouble when their van breaks down out in the middle of nowhere. They get help from a man named Arkan (Aldo Sambrell), who brings them to the castle of the 100 year old Countess Freguenmans (Mariangela Giordano) AKA actress and singer, Olga Lujan. What The Killer Barbys don't know is how utterly screwed they are because the Countess is actually a vampiric creature that needs their young blood to stay alive.

There is also a crazy legend of a satanic monk who tormented and killed a lot of little girls. He fell in love with a woman and tortured her to the brink of death. Then with a potion made of his blood and semen (?), saved her at the last minute. To this day, his image sometimes appears and disappears on the side of the castle. Sure! Why not? And I simply cannot talk about this movie without mentioning Baltasar the idiot (Santiago Segura) and his two dwarf minions (his "children"?) that help Arkan carry out his plan by slaughtering the band members. Could he be the satanic monk himself?

Much to my surprise, I love this film's atmosphere right out of the gate. Great lighting and smoke machines combined with extravagant sets make this an attractive film to look at. The copy of Killer Barbys I have is pretty dark so some of the outdoor nighttime scenes were kind of lost on me but other than that, the film looks great! The sequence of the band playing in an old concert hall reminded me of Franco's heyday filming jazz bands and nightclub scenes except with more moshing.

Much like his 80s splatter efforts like Faceless and Bloody Moon, I think Franco decided to just give the people what they wanted and we all have to suffer for that attitude; partly because "the people" are idiots and also because Franco didn't have a clue what in the hell they actually wanted. Maybe this is Franco trying to relate to 90s audiences and the rest is a happy

(?) accident. Take for example, the ubiquitous bad sex scene. The idiotic couple who stays in the van, going at it for hours (presumably) while the same Killer Barbys song plays over and over, is one of the dumbest and least inspired things I've seen in his filmography.

One of the things about this movie that impresses me is all the bizarre shit that happens. The script, partly in Spanish and partly in English, is terrible and is peppered with some seriously bad jokes. How much of it is meant to be taken seriously? Who the hell knows? The band drives around in their van, rocking out to their own music. That's pretty hilarious. In one scene, an unseen someone is singing out in the swamp. It sounds vaguely like Rick Springfield. When one girl gets beheaded, her severed head calls Baltasar a son of a bitch. I think that was meant to be funny. After killing one of her victims, the Countess rolls around on his naked body, gibbering like a dang loon. I don't think that was meant to be funny. But it is.

Italian horror fans will no doubt recognize Mariangela Giordano from Burial Ground: The Nights of Terror, Giallo a Venezia, and several other sleazy classics. Spanish character actor/director Santiago Segura has since gone on to do a series of comedy crime films playing Torrente, a private detective that excels in bad behavior and getting into ridiculous situations. He was also in Alex de la Iglesia's The Day of the Beast. Veteran actor Aldo Sambrell was in more spaghetti westerns than I care to delve into at this moment. Duder was prolific. As for the rest of the cast... the less said, the better.

Damn it, I like Killer Barbys! It's not a great film by any stretch of the imagination but I found it kind of fun. The acting from all of the band members is awful while the rest of cast (who are actual actors) do a decent job with the material. Some of the gore is pretty cool (the rotting yet living corpse of the Countess) and some of it really, really low budget (the bodies hanging up around the castle). Surreal, trashy, and astoundingly stupid, this is one of Franco's craziest films that I've seen; yet I'm not sure if I can exactly recommend it. Franco fans may get a kick out of Killer Barbys but the uninitiated will want to pass on this one. Where the hell did that steamroller come from anyway?

La Muerte Silba un Blues (1964)

Part-time musician and accidental smuggler, Castro (Conrado San Martín), gets busted at a checkpoint for hauling guns and ammunition which he didn't even know about. His friend, Julius Smith (Manuel Alexandre), also unaware of their cargo, is shot and taken into custody while Castro is shot as well while attempting to flee. 15 years later, Julius Smith sees Castro's wife, Lina (Perla Cristal), in a nightclub and performs "The Roof Blues", she and Castro's favorite song. Smith is run down by a car very shortly after that, confessing all he knows to the police before he dies. This gets the ball rolling as Castro returns to get revenge on Vogel (Georges Rollin), the man who ratted him out, profited greatly from the gunrunning, and even stole Lina. Castro, whom everyone believes to be dead, can't take any more of this bullshit.

Vogel has been living under the name Paul Radeck for the last decade and a half and pretty much owns a small seaside village. A cryptic letter arrives from Castro saying that he not only knows Radeck is actually Vogel but he has returned to take him down with his own secrets. On the case is Inspector Fenton (Fortunio Bonanova). He uses an undercover sexy lady named Moira (Danik Patisson) to get close to Radeck but her cover is blown ridiculously fast. Now everyone seems to playing their part in Vogel's little paranoid game as he tries to rub Castro out once and for all. But hold on! Not so fast, motherfucker. More secrets and twists will be revealed before this story is over.

La Muerte Silba un Blues is an engrossing but very relaxed noir crime film filled with equal parts melodrama and style. The music by Music by Antón García Abril is vibrant, classy, and never dull. This black and white film features some excellent, creative cinematography by Juan Mariné. The composition and the lighting are just wonderful and I can't even count how many of his shots are my favorites in this film. The screenplay that Jess Franco wrote with Luis de Diego is a little hokey but is intriguing and nicely nuanced at the same time. All of the characters, especially Lina and Vogel, are well written and multidimensional; and the cast is just so damn good that I was very invested in their stories.

When you've been watching as many Jess Franco films as I have and you've been watching them out of order as I have AND you also keep half-intentionally forgetting everything you've ever read about the man's work as I have, well you tend to get surprised a lot. All of a sudden, the very first Franco Friday, Kiss Me Killer, makes perfect sense. If nothing else, Franco was The Great Recycler of his own works and he returned to La Muerte Silba un Blues for a reason: it is one of his best films.

The use of Smith's song, "The Roof Blues", to drive Vogel bananas works great. I love the way Vogel is introduced, lounging by the pool with the wind blowing around him, trapping him in the loneliness of leisure. The life he's built for himself is all a lie and he knows it. The character of Castro, as portrayed by Conrado San Martín, is awesome. He's just a happy-go-lucky guy with a whole dimension to him that I won't spoil here. He makes friends with a black fisherman named Joe (Joe Brown) and these two actors have great chemistry onscreen together.

"A dead hero is more interesting than one hundred mediocrities alive."

Now I won't be returning to this to rewatch La Muerte anytime soon. Heck, I may never watch this again –because it's just not my style of film- but I'd be an idiot to leave without saying how impressive this film is and how entertaining. Granted, this was Franco's tenth feature length film so it's not hard to imagine that he could have his hand in something this good. Of course, there are some quaint gaffes like jump cuts and out-of-focus moments that became Franco's signature to nearly all of his later films but honestly, you won't care when you sit down with this one. The only thing I could find to criticize the film for is the damn disguise that Castro chooses for the big costume ball finale of the film. It is mind-bogglingly racist. Oh well, can't win 'em all, I guess. Keep an eye out for the director himself as a saxophone player near the beginning of the film.

The Hot Nights of Linda (1975)

Alice Arno plays Marie-France Bertrand, a nurse looking for work. The scumbag dude at the employment agency (Raymond Hardy) gets her a job working for the Raddick family as a teacher or something. After walking back to her apartment, she reads a book that sounds just like the plot of this movie and then she falls asleep. The next day, Marie-France goes to the family's villa and meets Abdul (Pierre Taylou), a mute servant, who takes her to meet Mr. Paul Raddick (Paul Muller). Paul tells her about his two daughters, Lina (Verónica Llimera) and Olivia (Lina Romay). According to him, Linda is paralyzed and needs special care and Olivia is obsessed with sex.

Meanwhile, the employment agent that got Marie-Franco the job in the first place and his photojournalist pal (Catherine Lafferière) are holed up in a nearby house, both having been paid by the police to spy on the Raddick family. Why would the police be involved? It turns out that Paul is obsessed with his dead wife Lorna (Monica Swinn) and has a locked room that he goes to in order to talk to the bed where he murdered her and her lover on years ago. Obsessed with not only sex but also with murder, Olivia goes on a violent rampage to get revenge for what happened to Lorna and no one is safe. Oh shizzle! I won't say anymore! This is too stupidly fun to spoil.

Much like Jess Franco's Sinner: Diary of a Nymphomaniac, this movie is just insanely sad, especially for Linda who is just so friggin' pathetic. When Lina Romay's character takes advantage of her, I actually winced with disgust at the cruelty onscreen. Romay appears playfully mean at first but then she just devolves into an evil jerk. I loved it! Don't let the banana eating and the champagne glass licking fool you, this bitch means business. Even Paul Muller's character who, despite being very cruel, is someone you can actually sympathize with on some level.

"I can't stand people that snore and you look the snoring type."

With atmospheric weirdness as the focus, the perfectly sleepy plot just drops out of the race almost immediately. This movie lulled me into a state of ethereal ennui and then I was honestly thrown for a loop in the last twenty minutes or so. That probably won't happen to you. Once the opening credits -with gorgeous music by composer Daniel White- played over a gloomy day in Paris as Alice Arno walked to her apartment, I just drifted.

Jess Franco drops you into this film right in the middle of a scene and thanks to the English dubbing, it is both mystifying and funny. There is also a great amount of post-synced dubbing. So many lines of dialog are playing while no one's lips are moving that I was just hypnotized. Alice Arno has a lot of dialog in the English version that she says telepathically. She's a talented mutant.

The plot is very dreamlike, slow, and convoluted but this is nothing new for Franco. If you're a fan of his work from this period then you'll be all over this one. The characters are, for the most part, well thought out, and the actors are all capable enough to make this erotically drowsy and perilously ridiculous crap interesting. A tragedy in the past plays itself out over and over again for Paul and Olivia. There's even some comic relief characters!

Okay, I admit it. I was avoiding this film because of its title. It sounds like a porno and that cover art with Lina Romay lasciviously eating a banana (a cover art promise is actually fulfilled!) just made me assume that I wouldn't enjoy this film. Lucky for me, The Hot Nights of Linda was made during an amazing period of Franco's work. Who would have ever guessed that even in 1975, he was still interested in making movies that were perverse without relying on endless shots of genitals? Is anyone surprised that there's a hardcore version of this film out there? No? I should hope not! Yeah, I didn't watch that cut. So I guess I learned a lesson here: Always judge a book by its cover!

El Siniestro Doctor Orloff (1984)

Dr. Orloff's son Alfred (Antonio Mayans) is pining over his lost love who also happens to be his dead mother Melissa. He keeps her body preserved so that he can revive her someday. Alfred needs the bodies of young and sexy women to make this terrible dream come to life so he sends his blind assistant Andros out to kidnap him some raw materials. Meanwhile, Inspector Tanner (Antonio Rebollo) is feeling the pressure as he hasn't been able to crack the case yet. His lovely wife Muriel (Rocío Freixas) wants to help so she gets mixed up in all this craziness too. This should turn out great for all parties involved.

As I was watching The Sinister Dr. Orloff (not to be confused with one of my favorites, The Sinister Eyes of Dr. Orloff), I thought to myself, "Could this be a nice throwback to his early 70s goodness?" The answer is yes. This kind of meandering pervy crap is exactly what I was hoping it would be. Not only are characters recycled from this storyline that Franco remade over and over again, the plot as well will be very familiar to fans of this disjointed series.

Antonio Mayans fans, rejoice! He is pretty frickin' great in this film. Alfred is a really, really pathetic male chauvinist psycho dickhead and his narration while he's cruising the streets with his robotic manservant is as lame as it is hilarious. Howard Vernon is back as the original Dr. Orloff and he looks truly insane in this. His hair was styled during a nuclear bomb test and his character spends the movie in a wheelchair trying to talk Alfred out of his insane plans. Jess Franco himself plays a ridiculous gay stereotype who witnesses one of the abductions. Lina Romay does some voice work but unfortunately doesn't play a character onscreen in this one. Rocío Freixas is very cute and all but she's clearly standing in for Romay. She even looks like she's borrowing Lina's blonde wig!

The Spanish seaside locale is beyond beautiful and there's some very familiar looking architecture on display (see Countess Perverse). This gets predictably trashy as there's plenty of utterly gorgeous female flesh on display but it only goes for extended onscreen sex once. Color me relieved. The real sleaziness happens when Alfred strangles one of his victims -who is EXTREMELY naked- to death and he seems to be really, really enjoying it.

"You can't atomize the soul of a human being."

The Sinister Dr. Orloff is a wonderful overdose of mad science, off kilter dialog, and jiggling boobies (and other body parts). It's good but definitely not essential for Franco fans but there's a whipping scene if you're into that kind of thing. There's also endless shots of Andros carrying naked women over his shoulder which I think is a fetish as well. The synthesizer music at the beginning is very subtle like a supernova smoking crack. Come to think of it, all of the music in this film is pretty deranged; and surprise (not really), it's all done by Franco under a pseudonym! My only major complaint about this one is that I really wish it was dubbed into English but I highly doubt this film got very much distribution beyond Spain.

Richard Glenn Schmidt

5 THE THEATER EXPERIENCE

Whenever I read books about people detailing the glory days of the grindhouse era and the splendor of drive-ins gone by, I get a little bummed out. Seeing a drive-in ad in an old newspaper with triple features like Fangs of the Living Dead, Crypt of the Living Dead, and Curse of the Living Dead (AKA Mario Bava's Kill Baby, Kill) make me yearn for the invention of the time machine. You see, I've only been to a drive-in once that I remember and a few ratty theaters that were slightly less spunk covered than the legendary ones on 42nd Street. I don't really want to get hit on by a junkie transvestite in a soiled raincoat or sit in my car for 2 hours unless I absolutely have to so I guess it all works out.

Even in this sadly digital era of the cinema, I still love going to the movies. While putting these memories together for this chapter, I really felt like the theater experience was in danger of going out of style. Nope. People still go to the movies. Pretty shocking! And really, why is film being replaced by digital really so bad? It's just another medium for transmitting stories. Human beings are still going to large buildings and staring at screens. I still get a hotdog and occasionally, a frozen Coke, before the show. What's the big deal?

So whether it's hearing the adorable joy of kids laughing at BB-8, seeing a 70mm print of Tarantino's newest splatter stage production, or watching Suspiria with a group of unsuspecting strangers in an event space that used to be an old bank, I still try to get up off my butt and go sit down on my butt so I can see some cool shit on a big screen. And since I'm forever obsessed with film, I imagine I'll still have a few chances to get spoiled (and hopefully not soiled) out there in the dark. This chapter is my collection of memories from going to the movies, some grand and some truly lame.

Richard Glenn Schmidt

The Best & Worst Theater Experiences

The Abandoned (2006)

The buzz around this movie was big and by "big", I mean almost nonexistent. I'd heard tiny little whispers about this movie from Spanish director Nacho Cerdà for a while and I was very surprised to find out (totally by accident) that it was playing at my favorite theater (Starlight 20). After work that same day, my wife LeEtta and I went to see it. Including us, there were 5 people in the auditorium. The film kicked in and the volume was up too loud but it didn't bother me at all. We were trapped in a super sensory overload attack for 99 minutes. This film is fucking amazing.

Coraline (2009)

Some dumbshit in the audience tried to ruin this one for LeEtta and I. As a pre-Valentine's Day celebration, we went to the theaters. Instead of the Friday the 13th remake (2009), which neither of us were all that excited about, we opted for Coraline in 3D. This was a very wise move. Coraline is one of those fun and scary kids movies filled with moments of transcendent beauty. So yeah, there was this one dumbass chick whose medication had either just kicked in or had just worn off and wouldn't shut the fuck up during the movie. Luckily, Miss Hot Topic 2006 was frightened into silence by many of the really freaky scenes hidden in Coraline and the rest of us were allowed to enjoy the film in peace.

Creepshow 2 (1987)

My sister Lora and her fiancé Steve took me to the drive-in one night. I was 10 years old and the triple feature was pretty strange: Italian exploitation master Ruggero Deodato's Cut and Run (1985), Hot Pursuit (1987) starring John Cusack, and Creepshow 2. This was truly a magical evening. I got to stay out way later than I was ever allowed to and I got to see two R rated films on the big screen. The John Cusack comedy was kind of the wild card but was just boring compared to the other two films. I remember Cut and Run unnerving and confusing me but then Creepshow 2 saved the night. "The Raft" was totally terrifying but exhilarating and I couldn't look away.

The Ring (2002)

I probably talk about this theater experience too much. You watch a videotape and then you die in 7 days. That's all I knew about this one when

LeEtta (before she was my wife) and I were going to see it. This should be a great date movie, right? Instead of a hot date, we were clutching each other in the dark out of sheer terror. Hours after we had seen Samara come out of that TV, we could still see her in the shadows lingering around the corners of our vision. I don't prefer Gore Verbinski's version to the original Japanese classic but I'll always cherish this wildly terrifying surprise first viewing.

Transformers: The Movie (1986)

My excitement combined with the mania of the other kids in the crowd was almost too much to bear. When this movie started, the place nearly erupted into a nerd frenzy. The biggest revelation: Transformers: The Movie is just like the show except its better animated and way more violent. When Weird Al Yankovic's "Dare to be Stupid" showed up on the soundtrack, it was a religious experience. Rest in peace, Ironhide.

Grindhouse (2007)

For anyone who didn't get off their asses and go see Planet Terror and Death Proof along with all the fake trailers, SHAME ON YOU! My friend Matt Torrence (who doesn't even like horror movies) and his wife Rubis were kind enough to pick me up when my car was on the fritz and take me to the movies. The only downside to this experience was that I, having just gotten over a cold, was "the coughing guy" in the movie and got up several times to go and hack my lungs out in the lobby. But it was worth it, by God. Seeing this on the big screen with a very vocal and jovial crowd was a friggin' riot. The experience was an invigorating rush of fanboy love for all things trashy and splatterific.

Taxi Driver (1976)

In 1998, while visiting some friends in Tampa, Mike Fusco and I went to the shitty theater (the one that did Rocky Horror every weekend) to catch a showing of Taxi Driver. This dump had posters up for upcoming showings of Alien and Clockwork Orange. In other words, this place was heaven for cinema obsessives like us. I'd seen this classic film on tape before but I had no idea what seeing it on the big screen would be like. I don't think I blinked during the entire film. The print was beat up and scratchy and it made the film feel even more unpredictable and dirty than I could have imagined. When it was over, I felt accelerated and oddly happy. That shitty theater is now an even shittier flea market.

Blair Witch Project (1999)

My friend Mike Jolley and I caught this one on a Saturday night after it had been out for a week or so and the word on the street was that this was THE SCARIEST MOVIE EVER. Well, it isn't but it was a great time at the theater. We had a great crowd that night and everyone was into the film. I remember a woman in the audience actually screaming for her mama. Classic. On the way back home, the foggy night surrounded my car while Mike and I talked about the movie. We were actually scaring ourselves silly by discussing what we had just experienced.

Wicked City (1987)

The dumpy theater in West Palm Beach that my friends and I used to go to (yet another one that did Rocky Horror every weekend) actually had a print of the animated film, Wicked City. This is perhaps the strangest experience I've ever had at the theater (based on the content of the film). At the time (around 1995), it was very hard to be obsessed with anime. You could go to the video store and rent Fist of the North Star, Akira, Vampire Hunter D, Crying Freeman, and that was about it. As this violent and kinky freakout exploded across the screen, a lot of people were giggling nervously, especially during the tentacle business. Needless to say, I'd never seen anything quite like this before. After the film ended, the audience, myself included, was confused and embarrassed. Good times.

Sling Blade (1996)

I don't know if my friends were drunk or just intent on getting on my fucking nerves but I actually ditched them at their seats in the back row and sat alone in the front to catch this great indie flick. Shortly before this movie got really popular, it was playing a limited engagement at the dumpy theater downtown. I hadn't heard anything about this film but something told me to get away from my cackling cronies and give it my full attention. Glad I did.

Alien 3 (1992)

My mom dropped my friend Vick and me off at the theater (Cobb, I think, in Jupiter, Florida) on a beautiful Saturday afternoon. It was just before the end of the school year and our spirits were pretty high. Neither of us had any clue what the new Alien film was like but we couldn't wait to see it. So yeah, holy shit, we were totally caught off guard.

Instantly, my most beloved characters from the first film were killed off before even showing up onscreen. Then the most grim and strange (until Resurrection) of the Alien movies got moving. Alien 3 is totally depressing and a very bizarre film. I had never seen anything quite like it. To this day, this is still my favorite of the series.

What makes this experience so great is my friend Vick. Despite being from different countries (he was born in India), we were both 15 years old and both shared a bizarre sense of humor. Anyway, in a very harrowing scene, Ripley is attacked by a group of prisoners but they are not trying to kill her. Oh no, these guys have been without the comforts of a woman far too long and decide to rape her. Before they can, Charles S. Dutton shows up and beats the shit out of these dudes.

So why were we laughing hysterically at this scene? Were we so relieved that the day was saved that we couldn't contain our joy? Not at all. For some reason, the 'leader' of the rapists, just before violating Sigorney Weaver's character, puts on his goggles, and makes this odd face like he's about to do a back-flip or something. Despite the obviously serious tone of this scene, Vick and I were in stitches. For days after we saw the film, Vick would imitate this rapist's trademark move and then do a booty humping gesture that was Oscar-worthy. We were very sensitive dudes.

Freddy's Dead: The Final Nightmare (1991)

By the time I was 15, I was pretty much obsessed with Freddy Krueger. My sister Lora and her boyfriend (at the time) had introduced me to A Nightmare on Elm Street when it first came out on video in around 1985. It was one of the most insane franchises in horror at the time and I had been a devoted fan (though it nearly threw me off with the abysmal 5th installment). Blame it on good marketing or something but my excitement for Freddy's Dead knew no bounds.

I was able to convince my parents to let me see this one (by myself since nobody wanted to see it with me). My mom had to buy me a ticket when she dropped me off. Enabler! Freddy's Dead is by no means the best in the series but you couldn't have told me that. This was the greatest horror movie ever made as far as I was concerned. Plus, I was really psyched about the 3-D sequences. With my 3-D glasses clutched in hand, I eagerly awaited the signal to be given to put them on.

When the 3-Dness kicked in and the dream-worms (or whatever the fuck they were supposed to be) came slithering off the screen, something in the back of my mind told me that this was all garbage. But it was also somehow a totally great moment. This was the first time I'd seen a 3-D film on the big screen (that I could remember) and it won me over despite the convoluted setup. The roller coaster had me and there was no backing out. I still really dig this film to this day.

Richard Glenn Schmidt

Candyman (1992)

In the fall of 1992, it was imperative that I go see Candyman. My mom drove my friend Vick and I to the theater and I believe she had to buy us tickets since we weren't quite old enough to get into an R rated film. We bought candy (I got Skittles) and sodas then settled in our seats and had the bejeezus scared out of us. Candyman is gory for sure but more importantly, it has an inescapable tension and fucked up atmosphere that pervades throughout the entire film. Hats off to British born director Bernard Rose (Paperhouse) for kicking ass and taking names on this one.

There is a funny scene buried in all the freakiness which comes after the lovely Virginia Madsen is assaulted by a guy posing as Candyman and his gang of thugs who don't want her snooping around in their neighborhood. The cops snag a bunch of dudes matching the description of her attacker and have a lineup where they have to say the line: "We hear you're lookin' for Candyman, bitch." To Vick and myself, who were 16 at the time, this was the funniest moment in film history. I have rewatched this scene and it's nowhere near as amusing as I remembered it.

Major Payne (1995)

Even though I have never been paid a penny for babysitting, it seemed like I was always taking care of younger cousins or kids that belonged to my mom's coworkers. This is how I ended up watching this horrid thing in a theater full of bored children. Unless you've seen this piece of shit then you have no idea just how mind-numbingly terrible this was for me.

Boogie Nights (1997)

This is a great film which is why I SHOULD NOT have gone to see this at the theater located in ground zero of retirees in Palm Beach Gardens. Imagine watching porn with your grandparents. Now imagine if you had 100 grandparents. Okay? Got it? I'll move on. This old bag behind me was totally offended by every frame of this movie and didn't hesitate to tell her husband every five minutes that she "can't believe they're showing that; why do they have to show that?" My friend Rocky and I are sitting there trying to enjoy the movie and this rude idiot wouldn't shut up.

Finally, we get to the donut shop robbery and right after the violent shootout takes place, there's this moment of calm. So what does this old bag do? She says, "Oh my, why did they have to show THAT?" I stood up, turned around, put my finger against my lips, and shushed this woman like a grade school teacher. I was very proud of myself but Rocky was trying to slink under his seat to get away from the scene. That was pretty fun.

Clifford (1994)

So I'm in Great Falls, Montana visiting family when the prospect of going to the movies pops up. At first, I'm relatively interested but then it dawns on me that I'll be doing this with my young cousins (ages 12, 8, and 5). The only safe movie playing is Clifford. I think if this movie was on TV right now, I'd probably get a laugh out of it. But being a crappy 16 year old with a chip on my shoulder and trying constantly trying to act cool, this experience was hell on earth especially if you consider the fact that this was the 3 hour and 17 minute director's cut.

The Transporter (2002)

So yeah, my friend Ryan Hastings (R.I.P.) and I go see this movie and it looked promising enough. I was thinking "Hey, that guy from Lock Stock and Two Smoking Barrels is in it. What could possibly go wrong?" I have been told that I am pretty much an idiot for not digging on The Transporter like I should. I admit the fight scenes are awesome but the rest of the movie pretty much blows. However, Crank (2006) redeemed Jason Statham for me which I really wish I had seen in theaters. Anyway, back to The Transporter…

The best of the worst moments was when Frank (Statham) and Lai (Qi Shu) escape from the bad guys by ducking into the water with scuba gear. They start swimming to safety and this beautiful music starts playing. Well, they keep swimming and swimming and swimming. I started giggling and then laughing out loud and Ryan starts telling me to shut up. Finally, he starts laughing. And they keep swimming and the other dozen or so people in the theater start laughing too. When the underwater sequence is finally over and Frank and Lai burst forth from the water, I started applauding. Someone in the back cheered and everyone was still cracking up. Yeah, I'm a douche. Sorry, everybody.

Lost in Space (1998)

Kim, my girlfriend at the time, and I were so unbelievably bored in Port St. Lucie, Florida one afternoon that we actually paid cash money to watch this fucking wretched sack of ass. I shouldn't have been surprised. I only ever watched the original show when I was bored out of my skull on Saturday mornings when cartoons were over. So why would a film version made over 30 years after the show went off the air be any better? Anyway, Kim and I were bored beyond belief and the only saving grace was the tremendously bad dialogue. We left the theater even more depressed than when we walked in.

Ballistic: Ecks Vs. Sever (2002)

Here is yet another piece of shit that LeEtta and I went to see while we were dating. Jeez, how desperate were we to go to the theaters? I think we should have stayed in and watched her VHS of Real Genius again or something. This film is unimaginably bad. For an action movie, it has the most pitiful pacing, stupid dialog, and a shitbox plot. Millions of rounds of bullets are fired into bodies but there's not a drop of blood spilled. Yikes.

McHale's Navy/Anaconda (1997)

Once again, boredom proves to be my undoing. My friends and I were desperate to see something, anything. Unfortunately, this was one of the worst weekends to go the theaters in cinematic history. Only ten minutes into McHale's Navy and we were immediately roaming through the theater looking for a better option. We busted in on the first 15 minutes of Anaconda and stayed for the rest of it. Do I need to say any more about this? Out of the frying pan and into the toilet.

Reality Bites (1994)

It's senior year of high school and I had just gotten dumped by my girlfriend (who wasn't really my girlfriend but had tempted me into dumping a really nice girl for her and then turned around and dumped me for my troubles). I finally had my own car (which I would wreck a couple of weeks later) and I decided to go to the theaters alone in order to prove that Mandy (her real name) didn't mean anything to me anymore. I run into a bunch of acquaintances from school and decide to join them to watch this film called Reality Bites. The trailers seemed to indicate that this film was speaking to my generation so I was pretty interested. Oh no. No. No. No.

After 20 minutes, I got up and walked out. I could not relate to these morons on the screen. They were too whiny for me (which is funny because, in fact, they weren't as whiny as I was at that age) and they didn't relate to me at all (oh, I wish that were true). Now I know that the rotten mood I was in affected my enjoyment of this stupid fucking movie and that I would fall head over heels for other pretentious indie dramas but damn, this just sucked. To this day, I have never revisited Reality Bites. (Ben Stiller would not be my friend until again until Zoolander.) Damn, the trailer makes this film look like the most un-entertaining thing ever made. What was I thinking?

Dawn of the Dead (2004)

For the record, I think that this is an okay horror film. My nerdy and tiringly familiar complaint -I'm really showing my age here- is that zombies are slow and they should NOT be fast. I know that in Return of the Living Dead, the brain-eating variety are pretty light on their feet but that film is just so great that I'm willing to let it slide. The remake of Romero's 1978 classic is not that great. When the zombies of the new Dawn of the Dead appeared to be taking performance-enhancing drugs, I was pretty annoyed.

That is a pretty weak complaint, I know. But the reason this goddamn movie gets on my list of worst theater experiences is because I had heard that I should stay after the credits to see the bonus footage. One of the survivors gets ahold of a video camera and starts filming. We are shown little bits and pieces of this footage while some shitty Nu-metal plays along in the background. Interspersed in between this are sped up shots of hungry zombies screaming at the camera accompanied by ungodly blasts of screeching noise. While trying to figure out what the fuck happened to these people at the end of the movie, I was getting beaten over the head with one idea: ZOMBIES. Oh really? Zombies!?!?! What? I didn't know that I had just watched a movie about zombies!!! Look here, Niven Howie (the editor), you fucking asshole, I GET THE POINT!

The Exorcist (1973)

God (or Satan) damn it! The re-release of The Exorcist in 2000 could have been so awesome. But no, they had to go and create some pitiful monstrosity called "The version you've never seen". While still astoundingly scary, Kim, my buddy Scott, and I were not pleased at all with the additional shitty audio effects and all the new digital tomfoolery mixed in to make the film scarier. All any of this did was annoy the fans of the original version and telegraph a few of the upcoming scares. Getting to see the infamous "spider walk" on the big screen almost saved this experience from being on my shit list. Almost.

The Crow (1994)

I saw this with my high school girlfriend. We were together for six whole months! That's marriage in high school terms. Anyway, I took my feisty (read as: Italian) lady to see this, the most emo-goth friggin' movie ever filmed, and she melted like butter. We were -I wish I was kidding- crying and declaring our undying love for each other the rest of the night. The clock was already ticking because we broke up a few months later.

Richard Glenn Schmidt

Out of Africa (1985)

Somehow I ended up watching this crap with my parents. I was 9 years old and bored out of my dumb brain!!! This is not a movie for children. This may not be a movie for anyone at all. What the hell else was playing? (I looked into this and I could been taken to see Clue, Young Sherlock Holmes, or even possibly Rocky IV.) Couldn't they have dumped me in some other theater? Oh wait, I just had a terrible thought. Did I want to see Out of Africa? Was this my own fault? Please God, don't let that be the case. All I can remember from this experience is Meryl Streep getting caught in a brier bush and me squirming around in my seat through the entire film from epic boredom.

Hamlet (2000)

I always call this 'Ethan Hawke's Hamlet' so people know which one I'm talking about. My friend Kelly Innes and I went to see this at Tampa Theatre. Kelly claimed it was for class credit and I believed him. What a fool I was! Things started out normally enough in this modernized Hamlet but we soon realized we were in great peril. In case you didn't know, this is a fucking piece of garbage. Standout scenes include the "to be or not to be" speech in a Blockbuster Video and Hamlet's father's ghost materializing in front of a Diet Pepsi machine. There is also an array of boom mikes in the shot and other flubs.

As we made our way through this steaming pile, I started laughing and goofing off. First Kelly was turning red with laughter then he began offering his own heckles. When we heard that other people were starting to pick at the film, it was all over. After that, I think everyone was then trying to laugh the film off the screen. It didn't work but a good time was had by all. When the film ended, sarcastic applause, whistling, and honest-to-goodness jeers abounded throughout the theater.

Crash (1996)

Once again, the Tampa Theatre screws me over. My friends Margarita Acevedo, Mike Fusco, Mike Jolley, and I went and caught David Cronenberg's adaptation of J.G. Ballard's book. Now I like Cronenberg but this is a terrible, terrible film. The theater was in complete silence during the film as everyone seemed to be completely enraptured by this SHOCKING and CONTROVERSIAL thing. All I could think of was, "Hey that dude just stuck his dingle in a scar on Rosanna Arquette's leg!"

So the film lets out and our gang is walking back to the car when Margarita blurts out something to the effect of "Wasn't that film beautiful!?" We all went completely bonkers and started giving her shit and she fell on the ground in protest. The consensus of the dudes in our party was that that was a SHITTY MOVIE. We dogged Crash all the way to the car and Margarita was (understandably) pissed at us. I think we probably ragged on the film during the drive home too. I emailed Fusco and he says he vaguely remembers some scar-fucking jokes taking place that night.

Passenger 57 (1992)

It took me years to figure out this simple rule: Do not under any circumstances go to the theaters on Friday night. Breaking this rule in Jupiter, Florida is especially heinous. However, I was 16 years old and didn't give a shit because at that age, I was usually part of the ruckus. I believe I was there with my buddy Scott and we were less than impressed with this action-packed offering from tax evader Wesley Snipes.

I like to call this film 'Wesley's Wandering Boil'. First, I noticed that Snipes had a big pimple on his face. Then it disappears. Then it came back bigger than before. Then it is covered with a band aid. Then it disappears again. However, this was not what makes Passenger 57 such a sensational theater experience.

While my friend Scott and I were watching this film, my attention was drawn to some yelling on the other side of the theater. This guy sitting with his wife is turned around in his seat and is yelling at some hoodlums sitting behind him. In the blaring gunfire and explosions, I can't make out what he's saying. The teenage jerks behind the dude and his wife are very amused by this man yelling at them and are just kind of staring and smiling back.

Once that incident ended, I went back to not enjoying the film. Suddenly, more insanity erupted as the guy, pushed too far by the fuckheads, grabs one of the teenagers by the collar and drags him out of the auditorium. He kicks the door open, throws the kid out, and comes back to his seat receiving a wave of applause from the packed theater. About two minutes later, two police officers, the douchebag kid, and an usher come in and the guy is removed from the screening of Passenger 57 with his embarrassed wife in tow.

Ponyo (2009)

So what was yours truly doing at a G rated film on a Tuesday morning? Well, aside from it being my wife's birthday, Ponyo is the new film by world-renowned animation director Hayao Miyazaki and we weren't going to miss it for the world. This breathtaking and fun film did not disappoint at all and I'm glad that somebody, somewhere is smart enough to realize that there is always going to be an audience for this stuff. During one of the trippy and fantastical underwater sequences, I leaned over to LeEtta and whispered: "This is the greatest drug movie ever."

The most notable and odious moment happened when the ending song caused some hilariousness. The fools at Disney decided to translate the lyrics to English and then do a painful remix with the American voice actors rapping about Ponyo. Everyone in the crowd friggin' bolted for the door when this unholy and shitty noise started. Now I've heard the Japanese version and I don't really like it either but the American one is like having your face bashed in with a candy hammer except less pleasant.

Daybreakers (2010)

My friend Stanley texted to inform me that Daybreakers kicked ass. So the wife and I took his advice and went to Regal Citrus Park 20 last night. I was kind of uneasy about this theater. It's attached to a mall way over in a part of town I don't know at all. I figured there would be some obnoxiousness from my fellow patrons. I'm still so terribly attached to Muvico Starlight 20 but that is quite a drive since we moved to the other side of town. Citrus Park mall has a wildly ugly color scheme going on. Everything is in mauve and teal. I know this is Florida and all but what year do they think it is exactly?

There were only about a dozen people in the theater to catch Daybreakers and of course, some loser couple decided to sit near us and talk their fucking heads off during the entire film. The girl was actually heckling the movie. Now I'm not saying you can't heckle Daybreakers but her method: repeating the dialogue back at the movie in a sarcastic tone. Let me tell ya, I was pretty impressed. My wife claims that she didn't even notice this couple. She's very lucky. I liked the film but I loved the experience! Oh wait, no.

Sucker Punch (2011)

I have noticed that this is a love it or hate it movie. Other than my wife and myself, I don't know anyone who doesn't hate this one. So maybe it's just hate it or hate it. Anyway, the wife and I thought we were pretty clever by having our date night on a Thursday, thus limiting how many people would be at the theater. While this imaginary algorithm did work in terms of numbers of people, an unfortunate drawback was that it spit out more shittily concentrated people.

Sucker Punch is a quiet/loud/quiet/loud film (like a Pixies song) and during the quiet moments I began to notice that there was a trio of teenagers having too much fun in the nearly empty auditorium. In terms of ages, these kids seemed to be in the latter half of their teenage years and the youngest of them looked around 16. If this guy and his two female companions were in their early 20s then -my God, I don't even want to ponder that. Anyway, they were talking real loud and it was very annoying but then the action scenes would kick in and no one is loud enough to rise about that. I guess that got too boring for these fucks because they started to chase each other around the theater.

No, I'm not talking about six year old children. I'm talking about people who can drive and possibly vote. They were chasing each other through the theater just hooting and hollering at each other. Finally, one of them ran behind us so fast that I felt the wind move the hair on the back of my head. I stood up, turned around, and bellowed at the top of my lungs, "Guys! We are trying to watch the movie! Will you please stop?!" These three morons were completely frozen in place. The girls were in mid-stride down two different aisles and the guy was climbing over a seat, totally freaked out. They sat down and almost made it through the rest of the movie before they started talking loudly again. At least I curbed some of their shenanigans.

Philadelphia (1993)

This is complicated. I went and saw this with several friends. We were all pretty ruined by this very sad and moving film. Our gay friend was particularly freaked out. Even in the 1990s, people actually believed that gay men were more likely to get AIDS than anyone else. This was the first Hollywood film I ever saw that said, "Hey everybody, AIDS is real." So the funny part about seeing this movie is that my friend Jay really hated that "Streets of Philadelphia" song by Bruce Springsteen, so we were heckling the song ever time it played. Just the song. Not the movie, I swear. Ah whatever, I'm definitely going to hell.

Threesome (1994)

I caught this film at a dollar theater and it was remarkable because, at the time, I loved this one (I have no idea why) and I remember yelling at this judgmental bitch who flipped out during the threesome sequence. She was whisper-yelling to her friend, "Oh my God! How can they show this?!?!", and I told her to shut the hell up. These kinds of incidents happened all the time when I was this age because I had a huge chip on my shoulder. I once yelled at a guy for having his kid on one of those kid leashes but that's a different story. Now I just glare at people and keep my secret hatred of them bottled up inside me.

Richard Glenn Schmidt

Rob Zombie's Halloween II – An Epic Story

I really wanted to see Rob Zombie's Halloween II and so I did my usual thing I do when I'm excited about a movie: I avoid as much online preview content as possible. The mostly lame trailer is pretty much the only thing I knew about the sequel to the remake. Well, that and the fact that Sheri Moon Zombie was playing the ghost of Deborah Myers in this one. It wasn't much to go on but something was calling to me. Something important.

I've always preferred Halloween II (the 1981 version) over John Carpenter's 1978 film. Halloween is amazing and obviously a better film but Halloween II is the one I reach for the most thanks to nostalgia. The hospital setting really got to me and after years of catching this film nearly every Halloween, it really turned into cinematic comfort food. The scene where Michael Meyers stabs that nurse and lifts her off the floor while a doped up Laurie watches in confused horror is some kind of devil-magic that still makes me smile. As to why I thought that this kind of beauty would somehow happen in the 2009 version; don't ask me. I was just hoping against hope.

My friend Nafa and I had been talking about going to see Halloween II since it came out back in August but we've both been pretty busy lately. He managed to go and see it and reported back to me that it was awesome. Nearly two months had gone by and I figured that H2 (yikes, that abbreviation) was just going to have to be a rental. Then Nafa reminded me that it would probably still be around in theaters through Halloween to pick up some more business. Duh, I didn't think of that.

Finally, our night arrived. We got off work and headed to the University Mall. I've been going to this mall since I first set foot in Tampa 17 years ago and it has been threatening to close ever since. Yet somehow the place keeps on truckin' by managing a few mediocre renovations and adding more dang shoe stores. I would hardly call the Regal University 16 Theater attached to the food court my old stomping ground. UPDATE: This theater is now a fancy schmancy place called Studio Movie Grill with a full bar and decent food though the mall is still crumbling around it.

I hadn't been to any screenings of a film at the old Regal since they opened the Muvico out in New Tampa (yes, we have a new one!). The place was always too trashy and too noisy for me to enjoy the movies there. Of course, any theater can be great if you avoid the crowds by choosing your show times wisely and not going to any opening weekend regardless of how excited you are to see a flick. I'm a friggin' expert on that shit now.

With over an hour to kill before the film started, Nafa and I headed to the Halloween store that used to be a Steve & Barry's clearance clothing store. This was a slightly half-assed affair but there were some highlights and lowlights nestled in retail hell. I keep hoping that Halloween will become the next big gift-giving holiday but that's a manifesto for a different day.

I was getting hungry but nothing in the food court inspired me. Nafa reminded me there was a Dairy Queen/Orange Julius near the middle of the mall. It had been many, many years since I had enjoyed OJ. When I was a kid, I used to frequent the Palm Beach Mall where I would get two bacon and cheddar hotdogs and a large Orange Julius. Then after checking out the death metal tapes in Camelot Music, I would circle back for a soda from OJ. One exceptional time, I picked up Peaceful Death and Pretty Flowers by Dead Horse.

Later, in the car, my mom actually asked to read Dead Horse's lyrics while we were stuck in traffic. She was infuriated by the violent and dark content of the lyrics and nearly confiscated the cassette from me. Thankfully, that was the last time she did that. Had my mom read lyrics from bands like Autopsy (disgusting) or Nocturnus (satanic) or Demolition Hammer (violent) or a hundred other bands I was into at the time, my metal days would have been over.

My appetite ain't what it used to be (thank God) so I just got one bacon cheddar dog and a small Orange Julius. The cost of this meal was over $6 (in 2009 money!) but no matter, it was delightful. Poor Nafa sat there watching me moan and eat like a total pig. I probably ruined his appetite. Sorry, duder. With still more time to kill, we ventured to Hot Topic, Spencer's Gifts, and a very bizarre dollar store called Kim's Dollar & More. Here's the surprise: we found cheapness everywhere!

We finally went to the Regal University 16 for show time and it was not nostalgic at all. I doubt the place has changed much over the years but nothing looked familiar. We got our tickets and Nafa got some crazy coupons. Apparently, he's a frequent Regal customer. We walk down the hall to our theater and –hey, what's that guy doing!! There was only one other dude sitting there waiting for the film to start and I swear he had to quickly adjust his pants when he heard us walking in. This was not a good sign. While having him behind us was a risk, I made sure to have at least 4 rows between us and the probably-masturbating guy. This piece of shit would be snoring soon (hmm, why's he so sleepy all of a sudden?) but he would be easy to ignore during Rob Zombie's flick.

H2 (I despise and love calling it that) starts us off with a great hospital sequence where Laurie (Scout Taylor-Compton) and Annie Brackett (Danielle Harris), who's still in a coma from the first film, are menaced by Michael Myers (Tyler Mane). But this all turns out to be a dream (get used to it). It's a year later and Laurie is all maladjusted and shit and is now living with Annie (who is scarred up but not in a coma) and Sheriff Brackett (Brad Dourif). She is plagued with nightmares, takes lots of pills, and dresses in torn and grungy clothes (awesome). Michael's body was lost and there is speculation that he's still alive. Of course, he IS alive and is slowly making his way back to Haddonfield (killing anyone who gets in his way).

A cynical and comically prickish Dr. Loomis (Malcolm McDowell) is making the lecture circuit with his newly released book about Myers. His book reveals that Laurie is actually Michael Myers' sister. Laurie reads this, spazzes out, and heads over to her friends' place. There she gets drunk, dresses up like Magenta from Rocky Horror (genius), and heads out to a wild Halloween party where she binge drinks and spazzes out again. Myers kills one of her friends at the party AND books it back home to attack Annie (finishing the job this time). A big showdown ensues between Michael, Dr. Loomis, Laurie, Sheriff Brackett, and the Haddonfield police department.

Thank you, Rob Zombie. Thank you for raping my eyes. Halloween II is so over the top and nuts that I can only describe it as taking a nauseous ride on a roller coaster made of circus peanuts as it zips through a universe of flickering fluorescent stars. The supernatural (I think) overtones and the gritty splendor are quite captivating. However, the film is also one of the most relentlessly violent and perturbing things I've ever seen in theaters. Every time I started to settle into a safe and comfortable place, the violence would come lunging back to plunge the knife in over and over again. And again!

I think Rob Zombie woke up last November 1st with a happy stomachache from too much Halloween candy and wrote down his nightmares. That's the real genesis of Halloween II. The director's obsession with the 1970s, characters who inhabit the fringes of society, and constant strings of expletives were in full force. More importantly though is the film's oddness. There are a handful of dream sequences, hallucinations, or whatevers that broke up the would-be monotony of all the violent setpieces. Remember in Halloweentown II: Kalabar's Revenge when the bad dude wanted to turn everyone's Halloween masks into their own real faces? No? Well, it's like that. Sort of.

As a horror fan, I have two ways of thinking. The first is this: okay, this movie is awesome. The second way of thinking: okay, everyone is going to fucking hate this movie and it's still awesome. There are so many of the latter that I can do nothing but mirth-sigh (whatever that means). Now I'm not just being contrary to any negative reviews this film received. I honestly feel that with every crazy turn Halloween II makes, I'm along for the ride. Contempt for the audience? Maybe. Contempt for the material? Probably. I heard rumors that Zombie didn't want to do this film. GOOD! He should only do projects he doesn't want to do from now. The proof is in the puddin'.

Forget the modern setting, Halloween II is a journey through a 1978 that never existed or perhaps one that's yet to come. Jason Vorhees gets resurrected by a bolt of lightning and Michael Myers gets brought back by a cow. That's impressive. I'm having a tough time communicating how important this film is. Purists concerned with deviations from the established rules of the Myers saga (yes, he takes the mask off in this one) can nitpick if they want to but I'm no purist. All I care about is mood (most important), gore (quite important), and boobs (least important) but Halloween II is more than all three.

Is this flick a thinker? Yeah. And why not? There is some heavy (not like highbrow literature or anything but heavy) shit happening here. Were the dream sequences there just to screw us up or is the whole thing a dream? Did Zombie go all Eyes Wide Shut on our asses? Could be. The film is very dreamlike and there are too many oddities for it to be just accidentally sloppy writing. Beauty is the key here and there are so many gorgeous shots burned into the back of my eyes. Plot and script were put in danger for aesthetics and that's all I ever ask horror movie directors to do. I don't give a double God damn about the mechanics. Just give me smoke machines and freaky lighting.

Rob Zombie's Halloween and Halloween II are just what I needed. They heal the damage done to me by House of 1,000 Corpses (which I actually like now) and The Devil's Rejects (that "heroic" death scene at the ending just ruined the whole thing for me). Both films had the atmosphere but failed in other ways. This is Rob Zombie really coming into his own. Malek Akkad, I implore you, keep throwing money at Rob Zombie projects. It's working and don't let anyone tell you it ain't. "Nights in White Satin" trumps "Free Bird" every time.

After this magnificent movie ended, I had to reenter society so that I could go home. This was not an easy transition. Rob Zombie had made my world a prettier place. Colors were more vibrant and I walked a little slower to catch all the details. On the way home, Nafa and I discussed the film the entire way. This was his third time seeing Halloween II at the theater but the film's frenzied energy still had him in its clutches. He dropped me off at home where I ran up the stairs to my apartment and started babbling about the film to my wife who nodded many times and thanked me for not taking her to see it.

Richard Glenn Schmidt

The Living Dead At Tampa Pitcher Show

Before I start badmouthing Tampa Pitcher Show, let me just say that I do think it's a cool place. Any old theater that still does The Rocky Horror Picture Show on a regular basis has something good going for it. My experience at their Dawn of the Dead (1978) screening was embarrassing and mostly terrible. You can probably write all of the following off as a weird old guy who should just the shut the hell up.

Sometime in 2010, I read somewhere that there was going to be a screening of the original Dawn of the Dead (oh, there was a remake?) accompanied by zombie video games, zombie strippers (I didn't expect this part to be true), and Mike Christopher AKA the Hare Krishna zombie from the 1978 film. I was really, really excited about this event. Seeing Dawn of the Dead -a movie that was hugely important to my development as a horror movie fan- on the big screen was paramount. Of course, I was headed for disaster.

Before we get to the screening, let me share this little story. My first encounter with this classic film was due to this stuttering kid at our school. Seemed like a nice enough chap so I would stand up for him when my loser classmates would make fun of his speech impediment. This kid was way into horror movies (or so he professed) and I was impressed as hell by his Dawn of the Dead t-shirt. It featured a person's exploding head.

When I asked this kid about what was going on with his t-shirt, he told me that in Dawn of the Dead there were all these zombies. Check. He then told me that the figure on his t-shirt was the king zombie. Um... wait a second. He related to me how bullets wouldn't stop this creature and that the heroes had to use a rocket launcher to destroy it. That's how its head exploded. Holy shit! I wish Dawn of the Dead had that in it! A couple of years later, when I finally watched Dawn of the Dead, I remembered that kid and just felt kind of stupid. In order to make up for his stuttering, he was just a bold-faced liar who'd probably never even seen the dang film.

Okay back to the DOTD screening. It was a Saturday night in early January and it was a friggin' cold night in Tampa. I know what you're saying, Florida gets cold? It does and when it does, us thin-blooded Floridians are screwed. Lows in the 30s might be nothing to a lot of people but it feels like the end of the world to us keepin' it real in the dong-shaped state. But more about that later.

I showed up too early to Tampa Pitcher Show due to my unbearable excitement. The ticket window was closed so I went inside. Sherlock Holmes (the one with Harry Connick Jr. and Rufus Sewell) was still playing on their only screen so I had to wait in the lobby for a while. I got something to eat and a soda. There were some teens playing zombie video games on televisions set up around the lobby. I didn't know anybody so I just kind of watched people playing for a while. At some point, the ticket window was open so I went outside and got in line to pay admission.

There were two odd dudes right in front of me in line. I'm pretty sure they were a couple and it was a May-December thing. Not judging but I was alarmed when the younger guy was behaving skittish as shit and I swear he looked at me about 90 times before he urged his partner to look at me. His request was so urgent that when the older dude turned to look at me, he was immediately confused. He gave his boyfriend a glare as if to say, "What the fuck is wrong with you?" Maybe the younger guy thought I was cute or especially ugly or maybe I had piss stains on my pants. Who knows? This probably sounds like homophobic paranoia on my part but it was just such an odd moment and a bad omen for the entire evening.

When I got back inside, Sherlock Holmes was still playing. The time for the event to start had already passed and one of the employees told me that the previous film had started late. For the next half hour, I sat and watched people playing video games some more. Folks started showing up dressed as zombie hunters with Nerf guns and plastic swords. I attempted to make small talk but I got the cold shoulder. Something was just wrong.

Finally, the auditorium emptied out and I got to go inside. A wave of nostalgia hit me like a ton of bricks. The cheap furniture and the garbage carpeting brought me back to every dollar theater I'd ever set foot in. I felt like I was right at home. Don't worry, that didn't last long. I marched right up front to a table, took off my jacket, and flopped down in a chair, giddy with excitement.

Someone rolled out a laptop and a projector and my heart sunk. No fucking way were they going to show DOTD with a tiny little projector when they had this huge screen. The urge to bolt was immediately quelled when a bunch of unfunny zombie memes started showing up on the screen. Whew, I thought, that was a close call.

So while these terrible zero-culture farts were just rolling along through a Windows slideshow of doom and my intelligence was being zapped from my brain, I noticed that I was sitting alone. Everyone at the theater except for me was sitting in the back. I was the only person who appeared to have arrived alone and the only one who doesn't know everyone else. That's when it hit me, I had stumbled into a clique-hole. The Rocky Horror kids wanted nothing to do with me! I was just some uncool dude who was crashing their party. Suddenly, I was very depressed and embarrassed. My body felt as heavy as a stone while a steamroller of social anxiety crushed me down into the filthy carpet.

Then the show started. Some ghoulish rock music kicked in and the zombie strippers came out to strut their stuff. Wow, there really is truth in advertising! Girls in zombie makeup, fishnets, frilly panties, strategically placed electrical tape, and very little else started doing their act. It wasn't just burlesque bouncing either, they actually had a victim whose guts they tore out. I had to applaud. This was good.

Once the strippers had done their bit, it was time for Mike Christopher to give a little speech. He seemed like a nice guy. He complained about how cold it was in Florida and that got a laugh. It would probably be 80 degrees in a few days. That's what makes all of us psychotic around here. When he was done, I should have left. I'm telling you, my friends, I should have walked right out the fucking door.

So the film starts. They were indeed using the laptop and the tiny projector. This resulted in DOTD taking up less than 20% of the available screen. The debate in my mind went like this: Is this an actual print of the film? Hell no. How important is that to me? Moderately. Is this bigger than my TV at home? Yes. Then fine, I'll stay.

Around this time, I noticed that I needed to put my jacket back on. Tampa Pitcher Show was probably trying to save money by turning the heat off. The temperature inside the place was starting to plummet. I had a wool cap in the pocket of my jacket. I took that out and put it on. Then I zipped up my jacket. Then I had to put my hands in my pockets. Holy shit, I was cold. Really, really cold.

Then the "your virus detection software is out of date" window popped up over George Romero's classic with a loud ding that echoed through the theater. My jaw dropped. That's right, the knuckleduck motherfucker who owned the shitty laptop in question was a complete asshole who didn't know his/her ass from a hole in the ground. I felt so stupid for sticking through this shit show that my urge to weep or start screeching at the top of my lungs in venomous rage was deflated. I just sat there and took it like a grownup -a thoroughly disappointed grownup.

When the film ended, I got up to leave with nothing in my heart but a feeling of profound foolishness and a love for DOTD that no crappy night out (and no shite remake) can shake. It was freezing outside. I ran to the car and hopped in. As the heat failed and only cold air was blowing out, I started laughing. It was after 2 in the morning, I was cold as balls, and I'd just wasted 4 hours of my life. I drove home shivering and making a pact with myself to never return to Tampa Pitcher Show ever again.

So in the end, Dawn of the Dead still haunts me. The film is urgently important to my heart. Seeing it when I was 13 and seeing it at that abominable screening were the same. The setting didn't matter. I was creeped out and depressed by the film. Even when I was a kid, it made me morose and I loved it. I'd never felt that way from a movie before. It made me listless and thoroughly freaked me out the more I thought about it. The world looked bent, distorted and yet somehow even more real afterward. This is what good horror movies do. Tampa Pitcher Show, leave me alone. I don't want to talk to you right now.

Fulci on the Big Screen!

In the fall of 2011, I saw on some website or other that Lucio Fulci's Zombi 2 (1979) was going to be making the rounds at theaters around the country. This news flipped me the fuck out. The thought of seeing The Fulch on the big screen really had me chomping at the bit. The closest that Fulci's classic was playing to LeEtta and I was in St. Petersburg at a place I didn't even know existed called the Beach Theatre (now closed, apparently). It was our anniversary so we decided to take a couple days off and stay at a hotel near the theater as well as attend the screening.

We arrived at the Beach Theatre about 5 hours early for the show just so I could scope the place out. I was a nervous wreck just expecting the whole night to be a disaster so this was the only way I could calm down with so long to wait for the movie. Then LeEtta found a little German restaurant that was completely empty save for us. The sole waitress was really confused by our presence and handed us the menus with much trepidation. We made her at ease once we started ordering some of the more traditional German items off the menu. The poor thing was probably hoping we'd bail after getting a look at the selections. We had a great time and having the whole place to ourselves made us feel like royalty.

Even after eating our scrumptious meal, there was still a lot of time before the movie so we walked around St. Pete and hit up an ice cream store as it was closing. There was a Temple of the Dog music video playing on a TV and suddenly, I had no idea what year it was. Back outside the theater, I saw a guy in a horror movie t-shirt and started up a convo with him. He was a really nice guy and I feel kind of bad because I can't recall his name. Sorry, duder.

When it was time for the film to start, we went in and I was a little bummed that the whole event wasn't better attended. Don't get me wrong, the Beach Theatre (which opened in 1940) couldn't have held a massive crowd but only about half of the seats in the theater were filled. We picked our seats and we were immediately struck by what terrible shape they were in. The armrest between LeEtta and I broke off and she spent some time trying to put it back into place.

The moment that made me realize that the year was indeed 2011 and not 1979 was when the movie started on the big screen but it was over a minute into the film. The projectionist tried to start the film over and that's when the Blu-ray player's menu flashed on the screen. My heart sunk. I guess you could call me naïve but I was pretty shocked that I was going to be seeing Zombi 2 from a goddamn Blu-ray and not on actual film. I suppose my Dawn of the Dead experience at Tampa Pitcher Show taught me nothing. All bitching aside, the movie looked AMAZING on the big screen and this is one of the moments that convinced me to buy my first

Blu-ray player.

The crowd was pretty sedate. No one dressed up like zombies and no one came in smoking pipes full of maggots or anything. Maybe that's going to happen at a City of the Living Dead (1980) event. There was one guy who showed up drunk with his lady friend. He was tall and lanky and made a big public display of affection for his poor companion as though someone there was questioning his sexuality. They served beer at the Beach Theatre and oh yes, he was partaking.

When the big splinter to the eye scene happened, this loud goofus started cheering and drunkenly clapping. He was actually offended when he looked around and no one else was going along with him. It just wasn't the crowd for that but I didn't hold that against him. Before the end of this movie, he had to leave very quickly nearly falling over several times while his girlfriend ran alongside trying to steady him. I'm probably lucky that he didn't puke or fall right on top of me.

When all is said and done, seeing Zombi 2 on a big screen with a modest-sized crowd was a huge deal even taking my minor complaints into account. Much like my lame Dawn of the Dead experience, the use of a DVD or Blu-ray for a film screening seemed like this huge letdown at first. But you know what? The power of the films I love transcend millennial disappointment. The miasma of horror that Fulci has shoved into the eye sockets of film audiences can be delivered by a laser very efficiently.

The Rocky Horror Memory Show

You should not under any circumstances go to an old rundown theater to watch The Rocky Horror Picture Show where the audience throws rice and toast and used condoms (regional) at the screen. Well, I guess you could. But you'd be going against the spirit of the film. If you're one of those folks who gets dressed up in lace and/or gold lame to reenact the film at a rundown theater, you too have got it all wrong. The whole point of The Rocky Horror Picture Show is that you watch it completely alone, locked in your room and then cry your eyes out when Columbia gets killed.

In 1990, there was all this hoopla about Rocky Horror's 15th anniversary and I decided to rent it. This was very odd experience. I was 14 years old and I had absolutely no idea what this film was supposed to be about. I assumed that it was a horror movie, which it is. But it's also a gender-bending camp fantasy fetish festival of gay. This is a good thing, obviously. To say that I didn't 'get it' would be an understatement. But I did fall in love with Columbia and Magenta instantly. There was something eerily comforting whenever they were on the screen. For a teenage boy, it was impossible not to notice Susan Sarandon jiggling about but Little Nell and Patricia Quinn stole my heart. I was crushed when Riff Raff guns down Columbia at the climax of the film. Nobody can get over that.

When I was a senior in high school, I was dating this teenage witch (I'm probably exaggerating her witchieness) who insisted that I go with her and see Rocky at the local almost-condemned theater in Palm Beach County. How could I resist? It was a reason to stay out until 2am and a reason get in good with this girl that I was head over heels in love with (after all, we'd been dating nearly 2 weeks). We went with her obnoxious friends and I got the 'virgin' treatment from the cast when we arrived at the theater. I'm sure this varies from state to state but I seem to remember getting on stage and... I don't know. There was whip cream involved. I've blocked the rest of it out and will need a therapist to uncover that particular public humiliation.

We had a blast throwing rice, toast and toilet paper, screaming at Brad and Janet, and dancing in the aisles. It was the best night. Plus I got to make out with my girl in the backseat of her gay friend's hatchback all the way home. She was wearing these bright red stockings and... I'm keeping those details to myself so you guys don't start throwing up on the book. So like a week later, she and I broke up. It was my first real heartbreak and I was totally inconsolable (for an entire day).

The next time I watched Rocky Horror, it was after my mom had bought me a copy for Christmas. Like most movies I owned on VHS, I proceeded to watch it over and over again. Oh, there's so much to love in every frame. The gay and cross-dressing themes don't really speak to me (I can hear you guys going 'yeah right') so much as the film's limitless love of bad sci-fi, horror, and rock and roll. I bought the cassette of the soundtrack and cruised around Jupiter, Florida blasting it from my car's speakers. Later in my senior year, when I was dating someone new, we went to another midnight showing at the same crap theater with a bunch of our friends.

While I sat there, watching the film with the crowd the second time around, I realized that I should have just left this experience alone with my 'virgin' run. It wasn't fun this time. It felt like a chore to get up and dance. I could tell my gf wasn't into it either (she was a dang stick-in-the-mud so that wasn't a big surprise) and I just wished I hadn't bothered. For me, The Rocky Horror Picture Show's real power lies in one's personal devotion to it. The public spectacle is an essential experience (if only once) but the movie was specifically written to be watched alone. How do I know that? Well, I read this interview with Richard O'Brien who said that "the musical play was only ever meant to be performed before one person at a time. I've always felt that the people who perform it live in front of a large audience are tainting my original vision. Please, I implore you, if you're a real fan of Rocky Horror, watch it all by yourself."

You should really Google that interview. It's fascinating AND it doesn't exist. Anyway, I guess I could launch into a diatribe about what exclusionary dicks the Rocky Horror cast and crew in your area are probably like. But I've heard they're not all like that. Florida tends to ruin everything. Meh, I'm kind of an asshole myself so I'll just shut up now.

6 MISCELLANY

All of the pieces in this second to last chapter just don't seem to fit anywhere else in the book. Maybe they don't fit anywhere else in the universe. That being said, I think they capture some of the utterly fascinating (just kidding) moments in my cinematic growth and experience. I kind of want to call it my "growthing" but that's gross and not a word.

Richard Glenn Schmidt

That Eurohorror Thang

Can you describe in 700 million words or less that European horror movie thing? I sure as hell can't. What is it about Eurohorror that makes it so friggin' addictive? Could it be the lazy menace or the incalculable morbidity? The feeling that something dark is lurking just around the corner or hiding just behind that tombstone is a big part of what makes horror so great. The European flair usually just means that the payoff will be bigger, brighter, or cheaper and yet somehow more endearing. This shit might bore Europeans to tears but for us kids over here on the other side of the pond, their films' alienness is intriguing if not utterly fascinating. Eurohorror has secret transmissions that awaken those happy (depressing) and morbid (ecstatic) neurons that destroy (invigorate) my dumb brain. I'm going to call this unique phenomenon, The Vibe.

I'm talking about white stucco walls, dirty floors, strange camera angles, overly bright blood, achingly beautiful actresses, claustrophobic spaces, ethereal music, ridiculous plots, etc. This all started in the black and white Italian gothics of the 1960s. The Italians were the kings of The Vibe until the late 80s. I blame it all on Mario Bava. Of course, ugly wallpaper helps too so things like the inept but strangely perfect Werewolf Woman (1976) make the list as well.

These characteristics were replicated (and in some cases even improved upon) very, very well by Spanish horror cinema in the 1970s. And speaking of werewolves, most of Paul Naschy's body of work (especially with directors León Klimovsky and Carlos Aured) contains this unique sensation as well. Check out any of his many performances as the doomed Waldemar Daninsky to see what I'm talking about.

I can't think of any one quintessential title that perfectly encompasses what it is that makes European horror so wondrous because I'm sure everyone out there has a different film in their heart. One of the first European horror films I ever watched that gave me The Vibe was Pupi Avati's Zeder (1983). Ohhhh, doctor! I tremble with joy just thinking about watching this movie. Every frame is filled with so much dread and the production design lays on the dull off-white and gray tones that just amp up the feeling that we, the audience, are alone and we're about to die horribly. I first caught this magnificent film on VHS when I was kid. It was retitled for the English speaking market as Revenge of the Dead with some hilariously misleading cover art. Zeder was one of my first Italian horror films and it remains firmly in my top 5 favorites from that magical land.

One fairly blatant example of that distinctly Euro-flava is the wacked out Vampyros Lesbos (1971). Jess Franco shot this little piece of brilliance in Spain, Germany, and Turkey. I'm not much for the softcore sex elements but this undeniably hypnotic film instantly grabbed hold of my soul when I

first took a chance on it. And while we're on the subject of lesbian vampires, there is also a very important and dreamy little number called Daughters of Darkness (also 1971), directed by Harry Kümel. If this soft focus gothic poem doesn't knock your socks off then you're not breathing, duder. And while I love the film, José Ramón Larraz's excellent Vampyres (1974) doesn't give me the same feeling. Strange, huh? It has all the required elements: buckets of blood, lesbian vampires, and a spooky cemetery but nope, The Vibe just ain't there for me. However, Larraz's Estigma (1980) is a Vibe classic of the highest order. Seek that one out!

Here are two more Italian examples, one from Dario Argento and one from Lucio Fulci. First up is Argento's Phenomena (1985). Most of this movie is so wild and bizarre that it's impossible without multiple viewings to pick up on The Vibe. Late in the film however, when Jennifer Connelly is trapped inside the killer's house, she finds a hole in the floor and descends right into what I'm freakin' talking about here. The catacombs beneath the Brückner house are starkly lit, gray, and insanely creepy. Lucio Fulci competes with Argento's sheer awesomeness with his own bizarre adventures in moody abstraction, The House by the Cemetery (1981) and City of the Living Dead (1980).

One Italian director that consistently delivers on The Vibe is the late, great Joe D'Amato. Before he disappeared forever into directing porno movies for a living, good old Joe was a cinematographer on the silly but very atmospheric The Devil's Wedding Night (1973). When he got a chance to direct his first horror film, the man made an art form out of style (and softcore sex) over substance with Death Smiled at Murder (also 1973). This film helps me escape the real world and threatens to never let me return. Even when he's wallowing in cheap crap, D'Amato still manages to deliver on that nearly indescribable gloomy goodness with Anthropophagus (1980) and Absurd (1981), a quasi-sequel to Anthropophagus. Absurd in particular is responsible for my current condition when it first entered my mind over 20 years ago after I caught it on late night television. This Halloween rip-off has piles of cheap atmosphere that never left my mind. I can't move on without mentioning that The Vibe is also very strong in D'amato's death-obsessed masterpiece, Beyond the Darkness (1979).

Usually, The Vibe comes from supernatural films but there are also several gialli that deliver what I crave. Whether it is through intent or accident, I get brief flashes of gray brilliance when I watch the yellow thrillers of Sergio Martino. I obsess over the tiniest scenes in everything from The Case of the Scorpion's Tail (1971) to Torso (1973) but I still can't quite put my finger on it. Other gialli that produce the same haunting reverberations in my soul include Emilio Miraglia's The Night Evelyn Came Out of the Grave (1971) and Armando Crispino's The Dead Are Alive (1972). It helps that both of these films have a dreamlike quality and a heightened sense of ghoulish improbability.

So do you get it too? Do any of you out there feel this thing? This unsavory and unwholesome longing for Eurohorror and you don't have a friggin' clue as to why? Or do you have a name for The Vibe? (I'm tempted to call it 'ghoulish improbability'.) Is there some obscure text out there that has coined a phrase for this stuff that I'm having a helluva time trying to describe? If you have an answer to any or all of these questions, please step forward. I'd love to commiserate with y'all. I know Riccardo Freda, God rest his soul, knows what I'm talking about. Just watch Barbara Steele in The Ghost (1963) and soak it up.

Graffiti Bridge! It's just Around the Corner!

Jason. Freddy. Michael. Prince. The halls of horror just got a little more purple (or purpler). What am I talking about? Ask yourself this: What am I not talking about? Graffiti Bridge (1990) is one of the most aggressively terrible and hurtful films I've ever watched. It's an ego-maniacal fairy tale in a horrible land where funk is the source of life. The fact that Prince wrote and directed this movie frightens me. The best thing you can say about this movie is that it's a collection of music videos tenuously connected together with filler material but you'd be wrong! The parts in between the songs are some of the most bizarre, childish, and quasi-religious load of claptrap (Funk is God!?) and tepid symbolism I've ever been stupid enough to sit through. Do you remember that scene in Batman where The Joker and his cronies trash an art gallery to Prince's "Partyman"? Imagine that scene stretched out for a half an hour film but with some PG-13 sex thrown in.

As you can tell, I love this friggin' movie. All I could think of was that this is Prince's Solarbabies. Okay, now I'm confusing myself. In Graffiti Bridge, Prince and Morris Day are competing for ownership of a club called Glam Slam and the affections of Aura (Ingrid Chavez), a poetry-writing angel. For some reason, Prince thinks the audience gives a triple fuck about this story. We don't. Why? First of all, how are we to believe that discerning nightclub patrons in Funk World (which looks a lot like a post-apocalyptic Minneapolis) would allow Prince's nightclub to falter when he's putting on a show? Morris Day and The Time marches in and steals Prince's fan base. How is this even remotely plausible? The fact that George Clinton has his own club begs the question: why the fuck isn't he the king of Funk World? Isn't that funk heresy?

There are no fat people in Funk World because Prince's drummer eats anyone who stops dancing, even if it's only for a second. Prince himself may look like an alien but Morris Day looks like something that MC Hammer coughed up. How would a woman -even one of the wretched 1990s- have trouble figuring out who to sleep with?

Ingrid Chavez has a penis. There's a scene in the film where she's in the men's room in Glam Slam and she stands up to pee. Okay, that didn't happen but the sex scene that she and Prince share is a clothed one. Yes, that's right. Prince humps her on his bike (or a brick wall or both) and they have their dang clothes on! I can't believe Prince couldn't go R for at least one scene in his movie.

If you're looking for your cult movie; something so unfathomably awful that you will scream at your TV and/or giggle until you shit your pants then check the $5 bin at your local Big Lots or Wal-Mart for Graffiti Bridge. If you hate movies like I do, then you will fucking love this. If anyone ever questioned Prince's sanity -and I'm sure many people did in his lifetime-then this could have been Exhibit A at the hearing. And if this is how (the artist formerly known as that symbol who was) Prince saw the world then he was clearly not a functioning member of society. Did I mention that I don't really like funk? The genre, I mean. It's better than blues music, I guess. Everything is better than blues music. So yeah, my name is not Prince and I am not funky. Thank you to my friend Nafa for introducing me to this splendorous film.

Buried Under the Cherry Moon

Back in January, my life changed forever when Nafa put on Prince's Graffiti Bridge as a joke and we ended up watching the whole thing. It turns out that the joke was on us. Last week, I demanded that we watch Under the Cherry Moon (1986). You see, Nafa is an ardent Prince fan but he hadn't until recently given his full attention to The Funky One's films. I used to think Prince was cool but then he scared me off with that hat with the friggin' gold chains obscuring his face. Plus, I kind of despise funk music. Okay, I appreciate the musicianship and the opportunity to be a music nerd about it but I promise you that I am not a funky person. At least not in a musical sense.

In Under the Cherry Moon, two Miami sleazeballs, Christopher Tracy (Prince), a complete douchebag ladies' man and his partner, Tricky (Jerome Benton), scam the rich ladies of the French Riviera to pay the rent. When Tricky learns of an heiress (Kristin Scott Thomas) who is set to inherit 50 million dollars, the two creeps move in for the kill. However, Tricky falls for Mary the heiress and ends up competing with Christopher for her affections. Their biggest obstacle (besides each other) is Mary's father (Steven Berkoff), who has his own scheme in place for his daughter's money. Throw in some murderous clowns and a doomsday device and you've got yourself a right kerfuffle! Yeah, I made up that last bit.

The first thing I noticed about Under the Cherry Moon (or UTCM for short) is that -and this was from just the first few seconds- it doesn't completely suck. For a second there, I was enraged. How dare Prince make something that wasn't insanely terrible and disastrously un-entertaining? I was accustomed to the atomic strength irony or unthinkable sarcasm that I felt when viewing Graffiti Bridge so I was taken aback by the similarities UTCM has with real movies. I mean, God help me, I really liked this film. Hold up. Wait a minute. Just because it isn't a total turd doesn't mean this movie isn't awful in its own way. The lines of what is meant to be a joke and what is meant to be taken seriously are so blurry, you'll get a migraine.

Get ready for the biggest piece of trivia about this film: before Prince took over the direction of UTCM, Mary Lambert was the director. Why is that name familiar? She directed Pet Semetary and Pet Semetery II. But here comes the big one: Mary Lambert directed Halloweentown II: Kalabar's Revenge! My mind is swirling now and I'm lost in the abyss. That's the one where people's Halloween masks become their real faces. Doesn't this explain everything? I'm channeling Joe Pesci in JFK with this one, kids.

The spotlight, which is supposed to be on Prince, is stolen by Jerome Benton. Not only is this guy a charismatic and handsome dude, he's also blessed with perfect comic timing. Every scene he's in makes the movie worth watching. He and Prince are a righteous comic duo and are totally fearless when it comes to getting a laugh. The gay over/undertones are jaw-dropping. I think Prince and Jerome are better in this movie than Morris Day and Jerome are in Graffiti Bridge. Even Kristin Scott Thomas gets in on the gags and she's totally brilliant. For example, the "Wrecka Stow" bit.

I determined that Graffiti Bridge was heavily influenced by Solarbabies. Well, UTCM wears its filmic inspirations on its frilly sleeve. I see lots of Charlie Chaplin and Groucho Marx in here. Plus, the place reeks with Fellini's 8½. One thing that really helps the film with its faux-classic vibe is the fact that it was shot in color but was released in black & white. The cinematography by Michael Ballhaus is incredible and even more incredible is Steven Berkoff's performance. Both Nafa and I were wracking our brains trying to remember where we'd seen this guy before. After the movie was over, IMDB told us it was the evil guy from Beverly Hills Cop. I was pretty embarrassed. How the fuck could I have forgotten that? Oh yeah, I'm trying to forget Eddie Murphy ever existed.

One part where the film fails miserably is Prince's and Kristin Scott Thomas' total lack of kissing chemistry. The minute these two lock lips, it's all over. It looks like Prince is trying to eat Thomas' face. Maybe that's not entirely accurate. He looks like he's trying to knock her unconscious with his beautiful lips. God help her, she's trying to keep up. I usually don't talk about a dude's kissing style but the Prince-ly duder needed to work on that action. Maybe he didn't practice with Apollonia enough. These are seriously uncomfortable scenes to watch. Speaking of discomfort, where are the fucking musical sequences? This movie only has three, I think. Lame.

The fatal flaw however comes during the final ten minutes or so when the pacing takes a total shit. Instead of ending gracefully, we get a hokey boat chase. When all seems lost, Prince goes for the tragic hero bit and it's a goddamned riot. When he falls to the ground after getting shot, we see that the son of a bitch has been wearing high heels during the entire film. Un-fucking-believable. This was probably the most important moment and not just in the film. I'm talking about IN MY LIFE. Let's put Robocop and Repo Man aside for a second here, Prince waits until the final moments of the film to reveal his footwear. Was this predicted in the book of Revelations 69:69 or what?

So what the hell is this movie? I'll tell ya. It's a serious arthouse farce that shouldn't be taken seriously, seriously. Or maybe it's a documentary. This is what Prince's life was like every fucking day. Now I really want to believe that Graffiti Bridge is a documentary. If it was, I might be able to find peace (not funk) before I die. I will say a couple of things on Prince's behalf. First of all, I can't wait to watch this movie again. And secondly, the scenes in Under the Cherry Moon not graced by the presence of Prince nor Jerome Benton are lifeless and lame. It's like those connecting bits in Fred Astaire and Ginger Rogers' movies where neither of them on the screen and everything comes to a complete standstill. So… hottest couple of 1986: Prince and Kristin Scott Thomas? WRONG! The answer is Prince and Jerome Benton, y'all. You need to see this shit.

Healing with Fellini

Federico Fellini has always been a tough sell for me. I always struggle to get through his films. They're beautiful, hilarious, haunting, and always about a half an hour too long. Satyricon was the impetus for me to nearly throw in the towel on art films altogether and get back, way back into horror movies. I've tried Roma (1972), Amacord (1973), La Strada (1954), and even 8½ (1963) but I find the guy's stuff impenetrably boring and repetitive with cool moments hidden in the running time.

My favorite aspect of his films are when characters in the periphery stare right into the camera and prattle off some nonsense at the audience. There's a lot of that in Satyricon (1969) and it's most unsettling. Hell, the whole thing is unsettling. There is tons of bloodshed, wild decadence, and enough kink to make you very, very uncomfortable. And just like the rest of his films I've seen, it's too friggin' long! I recently visited La Dolce Vita (1960) and it knocked me out! I was really surprised by that one. For some reason, I can handle Marcello Mastroianni being a dickhead in that film but not in 8½ which I have now tried to watch three times and still don't like it.

The one film that was a pleasant surprise when I first caught it on Turner Classic Movies is Juliet of the Spirits (1965), Fellini's first color film. While I was recuperating from my illness this past weekend, I noticed that TCM still had the film stashed away in its On Demand thingie. This film is full of ghosts and while I watched it on Saturday, I myself was haunting our living room. I felt like a husk of my former self and needed something to heal with. So, much to the confusion of my mother-in-law (who sat down long enough to catch about three-fourths of the film) and to the weariness of my wife (who was also sick and who just caught the last half hour), Fellini's phantasmagoric psychoanalytic pop masterpiece invaded our brains and took no prisoners.

"Our dear, happy Juliet, she sees magic everywhere."

Visions of ghosts haunt every corner of this film to the point where it becomes impossible to tell what's real and what isn't. Time itself is happily disorienting and it falls apart along with all the absurd and hilarious chaos while Fellini, drunk on color, holds it all together. Juliet of the Spirits is about a housewife (Giulietta Masina) who suspects her husband is cheating on her. She is visited by a number of spirits who guide her through this rough time (but in the end, she must choose her own course with or without the man in her life).

Yes, this movie is too long. In an instant, Fellini can communicate a memory or show what Juliet is thinking but that's not what he's going for here. He has to hammer his idea home through repetition. But his is an off kilter machine that reveals more with each turn. A Fellini movie is like a 2 and a half hour John Coltrane solo. The theme of the film is hidden within the notes and the distracting bleats of the horn. All that you need to know is revealed instantly yet the song becomes more and more dynamic with each measure. Little by little, it all comes together and your head feels like it's going to explode. But by the end of the film, you see Juliet's heart shining brilliantly and guiding you to safety with its perfect melody.

Whoa, did I just write that? I should probably stay away from artsy films. Anyway, I can't believe I found a Fellini movie I actually like! I haven't seen everything, obviously, but I take this as a good sign. There's still a lot of his works to go through but this portrait of Juliet is all aces. This petite woman with the thin smile is overlooked, left behind, and not good enough for her shitheel husband or the stuck up women in her family. But the spirits choose to speak to Juliet instead of her wacky friend Valentina (Valentina Cortese, my favorite actress in this film next to Masina). Everyone in the spirit world (even those with malicious or selfish intent) knows that Juliet is special. Every dream, disembodied voice, memory, and ghost is there to guide this woman who is so full of love she is about to burst.

I hope I don't seem as though I'm even pretending that I have a clue as to how to write about a film like this. Juliet of the Spirits is just a magical work of art that is so overwhelmingly beautiful and fun -okay, it's a lot of work- to experience that I just had to babble on about it. I've watched it twice now and I can't wait to watch it again. For any Fellini film to get to me like this one has is pretty special. There're so many more things to talk about. I didn't even go into the spirits (some of which are just creepy as hell) or Sandra Milo's frozen smile or the private eye (who dresses like a priest). This is just the tip of the iceberg, people. I think I'm gonna keep trying with this Fellini guy.

Last Dance with Prince

Every journey -even a purple one- has to come to an end. After subjecting ourselves to the terror of Graffiti Bridge and the accidental masterpiece that is Under the Cherry Moon, Nafa and I had to complete the Prince film cycle. The thing that worried us the most was that Purple Rain would just be a good movie. How the hell are we supposed to deal with Prince just being in a good film? Before we could know the answer to that, we dug on Sign 'o' the Times (1987).

So anyway, I was fully prepared to rename this film to Sigh... No... The Times(?). But I'll be damned if this isn't one of the best concert films ever made. It starts off all artsy fartsy like Graffiti Bridge and then it soars into an explosive funk sensory overload. As I've stated before, I don't like funk but I caught my foot tapping all by itself throughout nearly all of Sign 'o' the Times. Oh my God, that bass solo. Nafa, rewind that. Thanks to this film, I finally understand what the hell all the fuss is about.

The artsy stuff I mentioned are dramatic scenes featuring members of Prince's band acting out some lame ass poetry/dialogue. The funniest of these is when the guy in the fuzzy hat complains about his woman to the bartender. What's his beef? Well, his woman wants old fuzzy hat to talk to her. Oh wow, poor guy. Who talks to their women, seriously? And the weird thing is that the bartender totally understands! It's moments like these, hidden inside this wildly entertaining concert flick, that threaten to ruin everything. And yet, I must admit that Prince's nearly paralyzing pretentiousness is part of the reason why his films are so amazing.

Since we watched Graffiti Bridge back in January, Nafa and I have developed a perfect method for viewing Prince's films. I walk over to Nafa's place from my apartment around 5:30pm and we go out to Zaxby's. This is fine dining at its finest. Once we are stuffed with chicken and fries, we go to Wal-Mart. I'm not sure why but I think it's to get cheap snacks and drink. For Purple Rain, I got some grape Faygo (though I really wanted Mountain Dew Distortion) in order to have something purple to drink. The only other soul joining us on our funk sojourn is Nafa's cat, Buddha.

So Purple Rain (1984) begins with the fabulous and infectiously energizing opening montage where we get to see Morris Day picking out his outfit. Immediately, I realize what was wrong about Sign 'o' the Times, NO MORRIS OR JEROME! Well, this movie fixes that, thank Jesus. I still can't wrap my mind around the fact that we're back in Minneapolis again. Even stranger -once again- the lunacy of Prince's world is that his band is always competing against Morris Day and The Time. Yeah, I know, I'll talk more about this later. By the way, Prince's name in this movie is The Kid. Oh fuck. Not again. Oh hey, Jerome just threw a woman in a dumpster because she was annoying Morris. I can't even comprehend this moment right now.

Apollonia shows up wanting to sing in The Kid's band. She gets introduced to the man himself and he just fucking stands there staring at the back of her head. When she finally gets the courage to speak to him, he's gone. Unbelievable. The club owner (this morbidly obese black dude in a track suit) wants to ditch The Kid because he doesn't draw a big enough crowd. Sigh. What the hell? So The Kid goes home and his dad is beating the crap out of him mom. His dad is played by one of the most intense black actors in film history, Clarence Williams III. Now I didn't even spot this until IMDB pointed out this insanely obvious fact to me, The Kid's mom is played by Olga Karlatos from Zombie (1979). Holy crap, y'all. This is nuts. The Prince and Lucio Fulci connection is finally established. They said it would never happen.

"You have to purify yourself in the waters of Lake Minnetonka."

This movie has a potty mouth! There can be no swearing in a Prince film. Wait, why is Apollonia riding on the back of The Kid's motorcycle? Did I miss something? Are they dating now? The Kid convinces Apollonia to strip and jump in the lake. This caused a minor explosion of screams from me. First of all, NUDITY IN A PRINCE FILM!? Secondly, Apollonia has a superb rack. I mean, like outrageously nice. I could go on and on but I won't. Okay, I will. Great rack. I mean it. Even if you don't want to see this movie, you have to check her bobbins out.

So what happened to Prince in his other films? Did he mistake aloofness for charm or something? I mean, The Kid is a total dick in Purple Rain. He smacks around Apollonia and he treats his band like shit. Especially when Wendy and Lisa want to share a song THEY WROTE. The nerve of some people! If I wrote a song and The Kid was talking to me with ventriloquist dummy, I would be all like "Yeah, why don't you go back to your parents' basement, you fucking dick?" Yet, Prince is still charming as hell in this movie. Something that he would lose by the time he got to Graffiti Bridge.

The Kid's home situation is pretty bad. His dad is a failed musician and also insane. He beats his mom and then shoots himself in the head. The Kid nearly loses his mind and even has a vision of hanging himself. Geez duder, do you have to be just like your old man? He takes the music that the girls wrote and combines it with his dad's music to make the song "Purple Rain". So on the night of nights at the club, he has to prove to the club owner that he has what it takes to rock the joint. Morris Day teases him about his dad shooting himself but then feels really, really bad about it. Holy shit, Morris can act! So The Kid and the band get on stage and he surprises them all by busting out "Purple Rain". This is pretty much one of the most perfect moments in any movie ever. They play the song and practically the whole band is crying. It's nuts. Then The Kid comes back from cooling off backstage and tears the place apart with funk. Did I mention his guitar ejaculates on the audience? It does and it's brilliant.

So what's my problem with this movie? It's the same thing that's wrong with Graffiti Bridge. (Okay, EVERYTHING is WRONG with Graffiti Bridge.) The fact that Prince has to compete with Morris Day for two things, 1) the headlining gig at a nightclub and 2) a woman. Give me a fucking break! How is this even remotely possible? I'm not saying Morris isn't ugly and I'm not saying that Prince isn't short. So they're both equally freakish in their own respective ways. But Prince is obviously a hotter duder and his music eclipses anything The Time ever did. So aside from the fact that the plot hinges on something that doesn't make any dang sense, Purple Rain is totally great. Okay, Nafa and I agree that it's time to watch Graffiti Bridge again. Who's with us? Did I mention Apollonia's rack?

Richard Glenn Schmidt

The Horror of Gigi

Thanks to my wife, I have actually seen some decent musicals and Gigi (1958) is one of them. The film is charming, funny, beautiful, and totally disturbing. Here, let me show you. First things first, turn of the century France is a dangerous and terrible place. Then Maurice Chevrolet shows up and talks about how great little girls are. He says he means when they grow up but I think he's a pedobear. He casually mentions that the story we are about to see is about Gigi (Leslie Caron). Not Gigli. That's a different sicko freakfest. No, Gigi, my sweet. You are damned. You must run. Don't let the sugar magnate catch you.

Gigi is a happy go lucky schoolgirl with a miserable old biddy grandma for a guardian. Her name is Mamita and she sends Gigi to an old crone named Aunt Alicia who is training Gigi to be a classy lady (whore) because Gigi's mother is too busy with her acting (whoring) career to deal with her own daughter. Aunt Alicia wears a choker because she has to hide all the scars on her throat. So many assassination attempts... This old snobby slut feeds Gigi some dead sparrows and makes her chew on the bones. Aunt Alicia instructs her to look down her nose at everyone and instills in her an unhealthy appreciation of jewelry. Wow, Gigi's life really sucks. The whole point of all this is for her to land a man but not for marriage! This is just so she can be some duder's mistress. Keep your eyes on the prize, ladies.

Okay, I'm getting ahead of myself. That man-whore Maurice Chevrolet has a nephew (man-whore in training) named Gaston (Louis Jourdan) who is a rich and spoiled son of a sugar billionaire or some shit, I don't know. He thinks everything is a great big bore. But you know what? He's right. This is frickin' France. It is B-O-R-I-N-G! Gaston, please do us all a favor and fucking kill yourself.

"An ugly black cigar is love," Gigi says. She doesn't understand the Parisians. Don't worry, babe, no one else does either. Gigi and Gaston are like second cousins once removed or something like that. She cheats at cards but that's okay because Gaston is dating Eva Gabor (not the one that slapped the cop) so he's not all that bright in the first place. Eva Gabor is cheating on him with a roller-skating instructor (no, I'm not making that up) but he sees right through her lying Hungarian eyes. To keep his stupid male pride, Gaston confronts his woman about screwing Disco Stu. Through all this crap, we get to see the social structure of Paris back in the early 20th century. Holy shit, it's like The Crucible! All of these losers deserve a painful death involving white hot knives going into orifices that normally don't accept white hot sharp objects.

What is Maurice Chevrolet's advice to Gaston? What else would a man-whore tell a man-whore in training to do? Go screw every woman in France. That'll make you feel better! Gaston gets bored after a while and shows up at Mamita's place. They get Gigi drunk on champagne, sing a song about it, and then it's off to the seaside. Gaston and Gigi play in the water and ride donkeys while Chevy meets up with Mamita and they reminisce about when they used to get it on. So yeah, as I suspected, Maurice Chevrolet was a fucking dickhead scumbag and he just barely realizes that maybe, just maybe, he screwed up the only good and real thing that has ever happened in his life. Does he change his ways? No, he's a lecherous bastard the rest of the movie. Big shocker.

So Mamita and Aunt Alicia, the stupid old jerks, decide to intensify Gigi's training so that she can be Gaston's mistress. Notice how they're not even trying to get him to marry her. Ugh, the French are such sickos. Anyway, Gaston pays a visit and flips his lid when he sees Gigi dressed up like an adult. You see, he wants Gigi to stay a little girl forever. Yikes. Mamita lets him know that Gigi is on the market and he flips out... again. Gaston then sings a song about how Gigi is still a baby and a tot. Then he realizes she's a hottie. "Oh, what miracle has made you the way you are?" It's called puberty, dumbass. So he comes back and says "Uh yeah, I was just kidding, she's totally old enough."

They work out a financial arrangement for him to take Gigi to his bed. Mamita explains everything to Gigi and she's all like, "Oh thanks, asshole. Now I'm going to be Gaston's whore." Gigi flips out, understandably, and refuses Gaston. It gets worse when he admits that he loves her. We get more bullshit between Gigi and Gaston, Maurice Chevrolet sings a song about how he can't get it up anymore, and then Gigi gives in.

They go on their big date and things go wrong when Gaston realizes that that dumb idiot Mamita and perilous beyatch Aunt Alicia have totally screwed Gigi up. She acts too much like Eva Gabor now, damn it! As an added bonus Maurice Chevrolet is there and he's like "Nice job, I likes 'em young, too." Gaston drops Gigi like a bad habit and runs off to reflect for a while. Then he goes back to the apartment and asks Mamita if he can marry Gigi. Whoa, what a great guy! Although, I suspect that he just did it because it's cheaper to marry her then pay for an apartment where he can keep her chained up for sex and stuff. God, I love this movie! It teaches values that are completely lost on today's generation.

Richard Glenn Schmidt

Video Naschy

I wish I could say that I've been into the films of Spanish actor Paul Naschy since back in the day but sadly, I can't. It wasn't until about a year after my reconnection (I tried to use "reembracement" but it is not a word, duder) to the world of horror that I found out about Jacinto Molina and his life as a werewolf and other monsters in front of and behind the camera.

I've had man-crushes before but damn y'all, this is for real. Being that I'm a fat, breathless, and weakling loser-face, I'm just astounded by Mr. Naschy's screen presence. The duder was larger than life. His bodybuilding days weren't too far behind his film career and there are a few films where Naschy is just plain ripped. Let's face it, the guy was a movie star and the world sucks without him in it.

For fans of either 1970s or European horror films, it isn't long before one stumbles upon something magnificent and cheesy like Werewolf Shadow (1971). This is how I discovered Paul Naschy. And I had no idea what I was getting myself into. Nothing I had read could have prepared me for what I was about to see. Director León Klimovsky and his star create a strange and mesmerizing concoction of undeniable atmosphere and straight-faced camp that holds up to repeat viewings.

Horror Rises from the Tomb (1973) was soon to follow. This one is my favorite Paul Naschy film of all time. I've watched it over and over again and I can't shake the feeling that maybe seeing this film is the reason I was put on this planet. Cool, I can die now. Bye bye, everybody. But wait, there's more. I kind of liked Curse of the Devil (also 1973) but I was a little disappointed the first time around. My second viewing proved to me -not for the first time- that I had my head up my butt, cinematically speaking. Curse of the Devil rules. Deal with it, Richard.

My only speed-bump on my journey down Naschy Street is Crimson (1973 again!). I hate this fucking movie. I bought it because the DVD was cheap and I got rid of it as quickly as possible. Is there a chance that I need to revisit this film? I don't care. You can't make me watch it again. No sir, uh uh. It has all the elements for a trashy good time but sometimes a film rubs you the wrong way and there's no going back. Perhaps it's too French?

I was back on track by the time I witnessed Night of the Werewolf (1981) and Exorcismo (1975). I love clones of The Exorcist, so Naschy playing a priest who has to save a young lady from possession is right up my alley. A great movie? Not really. But Exorcismo does contain enough cackling insanity and head-scratching plot twists to make any bad film buff happy. Night of the Werewolf on the other hand, is just awesome all the way around. It's sort of like a remake of Werewolf Shadow but with more blood and hotter women (if that's even possible).

Some strange Naschy-ness came to me in the form of People Who Own the Dark (1976). This post-apocalyptic freakout is more about how human beings pretty much totally suck than it is about a bunch of murderous blind people driven mad by nuclear radiation. Paul Naschy plays one of the survivors of the bomb and he's a total dick. Naschy played total dicks very convincingly.

Now don't get me wrong, anti-heroes were this duder's specialty. Just watch Human Beasts (1980) sometime and tell me how in the world are we supposed to like his character? Or Blue Eyes of the Broken Doll (1974); in this Spanish giallo, Naschy plays a friggin' murderer who can barely contain his strangling desires when he gets aroused by a woman.

Speaking of the giallo genre, Naschy was in the problematic though occasionally entertaining 7 Murders for Scotland Yard (1971) where he plays a circus performer who after a "career ruining" injury, takes up drinking and is accused of being a modern day Jack the Ripper. The film is silly and mostly nonsense but the ending delivers. And while I'm on a silly tangent, there's always Vengeance of the Zombies (1973 yet again) where Naschy plays an Indian mystic named Krishna, his twin brother, AND the friggin' devil in the same movie. Wut?

A couple of the more obscure Naschy titles that have surfaced recently, The Hanging Woman and The Hunchback of the Morgue (both 1973!), are the cat's pajamas. In the former, Naschy doesn't have a very big part. But he makes the most of it and it's another atmospheric and odd film for his catalog of horrors. The Hunchback of the Morgue is a gory hodgepodge of ideas and Naschy gets the juiciest role as the titular hunchback, an outcast driven by impossible love and manipulated by evil.

Naschy wasn't content with just playing the werewolf either. He has also played a mummy in Vengeance of the Mummy and a vampire in Count Dracula's Great Love, both to great success (and both in 1973 like there was any doubt). Well, "great success might" not be the right term. Maybe he played them both to fan appreciation because I friggin' love those flicks.

I've seen quite a few Naschy films and luckily, I have many more to go. I feel special, like I'm in some secret club that I want everyone to know about. You say you're not a "Naschy type" of person? You think his movies are overhyped, boring, stupid, or not important? Just keep watching them, duder. And after you've seen about 10 or 12 of his films, let me know if you still don't like Paul Naschy and I just might consider letting you off the hook...

Richard Glenn Schmidt

7 NINETEEN SEVENTY-SIX

What year were you born? If you don't know, you should really look it up! I entered the world in 1976 and one of my favorite hobbies is watching films released that year. I highly recommend you do this with your own birth year. Or you could get really weird and see what films were in theaters around the time that you were conceived. That's when the thoughts of your parents getting it on actually invade your mind and you start crying blood.

So anyway, 1976 was weird as shit and the more I dig into it, the more fun it is. The giallo was dying down and the slasher boom was a few years away. Blaxploitation was already old hat and Jaws had studios scrambling to churn out another blockbuster. And yet, Star Wars hadn't come along and totally screwed up everything. So needless to say, it was an odd time in cinema. So anyway, here's a bunch of things I wrote about the films of Nineteen Hundred and Seventy-Six, the greatest cinematic year the world has ever known. BTW, if you've made it this far in this book, thank you so much! And don't feel too bad. It's almost over. This book will self-destruct in 17 pages.

Satan's Slave (1976)

Catharine Yorke (Candace Glendenning) is traveling with her parents to meet some estranged family members. After a terrible accident, Catharine is left orphaned and in the care of her creepy Uncle Alexander (Michael Gough of Horror Hospital) and her disturbed cousin, Stephen (Martin Potter). As mysterious and eerie events begin to occur, Catharine realizes that she is part of a satanic plot to resurrect a dead witch.

Well, this is a sleazy surprise! Satan's Slave has a weak plot and a weaker script but there is plenty of nudity, gore, and trashiness to keep just about any Brit-horror fan pleased. Director Norman J. Warren (Terror, Inseminoid) handles the pacing quite well and keeps this cheap junker from derailing completely. The author of the screenplay, David McGillivray, also wrote delightfully trashy titles such as Frightmare and The House of Whipcord.

What better choice than Michael Gough to portray the seemingly kind but conniving and malevolent uncle? As usual, Gough is great for playing an evil character because damn it, he looks and talks the part like it's nobody's business. Candace Glendenning is so beautiful that it's easy to forgive her character, which is too doped up half the time to react to her darkening situation. I'm not sure what to make of Martin Potter's acting. His portrayal as Stephen is only interesting when he's up to no good, which is most of his screen time, luckily.

I can't help but gush about Satan's Slave now that I've listed its faults. I was never bored during this little gem full of Satanists, psychic powers, a homicidal maniac, and even some witch burning. The cheesy gore effects and the trite dialogue only manage to warm my heart during the running time of this beautiful crap. Satan's Slave is a guilty pleasure and has all the ingredients to make a tasty bad horror movie stew and then some. Did I mention the nudity?

Plot of Fear (1976)

A sudden series of brutal homicides baffles the police but obsessive Inspector Gaspare Lomenzo (Michele Placido) is determined to catch the killer. Lomenzo also has to compete with Pietro Riccio (Eli Wallach), the head of a private detective agency who always seems to be one step ahead of his investigation. The only pattern for the crimes is that all of the victims were members of an exclusive sex club called The Fauna Lovers led by eccentric author Hoffmann (John Steiner). Inspector Lomenzo falls for Jeanne (Corinne Clery), a beautiful model who just happens to be involved with this club. She witnessed the accidental death of Rosa, a hooker who may be the key to cracking the case.

Paolo Cavara, you amaze me. After the excellent Black Belly of the Tarantula, director Cavara comes back with a vengeance with Plot of Fear. Whoa, dig that abrasive and frightening music score by Daniele Patucchi! One has to assume that Patucchi is also responsible for those horrid disco numbers as well. Wow. The prolific cinematographer, Franco Di Giacomo, responsible for other gialli such as Who Saw Her Die? and Four Flies on Grey Velvet, shines once again with his versatility. Whether it's a gritty and hooker-filled police station or a fog-enshrouded stretch of highway, the man has a beautiful eye.

"Criminals want to get caught. It's a macabre invitation to a treasure hunt."

Michele Placido's performance as Inspector Gaspare Lomenzo has instantly become one of my favorites in the entire giallo genre. Lomenzo is hotheaded, high strung, egocentric, and yet is a totally brilliant detective. The beautiful Corinne Clery (Hitchhike, The Devil's Honey) is excellent as Jeanne, the girl of questionable morals that Lomenzo falls for despite her involvement with the case. Eli Wallach (though hideously dubbed) is very good as the scheming and suspicious Pietro Riccio. An inexplicable American actor cameo in this film comes from Tom Skerritt (also dubbed) who does little more than wave his arms around in frustration. Last but not least, one of Italian genre flicks' elite, John Steiner of Tenebre and Mario Bava's Shock, delivers another fine performance.

Giallo fans will be quite pleased with this film as it has plenty of plot twists, a few brutal death scenes (immolation!), odious 70s fashion, garish set designs, beautiful ladies, sleazy sex, J&B sightings, and a slew of politically incorrect moments. Plot of Fear also sports a pretty dismal view of the world with its bleak snapshots of urban life and its rather sickening portrayal of the decadent wealthy. Sounds like fun, eh? Don't worry, the addition of some dry comedy and a fast-paced, entertaining mystery keep this one from getting too serious.

Dark August (1976)

I wanted to love Dark August but sadly, I don't. This film, released in the year of my birth and named after my (probably dark) birth month seemed like the most serendipitous horror movie event of my life. It isn't. The recurring 1976 theme of a cloaked figure (see Land of the Minotaur and a strange story my mom tells of my bizarre origin story) shows up and the main character smokes Vantage, my father's brand of cigarettes. Weird, right? Anyway, I fired this flick up on my birthday this year to see what all the fuss was about. Just kidding. There is no fuss anywhere about this movie.

After accidentally running over a young girl, artist Sal Devito (J.J. Barry) is haunted by three things: visions of the tragic incident, a strange figure lurking in the woods, and by Old Man McDermitt, the girl's grandfather. As Sal's mind is slowly coming unglued, his girlfriend Jackie (Carolyne Barry) tries her best to stand by her man. Jackie's friend recommends that Sal seek spiritual guidance from Adrianna (Kim Hunter), a witch who specializes in white magic. Adrianna discovers that someone has placed a curse on Sal which summoned a demon to torment him.

Director Martin Goldman attempts to make a classy horror film without an effects budget or a high body count (no proto-slashing here). Instead, he focuses on psychology, the performances of his actors, and the vaguely supernatural. The score by William S. Fisher is a jazzy synth mishmash with some wacko drums and piano (so of course, I dig it). The workmanlike cinematography by Richard E. Brooks has a few surprises stashed in the film in the form of some gorgeously composed shots.

Unfortunately, the entire film hinges on Sal, a friggin' unlikeable bastard. J.J. Barry (who co-wrote the film with Goldman and Carolyne Barry) turns in a great performance but his character is a selfish, smug douchebag. The only thing I liked about Sal's character is that it doesn't take him long to buy into the supernatural world around him. If this movie had taken an extra ten minutes while he moronically vacillated between faith and science, I would have given up. Other members of the cast do a fine job but the script has them caught in the mire of banal melodrama. Dr. Zira herself, Kim Hunter, is great and spouts some pretty crazy incantations during a séance which goes horribly awry.

Despite its Me Generation whining, ponderous pacing, and actors' workshop vibe, I have to admit that there is something special about Dark August. On the surface it feels like Savage Weekend but without the trashiness or the chainsaw. It does have a well-staged and surprising moment of violence that I didn't see coming. Another cool scene is when we first see the dark figure that's always watching Sal. It's chilling! Sal tries to catch this presence by following it deeper and deeper into the woods and his demon stays just out of reach and is always seen in a blurry haze.

Also in the film's favor: I watched Dark August on my beat-up Lightning Video VHS tape that lends a claustrophobic, anything-can-happen vibe to an old and justifiably unseen films like this one. Even though Goldman's film has some major strikes against it, I was left with a creepy feeling when it was over and a few things to think about. I can't recommend Dark August too much because I don't think horror film fans should go out of their way to find it. However, if this flick turns up on some 50 movie pack someday, patient folks should give it a spin.

Death Weekend (1976)

A dentist named Harry (Chuck Shamata) brings a model named Diane (Brenda Vaccaro) out to his vacation home out in the boonies. He claims that he's having a big get together but this sleazy duder only has one thing on his mind: banging Diane. On the way out to the house, Harry and Diane run afoul of a quartet of violent scumbags led by Lep (Don Stroud). Thanks to the help of some local yokels, the creeps manage to follow them to the house and they immediately start making trouble. You know this isn't going to end well. At least, not for Harry.

Home invasion horror meets rape-revenge thriller in Death Weekend, a nasty little piece of 1970s insanity that I like more than I should. Director William Fruet would go on to direct some other genre oddities like Funeral Home, Spasms, Killer Party, and Blue Monkey. I can't find who composed the score for this film but they did a fine job. The music is eerie, pretty, and very frickin' good.

"Jesus, that broad can drive! That pisses me off!"

I really like Brenda Vaccaro in this film but the script has some pretty terrible 'I will speak my thoughts out loud now' moments and even worse 'ooh am I enjoying this rape?' moments. As usual, her voice is so husky and breathy that it begs parody (not even SCTV could resist) but I really like her character when she gets pushed too far and starts mopping the floor with the baddies. The always dependable Don Stroud steals the film as Lep, a terrifying psycho fuckwad out looking for trouble with his horrible crew of shitheads. I like how Harry is not only a wimp but also a terrible pervert loser as well. I'm glad the script adds an extra sleazy vibe to the guy but Chuck Shamata barely holds his own and could have gone farther with his role.

While it turned out to be an engrossing and nail-biting film, I wouldn't call Death Weekend an essential piece of trash cinema. The menace, tension, and mayhem are all delivered successfully but there is little to elevate this above its place among other similar pieces of pointlessly offensive garbage. That being said, I found myself enjoying the film against my will. So if you're gonna watch this thing, trust me, the end is worth sticking around for. The finale makes up for the uber-unpleasant setup. I'm sure that super-producer Ivan Reitman is very proud of this film to this day.

Something to Hide (1976)

A drunken married couple, Harry and Gabriella (Peter Finch and Shelly Winters), are truly miserable together. Harry's big dreams have fallen flat and Gabriella is still bitter about giving up her stage career for marriage 26 years ago. One Christmas Eve, she leaves him. Left alone, Harry takes to the bottle even harder and is on thin ice with his boss. He continually skips going to the office in order to pick his wife up from the airport but she never shows. One afternoon, he picks up a young and very pregnant hitchhiker named Lorelai (Linda Hayden) and brings her home. She's a manipulative little parasite who worms her way into Harry's life and things quickly spiral out of control.

"Goddamn vegetarian creep!"

Something to Hide, from TV director Alastair Reid, is a very dark, offbeat, and melodramatic flick full of tension and a sense of terrible dread. The title song "How Can We Run Away" by Buddy Greco is as cheesy as it is perfectly ominous. Shelly Winters is completely obnoxious (but her part is little more than an extended cameo) and Peter Finch is excellent. Beauty Linda Hayden (Taste the Blood of Dracula) is made up to be so awful and unappealing in this movie that she's hard to look at. This won't restore your faith in humanity or give you a spring in your step but it's definitely worth a look. I don't think the writer likes women very much and you won't believe the freakin' ending!

Werewolf Woman (1976)

Daniella Neseri (Annik Borel) believes she is the descendent of a woman burned at the stake for being a werewolf. This leads her to all kinds of antisocial behavior, the worst of which is luring men to her bed and biting their throats out. Her father Count Neseri (Tino Carraro) and her sister Elena (Dagmar Lassander) put Daniella into an insane asylum before she hurts anyone else. She escapes the asylum and meets the man of her dreams, a sensitive stuntman (Howard Ross). Things start looking up until some rapist thugs take Daniella's newfound happiness away. Her wild side reemerges even worse than before but is it too late for Count Neseri to save his daughter?

Ah, finally an Italian film that I can honestly refer to as a complete clusterfuck. If any of the several plot threads of this film had been even moderately successful, Werewolf Woman might have actually worked. Part werewolf horror, part rape-revenge flick, part psychosexual exploiter... all bad. There are some bloody moments and the trashiness of the plot will surely earn an audience but this is one overly talky and uneven effort from exploitation director Rino Di Silvestro. The surprisingly good cinematographic duties are held down by two gentlemen, one of them being Mario Capriotti who worked with Ruggero Deodato on Waves Of Lust. Big points are earned in my book by the funky soundtrack.

The sexy Annik Borel puts forth an incredibly manic performance as Daniella. She's willing to go the extra mile and leave very little to our imagination as far as nude scenes go. Thank you for the bare crotch gyration, the film just wouldn't be the same without it. Oh, if only you'd stuck with the genre, you'd have made one hell of a scream queen. Despite some horrid werewolf boobs and a howl that sounds like a pigbird (a genetic mutation that hasn't happened yet), Borel is really friggin' awesome. The way I figure it, Daniella is doing the world a service by ridding the world of rapists and scumbags. The woman is a saint!

I love seeing Howard Ross (New York Ripper, 5 Dolls for an August Moon) in a completely likeable role. Doesn't it just tear your heart out when he -No! I can't bear to think about it! Dagmar Lassander (House by the Cemetery, The Black Cat) is pretty much wasted here as Daniella's sister, Elena. Her character just kind of disappears. The opportunity for a good old fashioned catfight is grievously overlooked here. Dang!

Werewolf Woman is yet another missed opportunity in Italian sleaze filmmaking. At least Di Silvestro tries (BUT DOES NOT SUCCEED) to satisfy every viewer. There are even some Exorcist-like moments thrown in for good measure. In some respects, I wouldn't change a single frame of this film if I had the chance and yet I can't recommend it. Look, just don't expect this one to be any good. If you're ideas of entertainment and fine Italian filmmaking are as bent as mine, then by all means, seek this badboy out. Otherwise, stay far away. Awoooooooooooooo, duder!

The Sexy Killer (1976)

When her sister goes insane after a heroin overdose, Wan Fei (Ping Chen) wages her own war against drugs, going undercover as a junkie/hooker and then shaking down (and killing) mofos for information. Her friend Wei-ping (Hua Yueh) is the only uncorrupted cop in the city but his hands are tied. Things get even more complicated when Wen Fei sets her sights on taking down Lung Tou (Shen Chan), a ruthless drug lord and S&M freakazoid, who has his hand in every pot of corruption in the city.

"Drugs! Drugs! I hate it so much!"

This Shaw Brothers' remake of Coffy (released in 1973) is a freakin' riot. It has all the cynicism, sleaze, and melodrama of the original Pam Grier vehicle plus the gratuitous and gleeful slow motion ultra-violence of They Call Her One Eye (also 1973). And oh my, it all works! The camerawork is perfect and the colors are vibrant and even occasionally searing. From the bombastic opening credit sequence to its awesome finale, The Sexy Killer's pacing is exceptional with tons of action, over-the-top acting, and disco fabulousness. This might just be my new favorite Shaw Brothers movie. All that's missing is Sid Haig. Highly recommended if you can track this one down in some dark alley or abandoned warehouse.

The Town That Dreaded Sundown (1976)

In 1946, the police of Texarkana, Arkansas are baffled by a rash of brutal attacks committed by a mysterious man in a hood. Luckily, the first two victims survive their ordeal but it isn't long before the brutality of the crimes increases and people start turning up dead. Captain J.D. Morales (Ben Johnson), a Texas Ranger known for always getting his man, is called in to help the local sheriff (Andrew Prine) capture or kill the evil bastard.

Thanks to the insistence of my good friend Brad, I am finally dipping my toes into the world of Charles B. Pierce. I started with the excellent Legend of Boggy Creek (1972) and then moved on to this little almost but not quite forgotten gem. Mr. Pierce's strongest asset is his constant attempt to create films that are both documentary and fiction. I thought this was a loose version of the Zodiac Killer story but The Town That Dreaded Sundown is based on a real case in Texarkana. The true crime business adds an extra layer of chill onto an already creepy film. The excellent score by Jaime Mendoza-Nava is also a plus.

There are shifts in tone in this film that could and most likely have thrown some people off. There are some comic moments of hillbilly slapstick which were probably meant to unsettle the viewer so that when the really shocking sequences come, they'd be that much darker. I've seen this method fail miserably in other films like the comedy cops from Last House on the Left but in Town That Dreaded Sundown, I swear it all works.

The cast is a mix of B movie folks and non-professionals. The most surprising casting choice comes in the form of Dawn Wells of "Gilligan's Island" fame. It's just mind-boggling to see Mary-Ann menaced by a psychopath. Where's the Skipper when you need him? Apparently, she was also in Return to Boggy Creek. Ben Johnson is very good as usual. He and Andrew Prine try to out-cool each other during their scenes.

So all in all, I'd say The Town That Dreaded Sundown is a tight little film. The fact this has been hard to find for so long is unfortunate because I'm sure a lot of folks expecting a different kind of film will say this is overrated. Don't let the hokey narration (which I love!) and some less than stellar performances from non-actors throw you. This one is worth sticking with to the end. Any film that features a killer in a white hood assaulting a victim with a trombone is worth checking out in my book.

Violent Naples (1976)

Commissioner Berti (Maurizio Merli) arrives in Naples to help the city fight against the mafia. Berti is a great cop; he busts a car thief and hauls him in on his way to his first day on the job. While uncovering several small time operations, Berti begins to work on a drug ring lead by Francesco Capuano (John Saxon) and a high level mafia man known as The Commandante (Barry Sullivan). When Capuano decides to rip off The Commandante, all hell breaks loose in the city. Berti soon discovers that the law isn't strong enough to control this quickly escalating situation, so he takes matters into his own hands.

The talented Umberto Lenzi (Almost Human, Eyeball) brings us Violent Naples, a gritty and bristling crime film as only the Italians can provide. Tight cinematography and a cool soundtrack are delivered as expected. However, what the damn hell is with the horrible closing credit song? "A Man Before Your Time" by The Bulldogs has to be one of the most God awful ways of closing a film. Ouch. The screenplay comes from Vincenzo Mannino, the writer behind works such as Syndicate Sadists and New York Ripper. The only issues I have with Violent Naples (other than that friggin' Bulldogs song) are some sped up action scenes.

The cast of Violent Naples is really a superb collection of actors. Man, I'm really diggin' on Luciano Rossi (Death Smiled at Murder) lately. I was hoping he'd be the main villain here but his gruesome (and well deserved) fate is too cool to miss. It's no surprise that Maurizio Merli (A Man Called Blade) is excellent in his role as Berti, a good cop who is frustrated by the powerlessness of the law he fights for. Merli was a fun action star with a relatively short list of credits under his belt before he passed away in the late 80s.

John Saxon (Tenebre) and Barry Sullivan (Take a Hard Ride) make a nearly awesome evil duo who can't stop trying to double-cross each other every five minutes. Elio Zamuto is seriously smooth as Franco Casagrande, bank robber extraordinaire. I find it odd that there's not even a whisper of a love interest in this one. Surprisingly, the movie lacks either some trashy nude scenes or one of those heartfelt moments where the woman begs her man not to go out onto those violent streets of Naples. What am I saying?

As usual, Lenzi displays his incredible knack for economical storytelling and staging breathless action sequences. Despite the violence on display here, Lenzi really wants to show the human cost and depressing outcome of the (sometimes frightening) brutality of the criminal world. Don't let Cannibal Ferox fool you, Umberto Lenzi is a pretty sensitive guy.

Richard Glenn Schmidt

Chinese Roulette (1976)

Angela Christ (Andrea Schober) is an unhappy little girl. She believes that her parents don't love her because she's handicapped. Unfortunately, Angela is also incredibly intelligent and bent on making her family pay through manipulating them at every opportunity. Her mother, Ariane (Margit Carstensen), suffers the most and is at her wits' end. When Angela arranges a little party for everyone at the family mansion and suggests a game of Chinese Roulette (a psychological guessing game), tensions rise and everything goes straight to hell. Along for the ride are Angela's father, his mistress, his mother's boy toy, and Angela's "friends" (who are actually servants): Taunitz (Macha Meril), a mute, and Gabriel (Volker Spengler), a pretentious writer. This isn't going to be pretty.

Chinese Roulette is almost exactly what I thought it was going to be. A name as heavy as Rainer Werner Fassbinder of the New German Cinema meant only one thing to me: obtuse. I had a feeling that I was just going to stare at the screen blankly until it was over and then throw my TV across the room. The film is so deadpan in its delivery that if one was looking for a parody of German arthouse cinema -well, here it is. But what saves Chinese Roulette, for me anyway, is an impeccable cast playing a handful of fucked up characters and filmmaker loading everything with tons of style. Fassbinder's ability to communicate a mood to the audience that is so tense and so dark that the animosity practically drips off the screen is really impressive.

Peer Raben's score is a wicked combination of brooding composing and discordant electronics. That beautiful score and the electric and dangerous cinematography of Michael Ballhaus are my favorite aspects of this cruel gem. The camera never misses a meaningful glance (of which there are many) and will sometimes move very purposefully, sometimes even jarringly, to meet every whim of the director. As I mentioned before, everyone in Chinese Roulette is superb. Frequent Fassbinder regular Carstensen is excellent here and Euro horror fans will no doubt recognize Macha Meril from Deep Red and Night Train Murders.

Entertainment value? Well, that's a tough one. Chinese Roulette requires all of your patience and your full attention. Light it is not. I got confused as to the rules of the game (the film's namesake) so I was totally lost until the end when I went back and re-watched the scene where the rules were explained. So yeah, the film is a lot of work for the viewer but if you're into it for the bleak atmosphere and the horror of human beings psychologically destroying each other, you'll love this film. Even though I'm not a fan just yet, I'm already looking into Fassbinder's other films. If they're all like this, I'm sold.

The Premonition (1976)

Andrea Fletcher (Ellen Barber) is a lunatic who travels with the carnival to look for the daughter she was forced to give up for adoption. She enlists Jude (Richard Lynch), an unbalanced mime (yes, you read that right), to help her accomplish her goals. Her daughter Janie (Danielle Brisebois) has been living with her new parents, Sheri and Miles (Sharon Farrell and Edward Bell), unaware that she's the progeny of a total nutburger. Andrea and Jude's first attempt to kidnap Janie go awry but it does establish a psychic connection between Sheri and Andrea. And this is the start of all kinds of paranormal bullshit and whatnot. All you need to know is that it all ends in an impromptu supernatural electric piano concert.

Well, this is... different. And I don't mean different good, I mean different bad. I had high hopes for The Premonition especially after the opening sequence with Richard Lynch in ballet slippers practicing his mime routine. That is sort of the highpoint of the film, I'm afraid. I did like the score by Henry Mollicone. Wait, what? That is seriously that dude's name? Thankfully, the cast are real people with real names. Lynch and Barber have some great scenes together. I liked Chitra Neogy and wish she had done more movies. Her burgeoning almost-romance with Edward Bell's character is good stuff. Character actor Jeff Corey steals every scene he's in as the befuddled detective.

A great cast, offbeat direction, and good camerawork just can't help the obvious and pretentious script. I will give The Premonition a little credit for its eccentricity and quirkiness but I barely got through this one. Okay, I didn't make it. I fell asleep but I did go back and pick up what I missed. On paper, this all sounds great but the more I think about this film afterwards, the more I just don't like it. Who knows? I usually like films that deliver the weirdness and the corny dialog but The Premonition left me stuck under the Ferris wheel. I should probably point out that I do think this film is worth checking out. I am sure that it will strike a chord (hey o!) with some adventurous viewers. Maybe I'll give this one another spin someday.

The House with Laughing Windows (1976)

Stefano (Lino Capolicchio) travels to a small town because he's been commissioned to restore a painting of St. Sebastian in the local church. The painting is quite disturbing and unique. It was done by a local artist named Legnani, dubbed "the Painter of Agony" by the locals. The whereabouts of Legnani and his sisters is a mystery which the town is tight-lipped about. After his friend is murdered while trying to reveal the secret of 'the Painter of Agony', Stefano decides to stay in town, finish the restoration, and solve the mystery himself.

Stefano begins to have an affair with a woman named Francesca (Francesca Marciano), the local schoolteacher who is willing to quit her job and flee the creepy town with him. The town drunk, Coppola (Gianni Cavina), reveals that he alone knows what's going on in the town and that the secret lies in a house with "laughing windows". It isn't long before both Stefano and Francesca's lives are in danger for getting too close to discovering the truth.

Pupi Avati (Zeder) directs The House with Laughing Windows, one of the best gialli ever made. This film is loaded with dread and foreshadowing while keeping a relaxed pace which only adds to the growing tension that keeps crawling toward the protagonist until the finale. The shots are gorgeously composed and the music by Amedeo Tommasi is haunting and sweet. From start to finish, this film sets a standard for the giallo that has rarely been reached since its 1976 release.

The acting here is all excellent, especially Capolicchio (The Blood Stained Shadow) whose character of Stefano becomes so obsessed with the horrors of the past that he will put his own life at risk to satisfy his boundless curiosity. Francesca Marciano is wonderful as the shy and headstrong Francesca. And Gianni Cavina is perfect as Coppola, the likeable but troubled town drunk. The rest of the cast come across superbly as a town full of eccentrics.

The film opens with a fantastic sepia soaked sequence depicting a brutal stabbing before the film downshifts to the quiet dread that plagues the rest of the storyline. The paranoia of the setting is easy to pick up on. It feels as though someone is always watching and a whispered word is never missed by prying ears. The tone of Laughing Windows is deadly serious tinged with strangeness and mystery.

Aside from being seemingly diseased or unhealthy, the decrepit small town in the film is riddled with complacency as well. Legnani's paintings (which pervade the minds of the town's inhabitants and Stefano's imagination) are very morbid and add to the bizarre atmosphere. Though it is bloody but hardly gory, Avati's film doesn't need spilled intestines or arterial spray to capture the viewer's attention.

For fans of Italian horror cinema, The House with Laughing Windows is a must-see and gets more rewarding with every viewing. Though not as violent as many of its contemporaries, this film is a stunning example of the giallo. Viewers will be surprised by the care and detail that Avati and company put into the film. They just don't make them like this anymore.

The Mysterious Monsters (1976)

Peter Graves narrates this delightfully clunky documentary on creatures unknown such as Bigfoot and The Loch Ness Monster. There are interviews with eyewitnesses, actors pretending to be eyewitnesses, researchers, and actors pretending to be researchers. Man oh man, 70s people were batshit crazy for legendary beasts! The Mysterious Monsters is incredibly entertaining and captured my imagination when I saw it myself in the 80s. It was impossible for my kid-brain to distinguish between the "real" footage and the reenactments. The phrase "psychometrize" is thrown around. Perfect.

Today, I love how this film provides "irrefutable" evidence of the existence of these monsters. Shit man, there is so much conjecture and not-so-subtle manipulation of footage going on that it is impossible not to get a kick out of The Mysterious Monsters. Despite some fun chills and effective moments, I remain skeptical. Oh, not of the Yeti. I believe in that! I remain skeptical that Graves didn't desperately need a paycheck.

Dr. Black and Mr. Hyde (1976)

Dr. Henry Pride (Bernie Casey) is a kindly physician working at a hospital in a poor neighborhood. He's always turning down the advances of Linda (Marie O'Henry), an attractive prostitute with liver problems. With his lovely associate, Dr. Billie Worth (Rosalind Cash), Dr. Pride is working on an experimental drug to cure liver disease. He notices that it turns black rats into white rats. Another side effect is that the white rats turn evil and kill all the black rats. After several failures with lab animals, Dr. Pride realizes he needs a human test subject. After testing it on a dying patient with less than stellar results, the good doctor uses himself as a guinea pig.

After his 'miracle drug' turns him into a big white creature filled with rage, Pride's evil side pursues Linda but she's terrified of him. The next day, when the effects have subsided and Dr. Pride is black to normal again, he reveals to Linda that he needs her to be a test subject for his drug. She declines but he tells her that refusal is not an option. Linda just barely escapes but others are not so lucky. Meanwhile, dead hookers begin showing up all over town.

"Well, you know if it had been the regular bit, like a murder, shooting, stabbing, beating -then we could understand it and have the proclivity to solve it. But this little lady has had her neck crushed like in a vice; meaning somebody has put some shit into the game. You know what I mean?"

Director William Crain (Blacula) takes some trashy and hilarious material and transforms it into something trashy and hilarious. Composer Johnny Pate keeps things funky and awesome. The script is filled with all types of ludicrously corny pimps, hookers, and drug dealers. It's also got lots of cursing, melodrama, violence, and jive talkin' that makes the blaxploitation genre so magical. But at the heart of it all, the story is a timeless one: a man with a hole in his heart uses modern science (and killing hookers) to fill that hole and comedy ensues.

There might be a message to this film but whatever it is, it's so heavy-handed that it's laughable. When Linda tells Dr. Pride that he isn't black enough, I just wanted to climb into a hole and die. The more he becomes like his evil white self, the more painful the story gets. An antidote to this schlock is my favorite character: Lt. Jackson, played by Ji-Tu Cumbuka. He's a super-cool detective who uses big words like "insalubrious" and cuts a very imposing swath through the neighborhood.

Despite its 'white people are evil' vibe, which I don't take personally (because I happen to be a pretty righteous dude), I really love Dr. Black and Mr. Hyde. Bernie Casey really goes wild as Mr. Hyde. My favorite moment in the film is when Dr. Pride -in Mr. Hyde mode, of course- throws a hooker across a parking lot and then runs over her with his Rolls Royce. You should definitely check out this crazy flick, it's a wild and entertaining monster romp for the ages. Okay, maybe just one age, the sweet, sweet 70s.

A Star is Born (1976)

Kris Kristofferson plays Eric Clapton, a washed up rock and roll star playing to stadiums of disappointed fans every night. His roadie and bestest pal, Bobbie Ritchie (Gary Busey), keeps Eric all fucked up on coke and booze and the tour is going to shit. One night, Eric stumbles into a bar where he sees a woman performing some fucking horrible songs. The woman's name is Bette Midler and she's played by Barbra Streisand. Eric discovers Bette, seduces her, and then gets her career started by forcing her to debut at a benefit for Native Americans. There's a joke there somewhere. How about this: "Haven't they suffered enough?"

Eric and Bette get married and they make love and stuff. She tries to get him to clean up his act. Oh shit, I forgot the motorcycle thing. Eric gets shitfaced at a stadium gig and drives a motorcycle off the stage. (Actually, his stunt double performs this moment.) It's pretty funny. Anyway, after Bette becomes a bigger star than Eric, he gets all jealous and stuff. Then he fucks a groupie -well, not really; he was too drunk to get it up -and Bette smacks him and bites his lip. Then he dies in a car accident and she stages a concert in his honor. Or whatever. Hey, Robert Englund is in this!

I first encountered A Star is Born when I was a kid. My parents rented it when it came out on VHS. While it was playing on our old TV, my parents took out sharp knives and stabbed me repeatedly while it was playing. Worse than that, my mom owned a copy of the soundtrack on LP. And I remember very, very well that a naked Barbra and a naked Kristofferson holding each other was about the least sexy thing ever.

The first thing you learn from A Star is Born is that all fans of rock and roll music are idiots, the lowest common denominator, and also scum. Okay, we've got that out of the way. Next thing you learn is that fans of motion pictures are even lower than rock fans. The fact that this shitbag pus-spewing visual rape was the second highest grossing film of the year in 1976 is baffling. Forget disco and bell bottom jeans, this is why the seventies sucked.

One of the worst aspects of the film, and I'm not joking here, is Barbra Streisand's dang afro perm thingie. She seriously looks like Barry Manilow. And when you have a love scene where one person looks like Barry Manilow and the other person looks a lot like Kris Kristofferson -because it happens to be Kris Kristofferson- well... you've got the worst gay celebrity fan fiction ever written.

When Gary Busey is the voice of reason in a film, shit just got real. You know what I'm sayin'? He provides Kristofferson with lots of coke but never takes any himself. Amazing. If you're at a concert and Busey offers you something he won't snort, smack it out of his hand and run like a motherfucker!

Barbra Streisand and rock and roll go together like those two great tastes... What were they? Oh yeah, peanut butter and kerosene. The songs are excruciating. And not just Streisand's shite either. The garbage they wrote for Kristofferson is just that. If this had been meant to be a fun, light movie where it was all tongue in cheek or whatever, I would feel awfully silly complaining about it. But no, this shit is meant to be played straight. More cocaine anyone?

Here are some lyrics for you:

I want to learn what my life is for
I don't want much, I just want more

And later:

Love; soft as an easy chair
Love; fresh as the morning air

This is a musical, damn it! The songs are supposed to be fucking good, aren't they? The whole songwriting process and then the recording process scenes are total crap. Everything is insanely awkward and just painful to sit through. But I would pay $80 million to have more of those scenes after not one but two horseback riding scenes and then the bathtub scene. Seeing Babs put makeup on Kris in the bathtub is pure, unadulterated cinematic agony.

So anyway, I did this little equation:

B-A-R-B-R-A S-T-R-E-I-S-A-N-D = 19 LETTERS
19 DIVIDED BY 3 = 6
666 = SATAN!

Don't believe me? Check this out: The last 10 minutes of this movie is Streisand singing. One camera. On her. For the rest of the movie. One fucking shot. SHIT! SHIIIIIIT! A Star is Born is fucking terrible and easily one of the most astonishingly painful movies I've ever sat through. But then again, I'd rather watch this again than watch Rocky ever again. There are some things that are just too horrible to contemplate. Note: I drew 11 sad faces on my notes during this viewing. This is the worst movie in this book.

Breaking Point (1976)

I first heard about Breaking Point over at the Bloody Pit of Rod blog and boy oh boy, I wish I hadn't. Apparently, big macho action movies weren't director Bob Clark's specialty. The film sports nearly constant logic problems, overacting from every member of the very irritating cast, and a layer of cheese so thick that the film is just freakin' ripe. The only things that work for Breaking Point are its excellent lighting and well-staged action setpieces. Bo Svenson does get to kick a little ass but it's not enough to save this ultimately unsatisfying piece of dumb schlock. And I love schlock!

Obsession (1976)

Every time I think I know what Mr. Brian De Palma has in store for me, I get totally suckered in and blown away. Notice that in that sentence there were the words "suck" and "blow". I really thought I knew where Obsession was going but I was way off. I think that several of De Palma's films are overrated. Sisters, Carrie, Blowout, and even Dressed to Kill have left me feeling empty and totally put me off at one time or another. Obsession made me realize that I have the guy all wrong and need to reevaluate pretty much everything. This film is sumptuously filmed and even Cliff Robertson is good. One more thing: the score by Bernard Herrmann is just astounding and gorgeous!

The Tenant (1976)

Speaking of directors surprising me, I also checked out Roman Polanski's The Tenant. Much like my feelings on De Palma, I find that most of Polanski's films just don't do it for me. This grotesque piece of paranoia is very, very good. Even though one of those "100 Scariest Horror Movie Moments" shows ruined the best surprise in this film for me, I still found a great deal to dig into with The Tenant. If phrases like "Kafkaesque" and "nightmarishly insane" describe your idea of fine entertainment, then check out this film immediately. Oh and it's funny too.

Image of Death (1976)

I had high hopes for Image of Death, an obscure Australian thriller. Other than the fact that I am obsessed with big-eyed Cathey Paine (Helter Skelter), I knew zilch about this film when the VHS arrived in my mailbox. And Cathey Paine is quite good in this probably made-for-TV flick but the script is awful. The writers insult their audience by explaining every single tiny nuance of the plot in great detail just to fill up its short running time. Instead of an unknown gem, I found a total dud that deserves to stay forgotten. In order to reach other markets, there are no Australians in this. Everyone has either an American or a British accent. Lame!

Mother, Jugs & Speed (1976)

When a film like MASH mixes comedy with tragedy, it works perfectly and it's because Robert Altman is a demented genius. When a film like Mother, Jugs & Speed mixes comedy with tragedy, the viewer ends up despising the film and it's because it was directed by Peter Yates, the guy who directed Krull. There are some fun, un-politically correct, and tasteless times to be had here but this film thinks it's pretty fucking clever and it's not. Bill Cosby is awesome and Larry Hagman is sleazy. I'm not sure what else to say other than I do applaud the director for taking chances with the tonal shifts. Look for the super cute Toni Basil. Yup, she's in this one.

Violent Milan (1976)

Director Mario Caiano delivers a pretty solid crime film with Milano Violenta. It's got the funky soundtrack, the bad dubbing, the brutal violence, the unlikable characters, and just about everything else one might expect from this sub-genre. Just a warning, the film does slow down in the middle quite a bit but makes up for it with some more ass kicking action near the end. There isn't much that separates this poliziotteschi from the pack (other than some soft focus cinematography and a somewhat strange tone) but it's definitely worth checking out.

Crypt of Dark Secrets (1976)

When it comes to the phrase, "What the hell is this?", Crypt of Dark Secrets is especially special. This silly shit has some hilariously delivered and idiotic dialog and an EXTREMELY NAKED witch in it. Every scene is awkward and nearly every actor has sunstroke or malaria or something. Whatever, this movie is pure fun and is filled with totally crappy magic that must be seen to be believed. If you can stay awake through this 71 minute marvel, it's probably because you are laughing your ass off at its inept genius.

Overlords of the U.F.O. (1976)

W. Gordon Allen, the writer, producer, and host of this documentary, takes himself and the material presented here VERY SERIOUSLY. This is the film that dares to ask the burning question, "Who are the overlords of the UFO?" Why is it worded that way? I don't know. While this is a rather dry presentation and gets a little dull at times, Overlords of the U.F.O. is pretty intriguing. There are some obviously kooky hoaxes that are presented here as evidence of the existence of aliens. The best moments are the artistic recreations of various incidents of sightings and abductions. However, my favorite bit is the information provided by communications from aliens of the planet Ummo. This stuff is so wild and just so much damn fun. Your enjoyment of this documentary will depend entirely on your interest in UFOs and the US government's attempts to cover up these incidents.

INDEX

7 Murders for Scotland Yard 235
99 Women 129
Abandoned, The 194
Absurd 220
Adventures of Buckaroo Banzai Across the 8th Dimension, The 44
Against the Drunken Cat Paws 20
Akira 99
Alien 3 196
American History X 38
Anaconda 200
Anthropophagus 220
Antichrist, The 30
Arang 83
Argento, Dario 55
Ariel 117
Arizona Dream 39
Arno, Alice 122, 160, 161, 175, 180, 189
Art of the Devil 2 71
Art of the Devil 70
Asami 72
Asato, Mari 96
Attack of the Robots 165
Aured, Carlos 218
Avati, Pupi 248
Awful Dr. Orloff, The 126
Baker, Rick 81
Ballistic: Ecks Vs. Sever 200
Barash, Olivia 49
Basic Instinct 46
Battle Angel 104
Battlestar Galactica 42
Bava, Mario 218
Bazelli, Bojan 80
Bertolucci, Bernardo 40
Beyond the Darkness 220
Beyond the Door 30
Black Hole, The 42
Blade Runner 7
Blair Witch Project, The 196

Blood of Fu Manchu, The 176
Bloody Judge, The 123
Bloody Moon 131
Blue Rita 147
Boogie Nights 198
Boogiepop Phantom 110
Boy From Hell, The 96
Brando, Marlon 40
Breaking Point 252
Breaking the Waves 38
Buck Rogers in the 25th Century 42
Buffalo '66 39
Burton, Richard 61
Busey, Gary 250
Bush, Dick 61
Caiano, Mario 253
Candyman 198
Caruso, David 46
Castle of Fu Manchu, The 178
Cat, The AKA Lao Mao 87, 97
Cavara, Paolo 239
Cheung, Jacky 74
Cheung, Roy 74
Chevrolet, Maurice 232
Chinese Roulette 246
Chung, Fat 84
City of the Living Dead 214, 220
Clash of the Titans 63
Class of Nuke 'Em High 57
Clifford 199
Color Me Blood Red 12
Conformist, The 40
Coraline 194
Corpse Packs His Bags, The 179
Count Dracula 130
Count Dracula's Great Love 235
Countess Perverse 180
Cox, Brian 81
Crabs crawling out of vaginas 148
Craft, The 24
Crash 202

Craven, Wes 8, 52
Creepshow 2 194
Crimson 234
Crow, The 201
Crypt of Dark Secrets 254
Curse of Kazuo Umezu, The 106
Curse of the Devil 234
Cyborg 43
D'Amato, Joe 220
Dario Argento's World of Horror 55
Dark August 239
Daughter of Dracula 143
Daughters of Darkness 220
Dawn of the Dead (1978) 210
Dawn of the Dead (2004) 201
Daybreakers 204
De Palma, Brian 252
Dead Are Alive, The 220
Death Smiled at Murder 220
Death Weekend 241
Demon City Shinjuku 104
Demon Prince Enma 115
Demoniac 167
Demons 2 28
Demons 26
Detective Story 89
Devil Came from Akasava, The 164
Devil's Island Lovers 174
Devil's Wedding Night, The 220
Diabolical Dr. Z, The 146
Digital Devil Monogatari Megami Tensei 106
Djalil, H. Tjut 95
Doctor Who 42
Dolls for Sale 169
Dr. Black and Mr. Hyde 249
Dr. Caligari 49
Dr. Orloff's Monster 134
Dracula, Prisoner of Frankenstein 136
Drouot, Jean-Claude 60
Ecco the Dolphin 49
Eddie fucking Constantine 166
Eerie Midnight Horror Show, The 30
Elephant 39
Eliminators 43

Empire Strikes Back, The 63
Enemy Mine 44
Erotikill 160
Estevez, Emilio 49
Eugenie de Sade 134
Eugenie… The Story of Her Journey into Perversion 171
Evil Dead II 41
Exorcism 168
Exorcismo 30, 234
Exorcist II: The Heretic 29
Exorcist III, The 29
Exorcist, The 29, 201
Faceless 153
Fantastic Planet 8
Fassbinder, Werner 246
Fellini, Federico 227
Female Vampire 162
Fight Back to School III, 46
Fonda, Bridget 46
Forest of Death 76
Franco, Jess 121-191
Freda, Riccardo 221
Freddy's Dead: The Final Nightmare 197
Friedkin, William 46
Fukasaku, Kenta 83
Fukutomi, Hiroshi 104
Fulci, Lucio 213, 220
Fusco, Mike 195, 202
G.I. Joe: The Movie 58
Gamera, Super Monsters 108
Ghost Ballroom 78
Ghost in the Shell 102
Ghost in the Shell: Stand Alone Complex 103
Ghost, The 221
Gigi 232
Girl from Rio, The 149
Gough, Michael 238
Graves, Peter 248
Great Horror Family, The 87
Grindhouse 195
Grudge, The 67, 92
Gummo 39
Halloween II (2009) 206
Hamlet 202

Hanging Woman, The 235
Hardware Wars 63
Harmagedon 113
Harris, Fox 49
Harryhausen, Ray 64
Hastings, Ryan 199
Headbangers Ball 55
Hellraiser 57
Heroic Trio, The 75
Hills Have Eyes Part II, The 52
Hino, Hideshi 96
Hogue, Brad i, 28, 40, 76, 165, 244
Hogue, Elizabeth i
Horror Rises from the Tomb 234
Hot Nights of Linda, The 189
House by the Cemetery, The 220
House with the Laughing Windows, The 247
How ot Seduce a Virgin 175
Howard Vernon's bare ass 170
Human Beasts 235
Hunchback of the Morgue, The 235
Hung Kam-Bo, Sammo 84
I Come in Peace 44
Ilsa the Wicked Warden 184
Image of Death 253
Ishigoru, Noboru 111
Ito, Junti 73
Jack the Ripper 144
Jason Leigh, Jennifer 46
Jigoku 90
Johnson, Steve 55
Jolley, Mike 196, 202
Kakesu, Shuichi 102
Kanbe, Mamoru 115
Karina, Anna 60
Kaufman, Lloyd 57
Kawai, Kenji 102
Kawajiri, Hideyuki 104
Kids 39
Kieślowski, Krzysztof 39
Killer Barbys 186
King, Stephen 57
Kinski, Klaus 43, 124, 130, 144 , 152
Kiss Me, Killer 122
Kiss Me, Monster 127
Klimovsky, León 218, 234

Kristofferson, Kris 4, 250
Kruger, Ehren 65
Kuroneko 77
Kurosawa, Kiyoshi 75
Kwaidan 66
Lai, Leon 74
Lam, Ngai Kai 88
Last Tango in Paris 40
Laughter in the Dark 60
Leda: The Fantastical Adventures of Yohko 109
Lee, Carmen 74
Lee, Christopher 123, 130, 171, 176, 178
LeEtta i, 65, 66, 81, 85, 108, 127, 179, 194, 195, 200, 204, 209, 213, 227, 232, 261
Legend of Boggy Creek 244
Lenzi, Umberto 245
Libert, Anne 125, 137, 143, 154, 170, 182
Lina Romay eating a banana 190
Loch Ness Horror, The 53
Locke the Superman 103
Lorna the Exorcist 148
Lost in Space 199
Love Ghost 73
Lucky the Inscrutable 175
Machine Girl, The 72
Macross: Do You Remember Love? 111
Macumba Sexual 133
Major Payne 198
Malicious 45
Marebito 94
Marquis de Sade: Justine 152
Mayans, Antonio 133, 141, 172, 190
McCrann, Charles 53
McHale's Navy 200
Medak, Peter 46
Megazone 23 110
Metal Skin Panic Madox-01 117
Midori - A First Taste of Midori 85
Miike, Takashi 89
Miranda, Soledad 128, 130, 134, 155, 157, 164, 182
Mishima, Yukio 4

Mitchum, Christopher 153
Mother, Jugs & Speed 253
Muerte Silba un Blues, La 187
Mysterious Monsters, The 248
Mystics in Bali 95
Nadja 24
Nafa 66, 206, 223, 224, 229
Nagai, Gô 115
Nakadai, Tatsuya 74
Nakagawa, Nobuo 91
Nakata, Hideo 81
Nakayama, Kazuya 89
Naschy, Paul 218, 234
NCIS 82
Nell 38
Nemesis 43
Neon Genesis Evangelion 119
Neri, Rosalba 130, 152, 175, 178
Ng, Christine 88
Night Evelyn Came Out of the Grave, The 220
Night of the Living Dead 10
Night of the Skull 150
Nightmare on Elm Street, A 8
Nightmares Come at Night 128
Oasis of the Zombies 172
Obscene Mirror, The 159
Obsession 252
Odin: Photon Sailer Starlight 116
Oldman, Gary 46
Olin, Lena 46
Onibaba 77
Ópalo de Fuego: Mercaderes del Sexo 183
Opper, Don Keith 42
Oshii, Mamoru 102
Otomo, Katsuhiro 113
Out of Africa 202
Overlords of the U.F.O. 254
Palance, Jack 152
Pang Brothers, The 77
Passenger 57 203
Patlabor 2 102
People Who Own the Dark, The 234
Peter Berg creeps me out 46
Phenomena 18, 220
Philadelphia 205

Pieces 12
Pierce, Charles B. 244
Pillow Book, The 39
Plot of Fear 238
Poison Ivy: The New Seduction 45
Polanski, Roman 252
Ponyo 203
Popeye 63
Pray 69
Premonition, The 247
Prince 222, 224, 229
Prous, Montserrat 162, 166, 170, 182
Queen Millennia 105
Queen of Black Magic, The 69
Quigley, Linnea 55
Reality Bites 200
Recorded Live 63
Reincarnation 94
Reis, Michelle 74
Repo Man 48
Requiem for a Dream 38
Return of the Jedi 63
Revenge in the House of Usher 141
Reynaud, Janine 127, 142, 158
Richard, Tony 61
Ring Two, The 82
Ring, The 65, 80, 194
Ringu 65, 80
Rintaro 108, 115
Rites of Frankenstein, The 125
Robocop 2 28, 32
Robocop 32
Robot Jox 44
Robotech 99
Rocky Horror Picture Show, The 215
Romay, Lina 122, 126, 133, 139, 141, 145, 148, 151, 154, 159, 160, 163, 168, 176, 180, 183, 185, 189
Romper Stomper 38
Rumble Fish 39
Sadistic Baron von Klaus, The 140
Sailor Who Fell From Grace with the Sea, The 4
Satan's Slave 238
Savalas, Telly 153
Saxon, John 245

Schneider, Maria 40
Séance 76
Séance on a Wet Afternoon 76
Seconds 23
Serial Experiments Lain 112
Sexy Killer, The 243
Shatter Dead 24
She Killed in Ecstasy 155
Shiina, Eihi 72
Shimizu, Takashi 93
Shock Labyrinth, The 94
Silencio de Tumba, Un 166
Single While Female 45
Siniestro Doctor Orloff, El 190
Sinister Eyes of Dr. Orloff, The 162
Sinner: Diary of a Nymphomaniac 182
Skerritt, Tom 239
Sleepy Hollow 25
Sling Blade 196
Slipstream 43
Soavi, Michele 55
Something to Hide 241
Spooky Encounters 84
Stanton, Harry Dean 49
Star is Born, A 250
Star Wars 63
Steele, Barbara 221
Steiner, John 238
Stephen King's World of Horror 55
Streisand, Barbra 250
Succubus 158
Sucker Punch 204
Sweet Home 75
Taxi Driver 195
Tenant, The 252
Terminal Justice 45
Texas Chainsaw Massacre 2 18
The Basketball Diairies 38
This is England 38
Thomerson, Tim 43
Threesome 205
Tokyo Gore Police 72
Tomie: Re-birth 93
Town that Dreaded Sundown, The 244
Toxic Zombies 53
Trainspotting 38
Trancers 43
Transformers: The Movie 58, 195
Transporter, The 199
Two Undercover Angels 142
Umezu, Kazuo 106
Vampyros Lesbos 156, 218
Van Damme, Jean-Claude 43
Venganza del Doctor Mabuse, La 168
Vengeance of the Mummy 235
Vengeance of the Zombies 235
Venus in Furs 124
Verbinski, Gore 65, 81
Vernon, Howard 123, 125, 126, 128, 136, 138, 141, 143, 152, 154, 155, 158, 159, 169, 174, 180, 182, 191
Violent Milan 253
Violent Naples 245
Virgin Among the Living Dead, A 154
Voltron: Defender of the Universe 99
Wallach, Eli 238
Walter, Tracey 49
Warren, Norman J. 238
Watts, Naomi 80
Werewolf Shadow 234
Werewolf Woman 218, 242
Wicked City (1987) 73, 196
Wicked City (1992) 66, 73
Williamson, Nicol 60
Windaria 109
Wishmaster 24
Women Without Innocence 139
Worst movie in this book, The 252
X 107
X from Outer Space, The 98
X312 - Flight to Hell 138
X-Cross 83
Yanni, Rosanna 127, 142
Yip, Gloria 88
Yoshioka, Takao 115
Yuyama, Kurihiko 109
Yuzna, Brian 55
Zeder 218
Zombi 2 213

ABOUT THE AUTHOR

Richard Glenn Schmidt is the author of Giallo Meltdown: A Moviethon Diary. He is the owner and operator of Doomed Moviethon, co-host of Hello! This is the Doomed Show, as well as an avid blogger at Cinema Somnambulist. A founding member of the pioneering realistic music band GYROJETS, Richard lives in Tampa, Florida with his wife LeEtta and their cats, Crisco and Sparkles. It is very likely that Richard is watching a movie right now. Okay, just kidding. He is definitely watching a movie.

Made in the USA
Coppell, TX
09 December 2022